TRIUMPH
BOOKS

ON THE CLOCK: CALGARY FLAMES

ON THE CLOCK: CALGARY FLAMES

Behind the Scenes
with the Calgary Flames
at the NHL Draft

RYAN PIKE

TRIUMPH
BOOKS

Library of Congress Cataloging-in-Publication Data

Names: Pike, Ryan, author.
Title: On the clock, Calgary Flames : behind the scenes with the Calgary
   Flames at the NHL draft / Ryan Pike.
Identifiers: LCCN 2023052920 | ISBN 9781637274002 (paperback) | ISBN
   9781637274026 (epub)
Subjects: LCSH: Calgary Flames (Hockey team) | Hockey
   Players—Alberta—Calgary. | National Hockey League. | BISAC: SPORTS &
   RECREATION / Winter Sports / Hockey | SPORTS & RECREATION /
   Business Aspects
Classification: LCC GV848.C25 P55 2024 | DDC
   796.962/6409712338—dc23/eng/20231117
LC record available at https://lccn.loc.gov/2023052920

This book is available in quantity at special discounts for your group or organization. For further information, contact:

Triumph Books LLC
814 North Franklin Street
Chicago, Illinois 60610
(312) 337-0747
www.triumphbooks.com

Printed in U.S.A.
ISBN: 978-1-63727-400-2
Design by Preston Pisellini
Page production by Nord Compo

CONTENTS

FOREWORD

I'VE KNOWN RYAN PIKE for 15 years. In the last few years of my play-by-play broadcast career with the Flames, I'd often spend time with him in the Flames dressing room after team practices and morning skates on the day of a Flames home game. Ryan was writing and reporting on the Flames then as he is now.

Since my retirement in 2014, I've followed Ryan on X and I've listened to his podcasts. He's a diligent and hard worker with intriguing insights.

His book offers a tremendous history not only of the Flames' player drafting over the years but also some interesting team history notations.

My time with the Flames started with the club's 1980 arrival in Calgary until I retired in 2014, and I was unaware of some of the historic tidbits Ryan reveals in the book.

No question Ryan put an enormous amount of time into researching information going right back to the franchise's early days in Atlanta. It makes for great reading—remarkable insights into the Flames drafting star players like Kent Nilsson, Al MacInnis, Mike Vernon, Theoren Fleury, etc., plus lesser-knowns, some of whom never made it to play in the NHL.

Explored are the positives, good fortunes, oddities, and pitfalls that the Flames, like most National Hockey League teams, experienced.

I had the good fortune of broadcasting all three Flames teams that made it to the Stanley Cup championships. This book explores how all those teams were built and later dismantled, as well as how different those teams were in terms of their style of play under the three different coaches—Bob Johnson, Terry Crisp, and Darryl Sutter.

Noted are insights into how the Flames' first general manager, Cliff Fletcher, through to most recent GM Brad Treliving were organized for the draft each year and the numerous changes in procedure over 50-plus years the franchise has operated.

Trading and securing draft picks are vital to a team's success, and these maneuvers are investigated with superb detail.

Team scouting for players has required much expansion over the years. In the Flames' early years, drafting Canadian and U.S. players with an occasional European player was the norm. Then numerous European countries started producing players with NHL potential. Russia was one of the last countries to permit players to come to the NHL, and the Flames were the first to have a Russian player in their lineup. Procedures for scouting potential players have also seen dramatic changes.

The business of the NHL has evolved over the years along with many variables, ranging from the value of the Canadian dollar, some Canadian teams like the Flames getting help from their U.S. counterparts, and having no salary cap to the complications that exist now with the salary cap. Ryan ventures into how those situations made an impact on the team.

I wholeheartedly recommend Ryan's work and know you'll thoroughly enjoy reading all the chapters ahead.

Peter Maher was the play-by-play radio voice of the Calgary Flames from 1981–82 until his retirement following the 2013–14 season. He also called games for the Toronto Maple Leafs for three seasons prior to his arrival in Calgary. Maher has called world championship games, six NHL All-Star games, the Stanley Cup Finals in 1980, 1986, 1989, and 2004, and the 2010 Winter Olympics. He was honoured by the Hockey Hall of Fame with the Foster Hewitt Award for excellence in broadcasting in 2006.

INTRODUCTION

THE WORLD OF professional sports can, at times, be unfair. While ideally that realm would be a true meritocracy, where the cream truly rises to the top on both the individual and team levels, unfortunately some individuals and teams enjoy baked-in structural advantages—often financial—that disrupt that meritocracy.

As aptly detailed by Michael Lewis in his 2003 book *Moneyball,* sports can be an unfair game, where rich teams have advantages over the teams that have fewer resources at their disposal. In this respect, even with attempts at leveling the financial playing field through tools such as revenue sharing and salary caps, the National Hockey League isn't quite a meritocracy, and rich teams still have advantages over the poorer teams.

But in an often unfair game, the annual NHL draft for amateur players—usually held in June—can act as a great equalizer. Even with a salary cap, rich teams can lure away free agents or players can simply opt to sign in locales closer to their families or ones that have more alluring geography or climates than other places—the sunbelt teams have that type of advantage over the likes of Edmonton and Winnipeg, unfortunately.

Every NHL franchise is allocated the same number of draft selections per year, one per round, with the draft order initially set in reverse order of the league standings from the previous season. How those picks are used is entirely the choice of each club. Some teams trade draft selections to bolster their NHL roster. Some teams keep their picks and use them to select new players. When a team drafts well, it can stockpile young talent, develop them into promising young professional players, and then either keep them or utilize them in trades. In a sporting world that can often be defined by money, draft picks are the only currency that is equal across the board.

As a team that has spent the entirety of its existence as a small-market hockey club, no matter where it's been located, success and failure for the Flames franchise has always come down to performance at the draft.

Despite having very little else in common, the cities of Atlanta, Georgia, and Calgary, Alberta, will be forever linked because of their shared hockey history—aside from perhaps major structural fires just 22 years apart during the 1800s that wiped out many of their prominent buildings, providing their NHL team with its shared nickname.

Very much a warm-weather city located south of the Mason-Dixon Line, Atlanta might seem like a pretty odd fit for a major hockey team, especially with the city already having big-league baseball (the Braves), football (the Falcons), and basketball (the Hawks) teams before the Atlanta Flames franchise was even awarded. And that's ignoring the box office competition the fledgling Flames would face from college football in the region. The expansion NHL club's survival in the Atlanta market would be determined by how good the team could get on the ice and how quickly, with the hope that a strong team would draw large crowds. Unfortunately, their rapid progression during the 1970s just wasn't enough to ensure their viability in Atlanta.

The Flames were purchased by a group of Canadian businessmen in 1980 and moved to Calgary, a Canadian farming town once best known for its rodeo that rapidly transformed into an oil and gas boomtown during the 1970s. The tools that the Flames had developed to attempt survival in Atlanta, particularly an organizational focus on scouting, drafting, player development, and the proper management of their young players as tradeable assets, became crucial components that contributed to their on-ice success upon their arrival in Canada.

Originally a southern hockey team grappling with low attendance in a major American market, the Flames moved to a small Canadian market and had to wrestle with exchange rate issues, attendance issues, competition with teams in larger markets (with more revenue), and then a transition to a hard salary cap system. In an existence that has been defined by various forms of financial challenges, the franchise's ability to find and develop young talent has been a necessity for the Flames since the beginning.

When the Flames have enjoyed on-ice success, it's usually because the team has built upon the foundation of strong drafting and development. Their glory days throughout the

1980s—where the club made the playoffs every season and advanced to the Stanley Cup Final twice—were driven by their ability to find value at the draft dating back to the club's days in Atlanta throughout the 1970s. When the Flames drafted well, those promising young players were able to help the team on the ice or as tradeable assets—often as both.

When the Flames have struggled over the years on the ice, that too has usually been as a product of struggles during the entry draft process to turn prospective picks into productive players. The club also struggled to retain their big-name, established stars throughout much of the 1990s. These problems were both products of off-ice economic pressures that drove up player salaries as the Canadian dollar was losing much of its value, making it challenging for small-market Canadian teams like the Flames to afford their best players. These challenges were made worse by struggles during entry drafts, resulting in the Flames having few blue-chippers waiting in the wings to step in for their departing stars.

The Flames' later resurgences—first in the mid-2000s and later in the mid-2010s—were fuelled in different ways by the draft. The former was due to the Flames utilizing picks as trade chips to upgrade the roster immediately; the latter was due to the club having a resurgence in their drafting and complimenting those efforts with strategic trading.

Some of the Flames' most impactful players over their history have been players they acquired via selection in the draft. From Al MacInnis, Gary Roberts, Mike Vernon, and Theoren Fleury to Mikael Backlund, Rasmus Andersson, Johnny Gaudreau, and Matthew Tkachuk, the Flames have done the majority of their team building through the draft—either by making picks, or trading picks for significant players. The best player who's ever played for the Flames franchise, 2020 Hockey Hall of Fame inductee Jarome Iginla, was acquired by the club in 1995 as part of a lengthy string of trades, all starting with the selection of Kent Nilsson by the franchise in the 1976 amateur draft.

Throughout their five decades in the NHL, the Flames have faced some challenges as a small-market hockey club—both in the Southern United States and Southern Alberta. When they've managed to overcome those challenges, it's been because of strong performances at the draft.

In *On the Clock: Calgary Flames*, we present an assortment of unique, memorable, and important stories capturing the Flames' history at the NHL draft, and how the small-market club used that annual event to level the playing field and build their franchise toward on-ice success.

1

THE SPRINT TO THE
FIRST FLAMES DRAFT

IT MAY BE a bit strange to consider, but in a very real sense, the Calgary Flames owe their entire existence to the American Basketball Association.

These days, the National Basketball Association is the undisputed top basketball league in the world. But that dominance used to be disputed by a laundry list of challenger leagues throughout the early decades of the NBA's existence—in part due to the explosion in basketball's popularity during that period and the relatively low barrier to entry for organizing another league and challenging the NBA's market share. In the 1950s and 1960s, several basketball leagues came and went— among the most notable being the American Basketball League, which folded in 1962. Arguably the most prominent, influential, and initially successful of those upstarts was the American Basketball Association, more commonly known as the ABA.

The ABA was formed in 1967 by Dennis Murphy, a former mayor of Buena Park, California, and Gary Davidson, an attorney from Orange County. After the duo went around drumming up interest and recruiting owners, the league began playing games in the fall of 1967 with 11 teams: the Anaheim Amigos, Dallas Chaparrals, Houston Mavericks, Indiana Pacers, Denver Rockets, Kentucky Colonels, Minnesota Muskies, New Orleans Buccaneers, New Jersey Americans, Oakland Oaks, and Pittsburgh Pipers. The ABA initially promised not to go after established NBA players to assuage concerns about them poaching players from the established league or diluting their talent base, but they ended up doing so anyway.

Attempting to paint the NBA as the more dull, stodgy brand, the ABA promised to provide a more energetic, hip brand of basketball. The circuit featured several rule tweaks designed to increase scoring—a longer shot clock and the three-point line were included—along with a funky multi-coloured red, white, and blue ball. The idea was to make ABA games fast-paced and colourful, and the gimmicks drew a lot of early attention to the league. It seemed well on its way to succeeding where other challenger leagues had failed.

Despite all the attention it garnered from the media and fans, especially in several of the league's home markets, the ABA had challenges translating their popularity into financial viability. After its exciting launch, the ABA ended up lurching along for a few seasons but experienced significant team turnover and eventually folded in 1976 with four teams—the Denver Nuggets, Indiana Pacers, New York Nets, and San Antonio Spurs—merging into the NBA.

But early in the 1970s, the ABA was performing well and seen as a potential blueprint for challengers to the other major sports leagues. Seeing another opportunity for a sport with a slightly higher barrier to entry—but still less expensive than challenging Major League Baseball or the National Football League—Murphy and Davidson turned their attention to hockey, and the National Hockey League.

At the time, the NHL was undergoing the first period of prolonged expansion in decades. The league had been comprised of just six teams for 25 seasons—to the point where that period has been referred to as the league's "Original Six" era—but the increased popularity of the sport led to fan demand for more clubs, leading to an initial six-team expansion in 1967 that saw teams emerge in Los Angeles (Kings), Minneapolis (Minnesota North Stars), Philadelphia (Flyers), Pittsburgh (Penguins), St. Louis (Blues), and San Francisco (California Seals). Plans were already underway for additional expansion rounds, including the placement of NHL franchises in Buffalo and Vancouver in 1970.

To the men behind the ABA, hockey's booming popularity and expansion to new markets meant there was money to be made. After recruiting former Western Canadian Hockey League executive Bill Hunter as part of their effort, Murphy and Davidson spent much of 1971 approaching potential investors and accumulating teams. In late 1971, they announced the World Hockey Association would be launching in the fall of 1972.

At the time, the NBA had its hands full with the ABA, and so their counterparts in the NHL offices were apprehensive about the WHA launch. Several established NHL owners were hesitant about entering into an expansion process in the first place, and the possibility of competing for potential expansion cities with the WHA only fed into existing fears of a weaker, more watered-down NHL product.

Concerned about the WHA beating them into prime markets, the NHL engaged in a rapid round of expansion, at least by the standards of the time. They were primarily focused on the brand-new Nassau Memorial Coliseum in Long Island, New York. While the area was considered the territory of the New York Rangers, the league was concerned about the WHA getting a foothold in the lucrative New York market with a prominent new building. Following some negotiations, Roy Boe—ironically enough, the owner of the ABA's New York Nets—was awarded an NHL franchise on November 8, 1971, to play at the Coliseum, with the Rangers being given a territorial fee in exchange for waiving their exclusive rights to the region.

In order to maintain a balanced schedule, an even number of teams, and to protect another new building the WHA might covet, the NHL also earmarked a team to play out of the brand-new Omni Coliseum in downtown Atlanta, Georgia. Atlanta Hawks owner Tom Cousins was awarded the franchise in December 1971. Both the Long Island and Atlanta teams were slated to begin play in the fall of 1972, the same month that the WHA was launching. The Atlanta team was dubbed the Flames, a reference to the burning of much of the city during the American Civil War in 1864, while the Long Island team was dubbed the New York Islanders.

"Giving NHL franchises to the Islanders and Atlanta was a last-minute thought because the WHA was starting up the next season, the same year we did, and the NHL didn't want the WHA in the two new rinks under construction, the one on Long Island and the one in Atlanta. So they granted franchises to them just before Christmas," recalled Cliff Fletcher, the Flames' inaugural general manager.

After a lot of scrambling and several proposed teams relocating before the season even began, the WHA ended up launching for the 1972–73 season with 10 teams: the Alberta Oilers, Chicago Cougars, Cleveland Crusaders, Houston Aeros, Los Angeles Sharks, Minnesota Fighting Saints, New York Raiders, Ottawa Nationals, Philadelphia Blazers, Quebec Nordiques, and Winnipeg Jets. Planned teams in Calgary, Dayton, Miami, and San Francisco never got off the ground for various reasons, primarily due to challenges in finding stable ownership or suitable arenas. With the Islanders beating them to a lease at Nassau Coliseum, the Raiders played out of Madison Square Garden as a tenant of the Rangers, who ran the building via their shared parent company. A challenging lease, competition in the hockey marketplace from the Rangers and Islanders, and low attendance led to the Raiders' owners bailing out mid-season and the WHA taking over control of the franchise.

At the time, short windows between NHL expansion teams being awarded, hiring their hockey operations staff, and then making a mad dash to the expansion and amateur drafts weren't uncommon. While the Buffalo and Vancouver franchises were a few years in the making, they weren't awarded until December 1969 and didn't officially hire their general managers until January 16, 1970, and February 25, 1970, respectively. So when the Flames officially hired St. Louis Blues assistant general manager and former Montreal Canadiens scout Cliff Fletcher as their GM on January 12, 1972, it provided the fledgling Flames (and Islanders) with essentially the same timespan to prepare as the Sabres and Canucks received two years prior.

The challenge facing the Flames was two-fold: existing NHL teams weren't keen on letting the Flames hire away their scouts in-season, so Fletcher faced challenges putting together a scouting staff. But time was also a big issue: the hockey season was already halfway completed by the time the Flames got rolling, giving them only about 10–12 weeks to view as many players as possible and put together a plan for the upcoming draft. (When the NHL added the Kansas City Scouts and Washington Capitals in 1974, the two expansion clubs hired their GMs over a year prior to their drafts and ended up having a full season of scouting to prepare.)

"I was hired as GM in January, and we had less than five months to get ready," said Fletcher. "I would have to say our knowledge of the players available in that draft was less than all the existing teams at that time because of our very late start."

The son of long-time NHL player and executive Bud Poile—at the time the Vancouver Canucks general manager, but who would ironically leave a few years later for an executive role with the WHA—David Poile was a recent college graduate looking for a job in hockey. Fletcher interviewed Poile in Vancouver for an administrative role and immediately hired him, leading Poile to hop into his car and make the lengthy drive from Vancouver to Atlanta to open the

Flames' offices with team president Bill Putnam. The Flames actually conducted their initial months of business from a trailer, as the Omni wouldn't be completed until a few weeks prior to the start of the hockey and basketball seasons. The staff in the Flames' initial draft preparations included three scouts: chief scout Don Graham, Aldo Guidolin, and Les Moore. (The club would briefly employ Al Arbour as a pro scout during the 1972–73 season before he would depart the organization for a head coaching opportunity with the Islanders.)

The major X-factor at play during the scouting process was the WHA. While the size of the Flames' scouting staff and the time they were given were pretty typical for expansion clubs at the time, the Flames not only had to compete with another expansion team when strategizing for the expansion draft, but they had to deal with 10 other teams vying for free agents, and 10 other teams conducting a parallel amateur drafting and recruitment process. Everyone was competing for the same promising young players.

The process surrounding the expansion draft largely followed the model used during the two earlier rounds of expansion in 1967 and 1970, which were crafted to assuage fears from existing NHL front offices that they would all lose their best players to these new teams. Each existing NHL club could protect two goalies and 15 skaters, and players who had only completed one pro season were exempt from the draft—they couldn't be selected and weren't required to take up a protection spot on their team's list. As a result, the Flames and Islanders were essentially limited to depth and fringe players in building their rosters.

"It was tough that first year," said Fletcher. "And the expansion team they gave us, they gave us nothing. I believe our whole expansion roster, the total number of career goals for the 20 players was less than 80. It was a challenge."

The tight expansion draft rules, and the lean rosters they produced for both the Flames and Islanders, put a big emphasis on the amateur draft to progress their team's development and help them field competitive teams.

The Islanders won a coin toss between the two clubs that determined the order in the various drafts they were involved in that year. As a result, the Flames received the first choice of goaltenders in the expansion draft and the first selection in the inter-league draft for minor league players. The Islanders received first choice of skaters in the expansion draft, and the first overall selection in the amateur draft held two days later—plus the first selection in each subsequent round, with Atlanta allotted the spot after them.

After the Islanders selected Billy Harris at first overall, the Flames selected forward Jacques Richard from the Quebec Major Junior Hockey League's Quebec Remparts at second. The remainder of the Flames picks were clustered across four leagues, with eight of the 10 players selected coming from either the QMJHL or the Western Canadian Hockey League—perhaps a product of the Flames having so few scouts and a short scouting window. As a matter of fact, half of their players were drafted from a pair of junior teams: the Remparts and the WCHL's Regina Pats.

The most successful player selected by the Flames in the 1972 draft was also the first: Richard played 215 games with the Flames between 1972 and 1975 and amassed 103 points in that span. He was traded following the 1974–75 season to Buffalo, along with cash considerations, in exchange for Buffalo's 1976 first-round pick and forward Larry Carriere.

Second-round selection defenceman Dwight Bialowas (18th overall; Regina, WCHL) played parts of two seasons with the Flames, generating 12 points in 48 games, before he was traded to the Minnesota North Stars midway through the 1974–75 season as part of a deal that brought Barry Gibbs to Atlanta. Third-round defenceman Jean Lemieux (34th overall; Sherbrooke Castors, QMJHL) served with the Flames for three seasons before he was moved mid-season in 1975–76 to Washington as part of a trade for Bill Clement. Fourth-round forward Don Martineau (50th overall; New Westminster Bruins, WCHL) played just four games with the Flames before he was swapped to Minnesota as part of a shuffle of depth players.

Defenceman Pierre Roy (130th overall; Quebec, QMHL) became a WHA regular with Quebec and New England, while goaltender Frank Blum (82nd overall; Sarnia Bees, Ontario Hockey Association) suited up briefly in the WHA with Ottawa and Toronto. Late-round picks Jean-Paul Martin (78th overall; Shawinigan Bruins, QMJHL), Scott Smith (98th overall; Regina, WCHL), Dave Murphy (114th overall; Hamilton Red Wings, OHA), and Jean Lamarre (132nd overall; Quebec, QMJHL), all forwards, never found their way to the major leagues.

The first Flames draft wasn't picture perfect and was conducted under fairly challenging circumstances for a first-time GM and a small scouting group with half of a regular length scouting season. But their inaugural draft landed the Flames several useful players who became assets for Fletcher to eventually trade for other pieces, as well as taught the club several lessons that they leveraged as they built up the hockey club over the next several years.

2

HOW JULIUS ERVING GOT THE FLAMES A 1974 DRAFT PICK

IN THE LENGTHY history of the Calgary Flames franchise, there have been quite a few complex transactions that require a bit of untangling to fully understand and appreciate. Possibly the oddest transaction they have been involved in was back during their Atlanta days, when they received a fourth-round pick in the 1974 amateur draft from the New York Islanders.

The draft pick changed hands because of a complex series of transactions involving the legendary basketball star Julius Erving, better known among fans as Dr. J.

It goes without saying, but Erving was really good at basketball. Playing primarily as a small forward, he starred at Roosevelt High School in New York and was recruited to the basketball team at the University of Massachusetts Amherst in 1968. Erving impressed in college, and after three seasons he had a strong desire to play pro basketball rather than continue in college.

Erving's pro aspirations carried with them some complications, though. At the time, the National Basketball Association's rules for eligibility for its amateur draft required players to be out of high school for four years before becoming eligible for selection—under these rules, Erving would be first eligible for the 1972 NBA Draft. But in 1969 the rival American Basketball Association created what was known as the "hardship" rule—a player could leave college early and petition the league to waive the ABA's similar eligibility rule if they endured unique financial challenges or familial needs. Erving sought, and was granted, eligibility for the ABA under the hardship rule and signed a four-year contract with the Virginia Squires that would run through the 1971–72 to 1974–75 seasons.

Erving played the 1971–72 season with the Squires and performed quite well, earning spots on the ABA's Second All-Star Team and All-Rookie Team. But late in the season, Erving made a discovery: while his primary advisor prior to signing with the Squires was Bob Woolf, another advisor, Steve Arnold, had worked for the ABA itself in the past as a player recruiter. While the ABA contended that Arnold's employment in that role had concluded before Erving's negotiations with the Squires unfolded, Erving felt it was a clear conflict of interest. Erving soon hired a new agent, Irwin Weiner, and, claiming that due to this situation he was pressured to sign a below-market contract by his old agent,

Erving filed a lawsuit in an effort to get himself out of his deal with the Squires.

As the situation surrounding his ABA contract got murky, Erving's new agent sought out playing options for his client in the NBA. This is where things got pretty complicated. Under the NBA's player eligibility rules, based on when he left high school, Erving wouldn't become eligible to sign or play in the NBA until after the 1972 NBA Draft. Additionally, the NBA announced that they would honour all existing ABA contracts, but that didn't stop Erving and the Atlanta Hawks from talking about a future together anyway—or eventually negotiating a contract.

The Hawks agreed to terms with Erving on a four-year contract on April 9, 1972, the day before the NBA draft—the first time he would be eligible for selection—but didn't announce the signing immediately because Erving and the Squires were still involved in the ABA playoffs. On April 10, the Milwaukee Bucks selected Erving at 12th overall in the NBA draft.

The case the Hawks made for why they felt they could sign Erving before his selection in the NBA draft relied on what they felt was a pretty clear precedent: Spencer Haywood. Thanks to an anti-trust lawsuit brought about by the player, Haywood had spent a year with the ABA's Denver Nuggets before seeking a contract with the NBA's Seattle SuperSonics, but the NBA had invalidated their deal because Haywood hadn't been out of high school for four years. The lawsuit argued that the NBA's draft policy regarding player age constituted an illegal restraint on trade under the Sherman Act and led to the NBA adopting a similar "hardship" rule as the ABA following a 1971 Supreme Court ruling (*Haywood vs. National Basketball Association*).

The Hawks and Erving's camp were of the mindset that Haywood's legal precedent and the creation of the NBA's own hardship rule fit Erving's circumstances, and so his signing with the Hawks should be valid. However, the NBA's perspective was that while the hardship rule would apply to someone of Erving's age and circumstances, they had agreed to honour existing ABA contracts. While Erving was eligible for selection in the NBA draft—both due to his age and due to the hardship rule, had he petitioned for early eligibility—he couldn't be signed to an NBA contract while his ABA contract was in force, even if the Hawks claimed the NBA deal wouldn't begin until his ABA deal expired. Quite simply, because of his ABA contract's existence, he could be drafted by an NBA team but not signed (either as a free agent or by the team that drafted him) until his ABA contract concluded, so the Bucks held his rights due to their draft selection.

Things got even messier in early September, when the Georgia Superior Court Justice George Ernest Tidwell ruled that Erving's ABA deal with the Squires was "voidable, terminated, and of no further force or effect." Because of that, the Hawks felt that they no longer had to wait until Erving's ABA contract expired, so they brought him to training camp— despite the NBA insisting that the Bucks had Erving's NBA rights. Three times, the Hawks planned to play Erving in exhibition games. Three times, the NBA told them that they would be fined $25,000 for having an ineligible player participate. Three times, Erving played and the Hawks were fined.

The Hawks refused to pay the fines and, along with Erving, filed a $2 million anti-trust lawsuit against the NBA.

As the Hawks and the league engaged in this battle of wills over Erving's NBA status, the Squires were involved in an appeal of the Georgia court's ruling on Erving's ABA contract. Eventually, a federal court judge issued an injunction declaring Erving's ABA contract valid and forbidding Erving from playing for any professional team except the Squires, as well as ordering the parties to resolve the dispute through arbitration. With his NBA options closed off to him, Erving begrudgingly returned to the ABA for the 1972–73 season.

However, following the 1972–73 season, the cash-strapped Squires were looking at their options to cut costs and deal with a disgruntled Erving at the same time, which resulted in a deal with the New York Nets. Following several weeks of complex negotiations with several parties involved, a deal was announced in July 1973:

The Nets received Erving and centre Willie Sojourner from the Squires.

The Squires received $750,000 cash, small forward George Carter, and the rights to power forward Kermit Washington from the Nets.

The Hawks received $425,000 cash (reimbursing them for legal fees and a bonus previously paid to Erving) from the Nets...and a fourth-round pick sent from the Islanders to the Flames in the 1974 NHL Amateur Draft.

After all of the dust settled, the Nets held Erving's ABA rights and the Bucks held his NBA rights. A couple years later, at the conclusion of a protracted arbitration and mediation process, Milwaukee received two 1976 second-round picks and $150,000 cash from the Hawks in compensation due to their signing of Erving violating league rules.

The Nets were part of the ABA merger with the NBA in 1976 and were permitted to enter the NBA with their roster kept intact, effectively voiding the Bucks' claim on Erving's NBA rights. But the financial terms of the ABA merger with the NBA were challenging for the Nets, who sold Erving to the Philadelphia 76ers in order to cover a penalty levied on them for entering the New York Knicks' home territory.

The Flames receiving a draft pick from the Islanders because of something that happened in the ABA was admittedly odd, but the Hawks and Flames were both owned by Tom Cousins while the Nets and Islanders were both owned by Roy Boe. Sending the draft pick to Atlanta was a unique way of further compensating the Hawks for abandoning their claim to Erving without Boe having to send any additional cash. Islanders general manager Bill Torrey was reportedly furious when he learned of the move, while Flames brass were initially fairly confused about what had transpired but happy to have another draft choice.

This was the first and only time a cross-sport draft pick transfer has occurred in NHL history.

"That was a unique situation," said Cliff Fletcher, the Flames' general manager at the time. "My counterpart with the Islanders was really, really upset. The same people owned the basketball and the hockey team in Atlanta, and Boe owned both teams on the island....We actually got a bonus fourth-round pick for a basketball player. It never happened before; it'll never happen again."

With the Islanders' pick, which ended up landing at 58th overall, the Flames selected defenceman Pat Ribble from the Ontario Hockey Association's Oshawa Generals. A burly two-way defender standing 6'4" and weighing more than 200 pounds, the hope was that Ribble could step into the Flames' blueline group and provide some size, physicality, and offence. He played his post-draft season (1974–75) with the Generals, then went pro with the Flames organization.

Ribble's tenure with the Flames was promising but also fairly short. He spent much of his first two pro seasons (1975–77) with the Central Hockey League's Tulsa Oilers, the Flames' top minor league affiliate, earning a look in 26 NHL games with Atlanta. He broke through as a full-time NHL player in 1977–78, playing 80 games and representing Canada at the World Championships in Czechoslovakia following the season. Once he gained a foothold in the lineup, Ribble began establishing himself as the player scouts hoped he would be— though perhaps less inclined to use his size to crash and bang along the boards than they had anticipated.

However, his tenure with the Flames ended prior to the 1979 trade deadline, after he had played 203 games and earned 43 points. Ribble was involved in an eight-player trade that saw Ribble, defencemen Greg Fox and Miles Zaharko, and forwards Tom Lysiak and Harold Phillipoff sent to the Chicago Black Hawks in exchange for defenceman Phil Russell and forwards Ivan Boldirev and Darcy Rota. The trade saw the Flames add a trio of experienced NHL players in exchange for five home-grown draft picks and some of their most exciting young pieces, notably Ribble and Lysiak. Russell became a pretty important player for the Flames, providing veteran guidance for the blueline group and serving as team captain for two seasons (1981–83) after the franchise relocated to Calgary.

The Flames received a 1974 fourth-round pick under incredibly odd circumstances, due to developments in a completely different sport (and two different leagues). But they spent that pick wisely, and Ribble became both a productive NHL player and a valuable trade chip for the hockey club.

3

HOW THE FLAMES DRAFTED THE WRONG NILSSON AND THEIR PURSUIT OF THE RIGHT ONE

IN THE 1970S, drafting, recruitment, and development of young hockey players was incredibly competitive for high-level teams. The National Hockey League was in the midst of expansion, growing from a dozen teams at the beginning of the decade to 21 teams at its close—with all those clubs drafting from the same relatively small pool of players. Factor in the World Hockey Association, which peaked at 18 teams in 1974–75, and there were a lot of teams clamouring for the same promising young players.

In this hyper-competitive environment, teams were seeking any kind of advantage. The Atlanta Flames got creative during this period, becoming one of the first teams to seriously scout Europe, building some drafting expertise in Sweden that ended up becoming one of the organization's hallmarks for decades to come.

The Flames fell in love with a Swedish prospect in the mid-'70s, and their successful pursuit of him over several years—and several drafts—enabled one of the most impressive series of asset flips in the franchise's history. It just didn't start out tremendously well, and the Flames ended up attempting to draft Kent Nilsson three times over a five-year period (and actually obtaining his rights twice).

A product of Nynashamn, Sweden, Nilsson emerged in high-level Swedish pro hockey with Djurgardens IF in 1973–74 as a 17-year-old. He scored nine goals and 17 points in 22 games, an impressive feat for a teenager in a tough league. In the 1974–75 season, just after he turned 18, he scored 13 goals and 25 points in 28 games, and also represented Sweden at the World Junior Championships. If his prior season was impressive, his follow-up was even more so. The Flames' part-time Swedish scout, raving about Nilsson's season, recommended they draft him at the upcoming 1975 amateur draft.

The Flames went to the draft and in the 12th round, 192nd overall, they drafted a forward with the surname Nilsson from Sweden's top division. Unfortunately for them, it wasn't Kent Nilsson, because he was too young to be drafted in 1975—to be eligible for that year's draft, players had to be born before January 1, 1956, and he was born on August 31, 1956.

"Our coverage in Europe was very minimal back then, the same as every other team," said Cliff Fletcher, the Flames' general manager at the time.

He summed up the situation succinctly: "We drafted the wrong Nilsson."

Instead, the Flames obtained the rights to Torbjorn Nilsson, a forward who played for Skelleftea AIK (and a teammate of Kent Nilsson on the Swedish national junior team) who was a year and a half older than Kent. Torbjorn Nilsson had nine goals and 13 points in 1974–75, just shy of half of Kent Nilsson's output that same season in the same league. Following his selection by Atlanta, Torbjorn spent four more seasons playing pro hockey in Sweden with low levels of success before moving onto other endeavours. He never signed with the Flames or played in North America.

At the time, scouting and drafting outside of North America was akin to the wild west. Few teams had full-time scouts in Europe and instead had to rely on a patchwork network of part-time bird dogs for information on up-and-coming hockey talents throughout the continent. While the quality of the scouting intelligence could be quite high, the quality of the more administrative pieces of information— such as birth dates that would be needed to confirm a player's eligibility for a particular draft—was spotty at best. Since reaching the NHL wasn't the end goal for many European players, who were often more focused on club success or being selected for their national teams for tournaments like the World Championships, individual players at that time often didn't explore NHL clubs' interests or confirm their own age eligibility for the draft. Ironically, the NHL's Central

Scouting Service—which has become a tremendous resource of consistent, centralized information for the scouting community—was established the following season.

The following season, Kent Nilsson played himself well out of the 12th round with a very strong performance. He had 28 goals and 53 points in 36 games in Sweden's elite league, and he made a second appearance at the World Juniors. The Flames tried again, selecting Kent Nilsson in the fourth round, 64th overall. However, the WHA's Toronto Toros had selected Nilsson in the second round of that league's draft a few weeks earlier. At the time Nilsson, like many Swedes of his era, was unaware of what had transpired with his North American playing rights.

"At that time, I don't think we even cared if we got drafted or not," said Nilsson. "My goal was to make the Swedish national team. I didn't know really if I got drafted, what number I got drafted, who drafted me, in the WHA or NHL."

After being selected by the Flames and the Toros, Nilsson opted to stay in Sweden for another season. He spent the 1976–77 campaign with AIK of Sweden's elite league. He had 30 goals and 47 points in 36 games that season, along with some impressive performances in international play. With the Toros letting his WHA rights lapse in the interim period—likely under the impression that he was going to be sticking in Sweden for awhile—Nilsson was lured to the Winnipeg Jets by fellow Swede Anders Hedberg (a former teammate in Djurgardens), signing as a free agent prior to the 1977–78 season.

Once he arrived in North America, Nilsson fit like a glove in the WHA. Nilsson thrived in the WHA and posted back-to-back 107-point seasons in 1977–78 and 1978–79. He was named the WHA's Rookie of the Year in his first season, its Most Gentlemanly Player in his second season, and the Jets won the Avco World Trophy as league champions. Nilsson established himself as one of the WHA's most creative and dynamic offensive players, just in time for that league to suspend operations and merge into the NHL.

Despite having popularity in a few key markets, the WHA's membership was constantly changing, with franchises folding or relocating with regularity. League revenues never quite reached what they needed to make the teams into sustainable businesses, and the large salaries offered to lure big names from the NHL (such as Hull to Winnipeg) soon became a financial drain on the league. Merger negotiations with the NHL occurred in both 1977 and 1978, at times involving as many as six teams merging into the NHL. Ultimately, a merger was agreed to in 1979 that would see the Edmonton Oilers, Winnipeg Jets, Quebec Nordiques, and New England Whalers (renamed to the Hartford Whalers during the merger) join the NHL for the 1979–80 season.

The addition of the four clubs was treated as a round of expansion by the NHL. The existing NHL clubs were given the opportunity to reclaim any former WHA players whose NHL rights they held, though the four former WHA clubs were allowed to protect two goalies and two skaters each from NHL selection by making them "priority selections" in the expansion draft. The rights of players not made priority selections by the former WHA clubs would automatically lapse and be reclaimed by the existing NHL teams.

The Flames had retained Nilsson's NHL rights during his time in the WHA and his contract with the Jets was about to expire, making him a pending free agent. Given those circumstances, the Jets opted to use their priority selections on goaltender Markus Mattsson, blueliner Scott Campbell, and winger Morris Lukowich. With Nilsson left unprotected by the Jets, the Flames received Nilsson's NHL rights via the first phase of the expansion draft and then protected him in the second phase where the four former WHA clubs could restock their rosters from the existing NHL clubs. The Jets also lost Bobby Hull in the first phase to Chicago but reclaimed him in the second phase when the Black Hawks left him unprotected.

After trying to select Nilsson in three different draft processes over a five-year period, and successfully claiming him twice, the Flames had finally acquired Nilsson. Nilsson soon agreed to a multi-year contract with the Flames. Ultimately, the persistence of Fletcher and his hockey operations and scouting staff paid off as Nilsson became tremendously valuable for the Flames franchise in two different ways.

In an immediate sense, Nilsson fit just as well with the Flames and their offensive systems as he did with the Jets. In the club's final season in Atlanta and Nilsson's first in the NHL in 1979–80, he led the club with 40 goals and 93 points. After the club's move to Calgary, he took another step offensively, amassing 49 goals and 82 assists for a 131-point season—the assist and point marks still stand as Flames single-season records. But for all his offensive prowess, Nilsson was a fairly limited player away from the puck and particularly in the defensive zone. While his ability to make superb passes and create offensive opportunities made him an easy player for

Drafted by the Flames in 1976, Kent Nilsson played two seasons in the World Hockey Association before joining the Flames in 1979 and establishing himself as their most dynamic offensive player.

coaches to like, his lack of defensive polish made him a challenging player to love.

Following a disappointing 1981–82 season, the Flames decided to shake up the coaching staff. Head coach Al MacNeil was moved into the front office, while University of Wisconsin head coach "Badger" Bob Johnson was hired as the club's new bench boss. Johnson focused on structure and defensive reliability, and the style of play he desired clashed with Nilsson's more free-wheeling, offensive-oriented stance on the game. During Johnson's tenure, Nilsson was moved from centre to the wing in order to provide his line with an effective two-way presence.

As the Flames found themselves plateauing somewhat in the Campbell Conference hierarchy—having established themselves as a regular playoff team but not yet one that could advance very far once they got there—they pondered the value of Nilsson as a potential trade chip rather than as a piece of their active roster. Nilsson missed the 1984 playoffs with an injury, but the Flames managed to advance to the second round before losing to Edmonton in a seven-game battle despite his absence. The following season (1984–85) the club disappointed, finishing third in their division and losing in the opening round to Winnipeg in a three-game sweep.

Fuelled by a drive to keep up with (and overtake) the Oilers, the Flames' desire to shake things up soon became a necessity. After entertaining a few different offers, Fletcher pulled the trigger on a trade at the 1985 NHL Draft that sent Nilsson to the Minnesota North Stars along with a 1986 third-round selection in exchange for second-round picks in 1985 and 1987. (The Flames also picked up a portion of Nilsson's salary.) While Nilsson's well-documented defensive challenges likely diminished demand for his services and drove down his price tag, the trade return of a pair of draft choices was seen as a disappointment by fans considering Nilsson's popularity and considerable offensive production during his time with the Flames—he scored at well over a point-per-game pace, even during two injury-shortened seasons. Nilsson was the Flames franchise's all-time leading scorer at the time of the trade.

Nilsson's departure was front page news in Calgary. Moreover, due to Nilsson's scoring prowess and popularity, fans were skeptical that the player selected in the second round of the 1985 draft could fill Nilsson's shoes: college centre Joe Nieuwendyk, selected at 27th overall. An Ontario product playing at Cornell University, Nieuwendyk went unselected in the 1984 draft but earned attention and accolades from scouts due to his impressive freshman campaign where he amassed 21 goals and 45 points in 29 games and was named his conference's top rookie. However, the premise of replacing the club's top scorer with a tall, skinny, fairly unknown college player led to headlines of "Joe Who?" in local newspapers. Following his selection, Nieuwendyk spent two additional seasons with the Big Red, amassing 52 goals and 106 points over 43 games, being named a first-team All-American each season. He represented Canada at the World Juniors and won a silver medal during his sophomore season and was named his conference's top player in his junior year. Nieuwendyk went pro after his junior year ended, playing 15 NHL games between the regular season and playoffs and not looking out of place.

With the other pick acquired for Nilsson, the Flames selected forward Stephane Matteau in the 1987 draft. A rugged two-way winger, Matteau experienced an offensive breakout during his draft year for the Hull Olympiques, scoring 75 points in 69 games after only amassing 14 points in his prior season. While he was highly regarded for his defensive acumen, his offensive growth pushed him into the first-round conversation that year. However, he slid into the second round, where the Flames nabbed him at 25th overall. Matteau was considered skinny for his height, and he quipped to newspaper reporters after his selection that he was planning on working in a Labatt's store the summer after his drafting to help build up his upper body. He ended up staying in major junior for two seasons following his selection, helping the Olympiques win a QMJHL championship in 1987–88.

While Matteau's arrival in pro hockey was delayed some-what, Nieuwendyk became a full-time pro in 1987–88 amidst much anticipation and fan anxiety following his 15-game appetizer the prior spring. Nieuwendyk had immense offensive success in his rookie season, scoring 51 goals and 92 points and being voted the Calder Trophy winner as the NHL's top rookie. The following season, he scored 51 goals again and was a crucial part of the Flames' 1989 Stanley Cup championship team as a 22-year-old.

Nieuwendyk spent nine seasons with the Flames, serving as captain for four seasons and winning the King Clancy Award for his humanitarian work. By the time he and Flames management reached a contract impasse during the 1995 off-season, Nieuwendyk was the club's all-time lead-ing scorer and most popular player, having accumulated 314 goals and 616 points over 577 games. But as negoti-ations on a restructured contract extension dragged into

Nicknamed "Joe Who?" upon his selection in 1985, Joe Nieuwendyk silenced doubters with back-to-back 50-goal seasons in his first two NHL seasons.

the 1995–96 season, Nieuwendyk sat out and refused to report to the club. Eventually, two months into the season, he was traded to the Dallas Stars for veteran forward Corey Millen and Western Hockey League forward Jarome Iginla, Dallas' first-round pick from the 1995 draft and a star with the Kamloops Blazers. Nieuwendyk won two more Stanley Cups—one with Dallas and another with the New Jersey Devils—before retiring in 2006. He was inducted into the Hockey Hall of Fame in 2011.

Matteau made his pro debut in 1988–89, following the completion of his junior season. While Matteau wasn't quite as good as Nieuwendyk, he emerged as a productive NHLer in his own right. He spent just one full season with the Flames, 1990–91, and he had 16 goals and 35 points in 82 games before being traded to Chicago early in 1991–92 in exchange for veteran blueliner Trent Yawney. Matteau carved out a 13-season NHL career and won the Stanley Cup with the New York Rangers in 1994. Yawney had 11 goals and 56 points in 274 games before departing the Flames organization as a free agent after five seasons.

Iginla emerged as a productive young NHL forward immediately upon his pro debut in 1996–97, but eventually he grew into the Flames' defining player of the 2000s and became one of the most successful players in modern Canadian hockey history. Iginla was the NHL's leading goal-scorer twice, won a pair of Olympic gold medals with the Canadian national team, and led the Flames to within a goal of winning a Stanley Cup in the 2004 playoffs. He eventually surpassed Nieuwendyk as the Flames' longest-serving captain and all-time leading scorer with 525 goals and 1,095 points over 1,219 games during a 16-season run with the Flames. Iginla was inducted into the Hockey Hall of Fame in 2020.

Iginla was traded to the Pittsburgh Penguins prior to the 2013 trade deadline for college forwards Kenny Agostino and Ben Hanowski, and a 2013 first-round pick. The Flames used that pick on Regina Pats forward Morgan Klimchuk, who played in the Flames farm system for several seasons but never became an NHL regular, only playing in a single NHL contest. Agostino and Hanowski both left the Flames as free agents after spending much of their time with the organization in the minors, but both made brief NHL appearances—Agostino had two points in 10 games with Calgary and 30 points in 86 career NHL games, while Hanowski had three points in a 16-game NHL career spent entirely with the Flames. The three assets that the Flames acquired for Iginla combined for just 103 career NHL games. Klimchuk was subsequently traded to the Toronto Maple Leafs for minor league defenceman Andrew Nielsen, who never played a game for the Flames.

In selecting Nilsson, then trading him for Nieuwendyk, then trading Nieuwendyk for Iginla, the Flames ended up trading their all-time leading scorer at the time for their next all-time leading scorer. Twice. The lengthy asset chain eventually ended when Nielsen left the Flames as a free agent in 2020, but a single draft pick in 1976 and two subsequent trades led to significant contributions on the club's roster almost continuously between 1979 and 2013.

The Flames' pursuit of Nilsson wasn't easy. Nilsson's on-ice contributions to the Flames alone would've made his time with the organization a net positive and justified the effort to select him in multiple drafts. When you consider that the Flames were able to transform Nilsson, as an asset, into a pair of Hockey Hall of Fame inductees in Nieuwendyk and Iginla, the sequence is an asset management marvel spanning multiple decades and general managers. In terms of value gleaned from a single asset, and the many pieces that asset later became, few draft selections have ever produced as much for a franchise as Nilsson did.

4

BUILDING A POWERHOUSE THROUGH THE DRAFT AND THE RISE OF "TRADER CLIFF"

IN THE FIRST several rounds of National Hockey League expansion throughout the 1960s and 1970s, the existing teams were concerned about losing their best players for nothing to the incoming expansion teams. As a way of assuaging the concerns of the existing clubs, the rules of the expansion drafts were designed to help teams keep their best players—between which players were deemed ineligible for selection and the number and composition of protection lists, most important players were off-limits for expansion teams.

And that created some challenges for those incoming expansion teams.

In the 1972 expansion draft, the Flames selected 21 players. In the season prior to their selection, 1971–72, those players combined for four wins and 56 goals in the NHL. Starting with their expansion season, the Flames increased goal-scoring output from the previous season every year—six seasons of continual offensive improvements—until a slight step backward in 1979–80, their final year in Atlanta. What began with 21 players who combined for four wins and 56 goals in the season leading into expansion turned into 41 wins and 327 goals at Atlanta's offensive peak in 1978–79.

Here's how Flames general manager Cliff Fletcher and his hockey operations group pulled off such an impressive feat.

Through the expansion draft itself, the Flames obtained the rights to two goaltenders, six defencemen, and 13 forwards. The goaltenders were Montreal Canadiens backup Phil Myre and Boston Bruins minor leaguer Dan Bouchard. The blueline group featured three established NHL depth players in Pat Quinn (Vancouver Canucks), Bill Plager (St. Louis Blues), and Ron Harris (Detroit Red Wings), along with minor leaguers Kerry Ketter (Montreal), Randy Manery (Detroit), and Larry Hale (Philadelphia Flyers). The most prominent player of the forward picks, and arguably the best player the Flames landed in their haul, was Pittsburgh Penguins centre Bob Leiter. Behind Leiter were established depth NHLers Billy MacMillan (Toronto Maple Leafs), Keith McCreary and John Stewart (Pittsburgh), Ernie Hicke and Frank Hughes (California Seals), Lew Morrison (Philadelphia), Lucien Grenier (Los Angeles Kings), and Rod Zaine (Buffalo Sabres).

The forwards were filled with minor leaguers Norm Gratton and Morris Stefaniw (New York Rangers), Larry Romanchych (Chicago Black Hawks), and Bill Heindl (Minnesota North Stars). Leiter, Hicke, and MacMillan combined for 35 goals in the season prior to their selection.

From there, the freshly minted general manager for the Flames began making moves, eventually earning a very appropriate nickname: Trader Cliff.

During the expansion draft process, the Flames acquired minor league defenceman Bob Paradise from Minnesota for cash.

A week after the amateur draft, the Flames sent a 1973 second-round pick and cash to Montreal for minor league forwards Rey Comeau and Lynn Powis. They also traded Heindl to the Rangers for depth forward Bill Hogaboam.

In August, they traded a 1973 third-round pick and cash to Montreal for minor league defender Noel Price.

During the 1972–73 season itself, Fletcher made four more trades.

In November, just a few months after acquiring him from the Rangers, the Flames sent Hogaboam to Detroit in exchange for depth forward Leon Rochefort. During that same week, Harris was traded to the Rangers for depth forward Curt Bennett. The Flames also claimed depth defenceman Noel Picard off the waiver wire from St. Louis.

Prior to February's trade deadline, two more trades were made. Gratton was sent to Buffalo in exchange for Butch Deadmarsh. Hicke was traded to the New York Islanders, along with a player to be named later, for blueliner Arnie Brown.

By the final day of the inaugural Flames' season, Fletcher had flipped four free assets from the expansion draft in exchange for future assets. MacMillan was sent to the Islanders in May as the previously-mentioned player to be named later to complete the Hicke–Brown swap, bringing the total to five expansion draft selections moved within the team's first year.

The Flames didn't get much established talent through the expansion draft and began their existence with a lean roster. As a result, the club had to lean on smart drafting and savvy trading in order to build their team. The first three Flames draft classes—1972, 1973, and 1974—provide some key examples as to how Fletcher and head scout Don Graham balanced the desire to package draft picks for established talent while retaining picks and using them well to draft promising young players. In short, the template for Fletcher's long-term strategy as a GM was established with those three draft classes.

The Flames held onto the majority of their 1972 draft choices, even adding a couple ninth-round picks through trades with Los Angeles and the NY Rangers where they agreed to avoid selecting certain players left exposed by those clubs. From the 1972 draft, second-overall pick Jacques Richard was able to jump into their roster immediately and was ninth for Atlanta in scoring in the 1972–73 season with 13 goals and 31 points.

A pair of 1973 draft choices—Atlanta's second- and third-round picks—were traded during the 1972 off-season to help acquire Comeau and Price, respectively. Comeau provided depth scoring, with 21 goals and 42 points in 1972–73 alone, and Price provided a steadying veteran presence on the club's blueline, with one goal and 14 points in 1972–73. The Flames had short-term holes to plug on their roster, and those draft pick swaps accomplished that goal and kept the team reasonably competitive in their first season without drastically impeding their accumulation of prospects in the future.

The Flames scouting staff liked the quality of the 1973 draft class, so Fletcher ended up making a swap with Montreal that essentially just allowed the Flames to get several draft choices a few seasons earlier than originally scheduled. The Flames moved up from fifth overall to second overall in the 1973 draft, while a second-rounder was moved up four years (from 1977 to 1973) and a third-rounder was moved up five years (from 1978 to 1973).

"That gave us an opportunity to move up from [pick] 5 to 2 to get Tom Lysiak, who was a slam-dunk to be selected at number one," said Fletcher. "The first pick in the draft was obvious; it was Denis Potvin. The Islanders got him because they had a very challenging and difficult first year. But we were able to get Lysiak number two and [Eric] Vail number 14. And number 22 we took a guy that we thought was going to be very good—Vic Mercredi from New Westminster, who tore up the Western Hockey League. He was a disappointment, but then Kenny Houston came on and had a great career. Those three players in that draft [were] as good as you could get."

The Flames agreed to terms with Lysiak very quickly, and he stepped in and led Atlanta in scoring in 1973–74 as a rookie with 19 goals and 64 points, finishing as runner-up to Potvin for the NHL's Calder Trophy as the league's top rookie. Vail, a second-round pick, didn't join the Flames until the following season (1974–75), but he won the Calder Trophy that season after scoring 39 goals and posting 60 points.

In 1974, for the first time in franchise history, the
Flames didn't control their first-round selection. They had
traded it to Montreal prior to the 1973–74 season for forward Chuck Arnason, then midway through Arnason's first
season in Atlanta subsequently traded Arnason and Paradise
to Pittsburgh for winger Al McDonough. Arnason spent
just 33 games with the Flames and had 13 points, while
McDonough spent the remainder of that season with the
club and played 35 games, where he had 19 points, before
departing to join the World Hockey Association's Cleveland
Crusaders.

Even without a first-round pick, the Flames still found
value in second-round selection forward Guy Chouinard and
fourth-round pick defenceman Pat Ribble, both of whom
quickly became NHL-level assets. Chouinard was a full-time
NHL player by 1976–77 and ended up becoming a star for
the Flames, straddling both sides of Atlanta's relocation to
Calgary and accumulating 193 goals and 529 points over nine
seasons. Ribble was a full-time NHL player by 1977–78 but
was traded to Chicago the following season.

Through this balancing act, the fledgling Flames quickly
became a team to be reckoned with. In their first season,
1972–73, they boasted three players who scored 20 goals or
more—Leiter, Comeau, and McCreary—and the club scored
191 goals and posted 25 wins. By 1977–78, just five seasons
into their tenure in Georgia, the Flames had one 30-goal scorer
(Bob MacMillan) and six 20-goal scorers (Guy Chouinard,
Tom Lysiak, Eric Vail, Willi Plett, Ken Houston, and Bill
Clement), and as a group scored 274 goals and won 34 games.
MacMillan and Clement were acquired through shrewd

trading of existing assists, while the other five goal-scorers were drafted by the Flames and developed internally.

Two asset chains show the subtle genius of Fletcher's penchant to constantly keep tinkering and tweaking his team's roster, even while his team and its players were performing quite well on the ice. One involved a couple trades over less than a decade, while the other sprawled out quite a bit longer.

Richard was the first-ever Flames draft selection in 1972, selected second overall after the Flames lost the coin toss to the Islanders. In October 1975, he was traded to Buffalo for forward Larry Carriere and a first-round pick in 1976. In January 1976, the Flames sent forwards Gerry Meehan and Jean Lemieux and Buffalo's first-rounder, previously acquired for Richard, to the Washington Capitals for forward Bill Clement. Clement spent seven seasons with the Flames before retiring after the 1981–82 season after scoring 85 goals and 224 points over 444 games with the franchise. Fletcher's tinkering allowed the club to leverage picks so they could upgrade on existing player assets, such as Richard, before they had a chance to drop in value.

The Flames selected forwards Don Martineau in the 1972 draft and John Flesch in the 1973 draft. In May 1974, the pair were sent to Minnesota in exchange for forwards Jerry Byers and Buster Harvey. Following the Byers side of the asset chain alone is pretty fascinating. Byers was traded to the New York Rangers in September 1975 for goaltender Curt Ridley. A few months later, in January 1976, the Flames traded Ridley to Vancouver for a 1976 first-round pick. They used that pick to select defenceman Dave Shand. Shand spent four seasons with the Flames before being traded to Toronto (along with a 1980 third-round pick) for a 1980 second-round pick they used to select forward Kevin LaVallee. LaVallee played several seasons with the Flames before being traded in 1983 with forward Carl Mokosak to Los Angeles for forward Steve Bozek. Bozek played several seasons with the Flames before being traded in 1988 to St. Louis, along with forward Brett Hull, for defenceman Rob Ramage and goaltender Rick Wamsley. He was re-acquired from St. Louis later in 1988 in a seven-player deal that brought forward Doug Gilmour to Calgary but was sent to Vancouver the same day with defenceman Paul Reinhart in exchange for a 1989 third-round pick.

The pick acquired from Vancouver was used on Finnish forward Veli-Pekka Kautonen, who never came over to play in North America. His selection ended an asset chain that stretched back to the very first draft class and saw Fletcher constantly trading assets in an effort to upgrade the club, and not being afraid to add components to a trade in an attempt to solve several roster issues at once. Ramage, Wamsley, and Gilmour ended up being key pieces of the 1989 Stanley Cup championship team, so it's tough to argue with the results of this strategy.

Due to the concessions made to the existing clubs around protecting their players, the expansion draft process didn't exactly set up Atlanta for success. In order to take the fledgling Flames from a ragtag bunch of odds and ends from other clubs and transform them into a success, Fletcher and his scouting staff had to make calculated gambles both on drafting and development but also on trading draft choices and players in an effort to upgrade the club's roster. For the most part, those gambles tended to pay off.

Head scout Don Graham didn't relocate to Calgary with the Flames, instead returning to the Detroit organization, but the work he and Fletcher did during their time in Atlanta created the foundation for the club's success following their move north.

5

LOOKING FOR
AN EARLY DRAFTING
EDGE BY EMBRACING
NEW SOURCES
OF PLAYERS

HOCKEY SCOUTING AND player development was relatively straightforward until the 1960s. Each of the league's six clubs had a designated territory of within 50 miles (or 80 kilometres) of their arena, and within that territory they had exclusive rights to scout and sign young players and send them to their designated local junior team. If a player came up within that area, they were essentially automatically property of a team. Amateur scouting wasn't a gigantic priority, and the onus was on teams to identify the right players within their territories and assist in their development and progression toward the NHL level. The Canadian teams (the Toronto Maple Leafs and Montreal Canadiens) and Canada-adjacent Detroit Red Wings had significant advantages due to their geographic proximity to big talent bases, but the American teams worked around this potential disadvantage by sponsoring individual junior teams and recruiting players from outside the other teams' territories to play on those sponsored clubs. For example, Bobby Orr was recruited by the Boston Bruins and played on one of their sponsored junior teams, the Oshawa Generals.

Things changed in a major way in the 1960s. The previous system of junior team sponsorship was phased out when NHL president Clarence Campbell instituted the amateur draft in 1963, giving all the league's clubs the same opportunity at acquiring players. However, the more significant change came in terms of the rapid and massive expansion of major league clubs looking for talent. In 1966–67, the NHL had six teams—Boston, Chicago Blackhawks, Detroit, Montreal, the New York Rangers, and Toronto—an amount they had sustained since 1942. That number doubled the following season, with the addition of six NHL expansion clubs: the California Seals, Los Angeles Kings, Minnesota North Stars, Philadelphia Flyers, Pittsburgh Penguins, and St. Louis Blues. With the introduction of the World Hockey Association in 1972, and subsequent NHL expansion to counter the WHA, the number of big-league teams peaked at 32 by 1974–75. After the WHA folded in 1979 and four of its clubs (Edmonton Oilers, Hartford Whalers, Quebec Nordiques, and Winnipeg Jets) joined the NHL, the number of clubs stabilized at 21—still a significant jump from where things had been when the expansion process began 12 years prior.

Needless to say, after a period of relative scouting detente, suddenly there was a significant amount of competition for promising young players. A club that found any inside track or inefficiency in the system that it could exploit would have a tremendous advantage. Against considerable odds, within this environment the Flames organization managed to thrive through their approach to scouting, drafting, and player development.

Under the guidance of general manager Cliff Fletcher and head scouts Don Graham (in Atlanta) and Gerry Blair (after the club's 1980 relocation to Calgary), the Flames were one of the clubs that found value in the draft by exploiting a few market inefficiencies and by going where others wouldn't or couldn't.

Once the NHL instituted the amateur draft in 1963, the primary focus of teams and their scouting departments was North America: the Quebec Major Junior Hockey League, the Ontario Hockey Association, the Western Canadian Hockey League, and a smattering of key players or teams from the smaller junior circuits. Zero selections were made from teams playing outside of North America until 1969. The players scouted, selected, and recruited were either Canadians playing in local junior leagues or Canadian university leagues, or they were Canadians recruited to play in collegiate teams in the United States. The only non-Canadian drafted between 1963 and 1967 was German-born Orest Romashyna, who was playing junior hockey in Ontario at the time. Michigan Tech forward Herb Boxer became the first American player drafted when he was taken by Detroit in 1968.

The reasoning for largely ignoring European players and trending toward taking American collegiate players only in the later stages of the amateur draft was pretty simple. Teams at the time were unlikely to get much value from those selections because of the players' lack of interest at immediately pursuing playing in the NHL. Especially prior to the NHL's expansion, big-league jobs in North America were sparse and players who had played in Canadian junior leagues were more familiar with the style of game NHL clubs valued. In turn, NHL clubs were more familiar with them, giving those players an inside track on the few roster spots that existed. As such, European players were unlikely to risk their familiar spots within their club team's system for the unlikely chance of an NHL job, and college players also had little incentive to leave school early to pursue big-league dreams.

But as the 1970s approached, and the number of teams and roster spots available in the NHL dramatically increased—and incentive structures for European and collegiate players changed in turn—NHL clubs slowly began considering players from outside their traditional regions. St. Louis selected Finland's Tommi Salmelainen at 66th overall in 1969, becoming the first European-based player selected in the NHL draft. But a second European had yet to be selected by the time Atlanta showed up on the NHL scene in 1972.

The 1972 edition of the amateur draft, the first for the Flames, was fairly representative of how drafting was conducted at the time—152 players were selected in that draft, with only 20 selected from outside the main Canadian junior leagues. Those 20 players were still all selected from within North American hockey: Canadian universities in eastern

Canada, collegiate players from schools in the northern United States, and a smattering of players from smaller Canadian junior leagues. Zero European players were selected. The league's clubs were fishing almost exclusively in the same over-subscribed pond, providing a big incentive to anybody who could find an inside track in Europe.

After the Flames got through their whirlwind inaugural draft, they shifted their focus to finding a competitive advantage. Europe quickly became a potential gold mine, if only they could find a pathway in.

There were challenges involved in building out a European scouting network. With the entirety of their scouting apparatus located in North America, the Flames had to go looking for individuals with sufficient knowledge and expertise not only in the various European leagues, but also knowledge of which players had skill sets that could translate effectively to the much different style of the North American game. Other challenges related to logistics and cost. The ongoing Cold War and the existence of the Iron Curtain between the Soviet Union's sphere of influence and the rest of Europe made a lot of extremely talented players from Russia and Czechoslovakia generally considered to be off-limits to NHL clubs—sure, they were technically available for selection, but they were extremely unlikely to defect from their home countries and therefore would be wasted picks. Additionally, players with contracts in Europe carried with them some complications, as NHL clubs would have to negotiate exits for those players from their club teams in order to sign them to deals in North American—usually by cutting a cheque to buy them out of their deals. Finally, building a network of knowledgeable full-time scouts in Europe comparable to the existing North American scouting infrastructure would be expensive.

In terms of the Flames, rather than replicate the scouting coverage levels they had in North America, they focused on a few key areas of Europe with part-time scouts and went from there. (They didn't employ a full-time European scout until the 1990s.) Their initial focus area was Sweden, but as they became more successful and comfortable in scouting European players, they built out their network of part-time scouts in places like Finland, Germany, and eventually Czechoslovakia and the Soviet Union later in the 1980s. Competition for the few European scouts with strong expertise likely drove up wages a bit, but utilizing part-timers instead of full-time scouts likely kept the value proposition for expanding scouting in Europe in the black.

A year after five Swedes were selected in the 1974 event, the Flames took their first European player, Torbjorn Nilsson, in the 12th round of the 1975 NHL Amateur Draft. That edition was the most international the NHL had experienced to that point, with six European-based players selected from Sweden, Finland, and Latvia. European influences in the NHL draft continued to expand from there, with the Flames firmly in the midst of that trend.

The next few drafts saw the Flames continue to dip their toe in the European talent pool. In 1976, a year after selecting Torbjorn Nilsson, the Flames selected Swedish forward Kent Nilsson in the fourth round. Two years later they selected German goaltender Bernhard Engelbrecht, their first non-Swedish European selection, in the 12th round. Swedish forward Hakan Loob was selected in the ninth round in

1980, followed by fellow Swedes Peter Madach in the fourth round in 1980 and Mats Kihlstrom in the sixth round in 1982. During those early drafts of their European experimentation, the Flames never selected more than one European in a draft class, but they took one in most years.

The proverbial floodgates opened in 1983 in terms of European selections by the Flames, starting a new status quo for the club where Europeans were a regular part of their drafting mix. In 1983, the Flames took three Europeans: a pair of Czechoslovakians—forward Igor Liba in the fifth round and blueliner Jaroslav Benak in the 11th round—and Russian star Sergei Makarov in the 12th round. The Flames selected four more Czechs in 1984—winger Petr Rosol in the fourth round, centre Jiri Hrdina in the eighth round, centre Petr Rucka in the 10th round, and defenceman Rudolf Suchanek in the 12th round—along with Finnish winger Joel Paunio in the fifth round and Swedish defender Stefan Jonsson in the 11th round. That made six Europeans in a dozen selections in that draft class. The 1985 draft class included four Europeans from four different countries: Sweden's Roger Johansson (fourth round), Finland's Esa Keskinen (fifth round), Germany's Peter Romberg (10th round), and Russia's Alexander Kozhevnikov (11th round).

During this period, the Flames were making calculated gambles on European players at different points during each draft. With increasing competition for players throughout the world, the challenge was to find the proverbial sweet spot in the draft order where a few factors were key—the player's perceived skill and ability to translate what made them effective at previous levels of hockey to the NHL style of game, along with the perceived likelihood that they would be available to play in the NHL within the near future. North American players faced few, if any, barriers to their availability to NHL clubs, but their talent may be variable. Meanwhile, European leagues had a high level of talent, but a bevy of obstacles existed to their availability. In addition to the previously mentioned contractual entanglements they may have had, players plying their trade in Eastern Europe behind the Iron Curtain—most notably in Russia or Czechoslovakia—and their families potentially faced harsh legal and political consequences in their homelands had they attempted to defect to the west to play hockey. While that factor became much less of a challenge after the collapse of the Soviet Union in the late 1980s, political challenges remained an issue regarding Russian players for years to follow.

Despite all the challenges and complications regarding scouting, drafting, and recruiting European players throughout the 1970s and 1980s, several players drafted from outside North America became very successful players for the Flames.

Kent Nilsson, the second Swede ever drafted by the franchise in 1976, became an instant scoring sensation after he joined the club in 1979. By the time Nilsson left the club via trade with the Minnesota North Stars in 1985, he was the Flames all-time leader with 562 points over six seasons. In 1983, Loob arrived in Calgary and became one of the most beloved players on the club, with his time with the Flames overlapping with Nilsson's for two seasons. Loob became known as one of the most effective goal-scorers in the league, standing as of 2022–23 as the lone Swede to ever score 50 goals in a single season. Loob had 429 points over six NHL seasons, all with the Flames. He won the Stanley Cup with the Flames in 1989 and then returned to Sweden to continue his playing career.

The Czech national team allowed Hrdina to join the Flames following the 1988 Winter Olympics, which was considered a major coup for the club at the time—virtually all Czechs who had made the move to the NHL prior to then had done so under dramatic, often dangerous, circumstances. Hrdina had a brief but important career in North America; he won the Stanley Cup in 1989 and had 94 points over parts of four seasons with the Flames. He was traded to the Pittsburgh Penguins in 1990 in exchange for defenceman Jim Kyte, with the Penguins hoping he could help young Jaromir Jagr adapt to the United States. The gambit worked, and Hrdina won two more Cups with the Penguins before returning to Europe.

After lengthy negotiations, Sergei Priakin was permitted by the Soviet national team to join the Flames late in the 1988–89 season and played just a handful of games—two in the regular season and one in the playoffs—during the club's Stanley Cup run. He had just 11 points in sporadic use over three seasons before returning to Europe. However, Priakin's arrival in Calgary paved the way for the arrival of Sergei Makarov the following season. Makarov was already a legendary figure in international hockey due to his role on the Soviet national team's KLM line—alongside Vladimir Krutov and Igor Larionov—but there was some question regarding how his skills would translate to the NHL style of game. Makarov quickly silenced doubters, winning the Calder Trophy as top rookie in 1989–90 as a 31-year-old, prompting a maximum age provision to be added to the award's rules, which has become known as the Makarov Rule. Makarov had 292 points over four seasons with the Flames and was inducted into the Hockey Hall of Fame in 2016.

"We felt it was an opportunity," said Fletcher, of the Flames' broadened drafting focus. "There was only a small percentage of teams in the league that were really focusing on [U.S. colleges], and we did that. And we also hired a top guy in Europe. We got Hakan Loob, and we got Kent Nilsson and later on we got Sergei Makarov, who was the Gretzky of Russia back at that time. We were early into the European and college markets, and we felt that gave us an edge in those two places because the junior leagues in Canada were scouted to death. I don't think there wasn't a player who any team didn't know. But there was an opportunity in Europe and at U.S. colleges, and a lot of teams didn't know a lot of the players."

Not every European player selected by the Flames became a star. But their willingness to gamble on European talent and eagerness to give their European draft choices a chance to compete for NHL roster spots definitely gave them an edge in drafting, development, and recruiting. It undoubtedly helped the club in their ascent up the standings during a challenging, competitive, tumultuous time in the hockey world.

6

1984: THE BEST
FLAMES DRAFT
CLASS EVER

THE 1972 AMATEUR draft process was a sprint for the Flames. Several of the subsequent early Atlanta draft classes saw elements of experimentation in them, with general manager Cliff Fletcher and head scout Don Graham testing out theories, examining market inefficiencies, and attempting to exploit scouting market weaknesses during the 1970s. After the Flames moved to Calgary in 1980, Graham opted to return to the Detroit Red Wings organization and Gerry Blair became head scout.

Because of the many variables involved—both controllable and uncontrollable, anticipated and unanticipated—drafting and development has elements of both art and science involved in its success or failure. But after years of trial and error, through the application of the organization's methods and guidelines, and some advantageous luck, the 1984 NHL Draft will go down in history as Fletcher's finest work as a manager during a draft.

Two other Flames drafting performances deserve honourable mentions for how well their selections turned out for the club: 1979 and 1981.

The 1979 amateur draft saw the Flames select defence-man Paul Reinhart in the first round (12th overall; from the Kitchener Rangers, Ontario Major Junior Hockey League); defenceman Mike Perovich (23rd overall; Brandon Wheat Kings, Western Hockey League) and goaltender Pat Riggin in the second round (33rd overall; Birmingham Bulls, World Hockey Association); forward Tim Hunter in the third round (54th overall; Seattle Breakers, WHL); forward Jim Peplinski in the fourth round (75th overall; Toronto Marlboros, OMJHL); forward Brad Kempthorne in the fifth round (96th overall; Brandon, WHL); and forward Glenn Johnson in the sixth round (117th overall; University of Denver, NCAA).

Reinhart was a great skater who moved the puck well and basically played as a fourth forward much of the time. He had 445 points for the Flames over nine seasons. Riggin was a solid goaltender. He played three seasons for the Flames, winning 51 games, before being traded to Washington with Ken Houston in 1982 for three draft picks and two players. Hunter became a reliable defensive forward and one of the most feared enforcers in hockey. He posted 108 points and 2,405 penalty minutes—still an all-time franchise record—over 11 seasons with the Flames. Peplinski could fight, score, or shut down the opposition. He posted 424 points over parts of 11 seasons with the team. Peplinski served as co-captain of the team for five seasons, and both he and Hunter were part of the 1989 Stanley Cup–winning team.

The 1979 draft produced four NHL regulars, three of them quite long-term regulars, in seven draft selections.

The 1981 amateur draft saw the Flames take defenceman Al MacInnis in the first round (15th overall; Kitchener, Ontario Hockey League), goaltender Mike Vernon in the third round (56th overall; Calgary Wranglers, WHL), forward Peter Madach in the fourth round (78th overall; HV71, Sweden), forward Mario Simioni in the fifth round (99th overall; Toronto, OHL), forward Todd Hooey in the sixth round (120th overall; Windsor, OHL), defenceman Rick Heppner in the seventh round (141st overall; Mounds View, high school), defenceman Dale DeGray in the eighth round (162nd overall; Oshawa, OHL), defenceman George Boudreau in the ninth round (183rd overall; Matignon, high school), and forward Bruce Eakin in the 10th round (204th overall; Saskatoon Blades, WHL).

Compared to the 1979 class, the 1981 class was better at the top end and much leaner later on. MacInnis was one of the premier offensive blueliners of his era, with a slapshot that was both feared and revered league-wide for its velocity and accuracy. He played 13 seasons with the Flames, won the Conn Smythe Trophy as most valuable player during the Flames' Stanley Cup win in 1989, and left the organization— via a trade to the St. Louis Blues—as the club's all-time leader in points. He was inducted into the Hockey Hall of Fame in 2007 and his number was honoured by the Flames in 2012.

Vernon played 13 seasons in the Flames net—an 11-season initial run, followed by two more seasons late in his career—and was the team's starting goaltender throughout essentially the most glorious parts of their glory years, two Presidents' Trophy seasons (1987–88 and 1988–89), and trips to the Stanley Cup Final in 1986 and 1989. Until the emergence of Miikka Kiprusoff in the mid-2000s, Vernon owned all of the franchise's goaltending records. His number was retired by the Flames in 2007 and he was inducted into the Hockey Hall of Fame in 2023.

Long-time hockey executive David Poile, then an assistant general manager with the Flames, recalled seeing Vernon play with the WHL's Calgary Wranglers in a unique set of circumstances.

"Atlanta was not the hotbed of hockey," said Poile. "We didn't have a fantastic following at that time of course; that's why we moved. When I get to Calgary, it was everything. Night and day, 24 hours a day, hockey, hockey, hockey. I was married, two young kids, so our date night was going to a Calgary Wranglers game. They had a goalie by the name of Mike Vernon, and I'm not taking any credit for this, but if you ask my wife, one player she feels responsible for, she'd probably say, 'We scouted Mike Vernon.' And then we drafted him in the third round."

DeGray and Eakin both had minimal NHL careers. DeGray played 28 games with the Flames, Eakin just nine, with DeGray's 153-game NHL career lasting parts of five seasons and Eakin's lasting parts of four seasons.

The 1983 draft class also deserves some praise. Arguably none of the players selected became bonafide stars in the NHL; 12th round selection Sergei Makarov was probably the best player the Flames selected, and he was already a legend from his time in the Soviet Union before he arrived in North America and played for seven seasons in the NHL. Despite the lack of star power in the 1983 class, six of the players selected by the Flames made it to the NHL, with three of them playing more than 300 games in the league in addition to Makarov.

First-round pick Dan Quinn (13th overall) played more than 800 NHL games, splitting his 14 NHL seasons across eight different teams.

Third-round selection Brian Bradley (51st overall) spent 13 seasons in the NHL, including playing for six seasons at nearly a point-per-game pace for the expansion Tampa Bay Lightning.

Third-round pick Perry Berezan (55th overall) played nine years in the NHL, including five in Calgary. He was the player credited with scoring Steve Smith's infamous "own goal" in Game 7 of the 1986 Smythe Division Final, which saw the Flames eliminate the Edmonton Oilers in the playoffs for the first time.

Fourth-rounder Kevan Guy (71st overall) and fifth-rounder Igor Liba (91st overall) also made the NHL, but neither had particularly significant careers once they arrived in the league.

The 1979 and 1981 draft classes were definitely notable, and the Flames landed good players who had lengthy NHL runs, and the 1983 class had a lot of strong depth players selected. But the 1984 crop takes the cake for the amount of value the Flames found across the entire draft.

At the time, the club's general draft philosophy was to take their big swing in the first round, going for the player with the most upside and overall potential. Subsequent to that, usually in the second round, they aimed to grab a player who was a bit more of a sure thing—a player who was more mature and developed and may not have as much pure upside but would likely be somebody who was able to contribute at the NHL level. The idea was to use the early picks to balance between the two players' potential upsides and downsides; by selecting a player who was closer to their developmental potential with their second pick, the Flames ensured that their farm system kept getting replenished. After that, the team went through the remainder of the draft, selecting from its draft list while attempting to address the organization's positional needs, the upside/downside balancing act, and attempting to take different types of players from throughout the hockey world.

The 1984 class represents the Platonic ideal for what the Flames were trying to accomplish with their drafting. The club made 12 selections. Six of them, exactly half, ended up playing NHL games. Four of those six played more than 1,000 NHL games, and one of those four was inducted into the Hockey Hall of Fame. The players selected in 1984 played 1,770 regular season games for the Flames and three played a major part, in one way or another, in the franchise's first (and only) Stanley Cup victory in 1989.

Ultimately, the Flames left that draft in Montreal with a dozen new players:

- Ottawa 67's (OHL) left wing Gary Roberts at 12th overall (first round)
- Sault Ste. Marie Greyhounds (OHL) defender Ken Sabourin at 33rd overall (second round)
- Edina High School left wing Paul Ranheim at 38th overall (second round)
- HC Dukla Jihlava (Czechoslovakia) right wing Petr Rosol at 75th overall (fourth round)

- HIFK (Finland) left wing Joel Paunio at 96th overall (fifth round)
- Penticton Knights (British Columbia Hockey League) right wing Brett Hull at 117th overall (sixth round)
- Red Deer Rustlers (Alberta Junior Hockey League) defender Kevan Melrose at 138th overall (seventh round)
- HC Sparta Praha (Czechoslovakia) centre Jiri Hrdina at 159th overall (eighth round)
- University of Wisconsin (NCAA) defender Gary Suter at 180th overall (ninth round)
- HC Sparta Praha (Czechoslovakia) centre Petr Rucka at 200th overall (10th round)
- Sodertalje SK (Sweden) defender Stefan Jonsson at 221st overall (11th round)
- Motor-Ceske Budejovice (Czechoslovakia) defender Rudolf Suchanek at 241st overall (12th round)

Roberts was the Flames' annual big home run swing early in the draft. A product of North York, Ontario, Roberts played his major junior in Ottawa of the OHL. Roberts' draft-eligible season with the 67's was his second with the club, and he emerged as a rugged power forward who was equally likely to get into a scrap as score a key goal—he had 27 goals and 144 penalty minutes in the regular season, and his 57 points ranked ninth on his team.

What likely elevated Roberts's draft stock in a major way was his postseason performance. The 67's had an excellent postseason in 1983–84, beating the Kitchener Rangers in five games to win the J. Ross Robertson Cup and then beating Kitchener again two weeks later to win the Memorial Cup. Roberts had a strong postseason, with his 10 goals in the OHL playoffs standing tied for second on his team, though his Memorial Cup performance was comparatively quiet with one goal and five points in five games. But Roberts' rugged playing style— he was termed as "aggressive," "nasty," and "antagonistic" by Fletcher in his comments to the media following the pick—fit the Flames' needs like a glove. The only real gamble was if Roberts could refine his game enough to be a successful offensive player at the next level. Roberts was reportedly 10th on the Flames' list, per a report at the time from the *Calgary Herald*.

A defensive specialist with Sault Ste. Marie, Sabourin was praised in his draft year for his strong two-way game and how well he utilized his size. His offensive potential was seen as rather moderate at the pro level, but the maturity of his game relative to other blueliners of his age had him perceived as a relative safe selection in the second round and well in keeping with how the club tried to hedge their bets after their first-round pick.

The star player for the Minnesota high school state champions from Edina in 1983–84, Ranheim was a player lauded by scouts during his draft year for his size, passing ability, and using his size to score around the net. He was touted by some scouts as a potential second-round selection and went toward the end of that round. His draft stock may have been slightly diminished by a combination of concerns about the quality of competition he faced in high school, questions about how much of his offensive success was due to his size advantage and how that might translate to the pros, and indications that he would play the full four years in college with the University of Wisconsin. According to a *Calgary Herald* report from prior to the draft, Ranheim was 14th on the Flames' pre-draft ranking.

The remainder of the 1984 crop featured the usual slate of developmental gambles, often in the form of players selected outside their first year of draft eligibility. Beyond the first two rounds, the Flames made a trio of later selections that seemed like prudent uses of their picks. Hull, the son of long-time NHL star Bobby Hull, was a fairly raw 20-year-old player away from the puck but had goal-scoring talents in the BCHL that had scouts buzzing. He broke the BCHL's goal-scoring record in 1983–84, his third year of draft eligibility. He had committed to Minnesota–Duluth for college, making his sixth-round selection more of a long-term investment, with the hope that he would mature physically and round out his defensive game in college.

Hrdina and Suter were both calculated, later-round gambles. Hrdina's talent was unquestioned, and he had multiple medals from major international events such as the Olympics and World Championships. But the combination of his age (26) and the questions concerning his availability to NHL clubs as a Czechoslovakian player pushed his selection to the late rounds. Suter was a late-blooming 20-year-old freshman at the University of Wisconsin who didn't have a huge role for his team, but the Flames became convinced of his talent after their scouts viewed him in the Badgers' practices and decided to take a flier on him in the late rounds.

There are no sure things in any draft class, but what set the 1984 Flames draft crop apart from others is how many of Fletcher's rolls of the dice turned out favourably over the course of the years that followed.

"The thing about scouting and drafting, it's quite a few years before you realize the impact that those draft picks had or didn't have," said Fletcher. "When I looked back in the '90s at how we drafted in the '80s, and I was gone, I had gone to Toronto, and I looked back on how Calgary had drafted in the '80s, I thought we did a remarkable job there. But you don't know that at the time, you don't know that for five years, even.... So to get a full reading on how you did in the draft, it's seven or eight or nine years."

Roberts disappointed in his first NHL training camp as an 18-year-old; he was criticized at the time by head coach Bob Johnson for his skating and overall fitness level. Roberts returned to the OHL for the next two seasons and dominated. He debuted with the Flames midway through the 1986–87 season and over the course of the next several seasons continued to refine his game, his increased fitness—as a response to Johnson's criticisms—helping him gradually emerge as a unique blend of pace, physicality, and scoring prowess.

The club's depth in the mid-to-late '80s allowed them to bring him along slowly rather than throw him right into the deep end of the pool, which gave him the ability as a fairly raw young player to learn the various facets of the NHL game from his coaches and veteran teammates and find ways to refine and fill out parts of his game. Over time, Roberts emerged as a really important player for the Flames, particularly in the early 1990s as more veteran members of the 1989 Stanley Cup championship team gradually moved on to other clubs.

At the peak of his tenure with the Flames in the early 1990s, Roberts formed a really effective trio with Joe Nieuwendyk and Theoren Fleury that had the ability to be a thorn in the opposition's side regardless of the zone they were playing in or the game situation. However, Roberts' playing style gradually took its toll on his body, as years of crashing and banging in the corners and battling with the opposition around the front of the net led to injuries that piled up and limited his effectiveness. A degenerative injury involving nerves in his neck limited him to just eight games in 1994–95 and required two surgeries. He missed the first half of 1995–96, returning to play 35 games and being voted the winner of the Bill Masterton Award (for perseverance and dedication to hockey) for his comeback. However, the neck injury recurred, and he missed the entire 1996–97 season and briefly retired before a chiropractic treatment was found that drastically improved his condition and allowed him to return to play.

In an effort to manage Roberts' ongoing health by limiting the amount of travel mileage he would have to undertake, the Flames worked out a four-player swap with the Carolina Hurricanes. The Flames received two-way forward Andrew Cassels and young goaltending prospect Jean-Sebastien Giguere in exchange for Roberts and incumbent netminder Trevor Kidd (the club's first-round pick from 1990). The move to the east, with shorter and less frequent plane travel involved in their seasons, helped give Roberts a new lease on life. He played another 11 seasons, all in the Eastern Conference, before retiring in his early 40s and transitioning to become a fitness consultant for NHL players and teams. Roberts had 505 points over parts of 10 seasons with the Flames, and injuries likely robbed him of reaching 1,000 points over his full career—he finished with 910 points.

After a solid, if unspectacular, freshman season at the University of Wisconsin, Ranheim played three more seasons for the Badgers and developed into one of the better all-around forwards in college hockey by his senior year. He spent the 1988–89 season primarily in the minors, where he was a standout for the International Hockey League's Salt Lake Golden Eagles, the Flames' top affiliate. Ranheim made the Flames out of training camp the following fall and established himself as a really effective second-tier forward. He never reached the lofty heights that Roberts did, but Ranheim was a strong depth piece for the club, amassing 194 points over six seasons. He was traded to Hartford at the 1994 trade deadline as part of a six-player trade involving another Flames selection from the 1984 draft.

Brett Hull spent two seasons at the University of Minnesota–Duluth, establishing himself immediately as one of the top offensive forwards in the entire NCAA. He signed with the Flames following his sophomore season, making his NHL debut at the tail-end of the 1985–86 season and playing five games (scoring one goal). He spent most of the 1986–87 campaign with Salt Lake in the IHL, again posting strong scoring numbers. He became a full-time NHLer in 1987–88, where he scored just shy of a point-per-game pace with 50 points in 55 games, establishing himself as one of the best young players in the NHL. With Hull excelling offensively and the Flames in the middle of a march to their first Presidents' Trophy as the league's best regular season team, Hull was traded to the St. Louis Blues prior to 1988's trade deadline.

Trading Hull raised some eyebrows around the hockey world, and curiosity about the move only increased in subsequent seasons as Hull became every bit as strong an NHL goal-scorer as he was in junior-A, college, and the IHL. The Flames of that era had no trouble scoring lots of goals but needed some help away from the puck to ensure that their opponents had fewer chances to score against them. As such, Fletcher was able to package Hull and veteran forward Steve Bozek to the Blues in exchange for steady backup goalie Rick Wamsley and sturdy defence-first blueliner Rob Ramage. Wamsley helped spell Mike Vernon for the next several seasons, while Ramage provided much-needed leadership, maturity, and physical presence on the blueline. Wamsley and Ramage were key parts of the Flames' 1989 Stanley Cup team, while Hull played for another 17 NHL seasons, won two Stanley Cups, and was inducted into the Hockey Hall of Fame in 2009. It could be argued that both teams got what they needed from the swap—though it must have been awkward for the Flames to watch how great Hull turned out to be as an NHL goal-scorer in the years that followed their championship victory.

Suter played his sophomore season with Wisconsin, where the Flames' predictions of his offensive breakout proved prudent. He doubled his production from his freshman year, jumping from four goals and 22 points to 12 goals and 51 points. He signed with the Flames following the season, earned a roster spot with an excellent training camp, and immediately emerged as a top-flight blueliner in the NHL, winning the Calder Trophy as the league's top rookie in 1986–87. From his arrival, he was a part of a tremendous one-two punch alongside Al MacInnis on the Flames' power play, and became one of the better offensive defencemen in hockey. The only knocks on Suter's performance were related to his rough injury luck, as he tended to get hurt at the worst possible times—he missed big chunks of the Flames' long playoff runs in 1986 and 1989, not appearing in either trip to the Stanley Cup Final due to injuries. He had 564 points over nine seasons with the Flames. Eventually he was sent to Hartford in the midst of his ninth season with the Flames, with Suter, Ranheim, and Ted Drury going to the Whalers in exchange for James Patrick, Michael Nylander, and Zarley Zalapski. Suter was subsequently traded to the Chicago Blackhawks the following day.

There is no such thing as a "perfect" drafting performance by a club. All a team and its scouting staff can attempt to do is provide the hockey operations group with depth and options, and perhaps a difference-making on-ice performer in the earlier rounds of the draft. The 1984 NHL Draft represents perhaps the closest the Flames have come to a "perfect" draft, with several difference-making players, a few effective depth players, and a draft performance that gave the club significant assets and flexibility to maneuver in the future.

7

GONE BUT NOT FORGOTTEN: THE LIVES AND LEGACIES OF GEORGE PELAWA AND MICKEY RENAUD

IN EVERY DRAFT class, there are promising players who don't pan out as their drafting club expected. After all, when you're looking at young men aged anywhere between 17 and 20 in their draft years, it's challenging to project how they will develop as hockey players or as people. Sometimes players get injured and their development derails as a result. Sometimes players see their development simply plateau. Sometimes, very rarely, players unfortunately pass away.

Out of hundreds of draft selections made by the Flames over nearly five decades in the National Hockey League, two promising young players tragically passed away before they had the opportunity to play professional hockey. Despite their deaths, each player left a strong, positive legacy behind in their local community.

Growing up, George Pelawa was the kind of kid that excelled at nearly every sport. Born and raised in Bemidji, Minnesota, Pelawa was known for his outgoing, boisterous personality and his competitive spirit. That spirit drove him to become a high-level competitor in baseball (as a first baseman), football (as a linebacker), and in hockey, where he was a star right wing growing up. He was scouted by the Minnesota Twins for baseball and recruited by several college football programs, but his primary sports love was hockey. And he was excellent at it.

Playing for Bemidji High School, Pelawa obliterated his school's scoring records. He was the team's star attraction, leading them to state championships in both his junior and senior years. Listed at 6'3" and 245 pounds, Pelawa would have been the largest player in NHL history at the time, and local fans and big-league scouts alike came to Minnesota high school hockey games to get a look at a big-bodied teenager hit, score, and somehow move around the ice like somebody 30 pounds lighter. Whether it was because of his size or his skill, Pelawa's prowess was surrounded by a certain mystique in terms of how he played the game. In one game, legend had it, Pelawa knocked an opposing player unconscious with his chest. In another, the normally gentle giant got knocked down by an opponent and threatened to break that player's arm after he got back up.

Pelawa was named Minnesota's Mr. Hockey—an annual award given to the top senior high school player in the state—following the 1985–86 season and had committed to the University of North Dakota. Pelawa, a massive hockey fan in addition to being a great young player, idolized Joel Otto, a fellow Minnesotan seven years his elder. Otto had been a star player at Division II Bemidji State and a Hobey Baker Award finalist in 1983–84 and had signed with the Flames as an undrafted free agent, making his NHL debut during the 1984–85 season.

At the NHL draft that year in Montreal, Pelawa was one of two highly touted high school players expected to be selected early. After Connecticut defenceman Brian Leetch went to the New York Rangers, the stars aligned, and the Flames selected Pelawa at 16th overall. The Flames highly valued Pelawa's overall package—his size, his maturity, his enthusiasm, and his skill—and were optimistic about his future development. At the time, general manager Cliff Fletcher declared to the *Calgary Herald*: "We wanted a big winger and we got one."

Pelawa's summer involved him training with Otto and participating in the Olympic Sports Festival in Houston, where he impressed during on-ice sessions involving some of the top young hockey players in the United States. His future seemed extremely bright, with a couple seasons projected at North Dakota along with the potential of a spot on the United States Olympic team at the 1988 Olympics hosted, coincidentally, in Calgary. An NHL contract, while never a certainty, seemed like a very strong possibility. The running joke was that the only thing that could stop Pelawa was a knife and fork, as the main criticism scouts had wasn't about his game, but rather his fitness level—he was "farm strong." But Flames brass was confident that a season or two in college would teach him the good training and nutrition habits necessary to whip him into NHL shape.

Unfortunately, that's not how things turned out for Pelawa. On the night of August 30, 1986, Pelawa and his older brother, Joe, were out visiting friends because it was the last weekend before the school year began. In fact, Pelawa had already moved into his dorm at North Dakota. They were driving back home—Joe in his car and George in his— until George's car got stuck at the side of the road after he pulled over to use the bathroom. They headed home to grab a towing chain and as they were returning to George's car, their car failed to yield at a T intersection and was struck by another vehicle on the passenger side. While Minnesota had recently instituted a mandatory seatbelt law, Pelawa was not wearing one. He suffered a severed artery as a result of the whiplash from the collision and was declared dead at the scene.

Pelawa's funeral was attended by an estimated 1,500 people, who packed into the Bemidji High School auditorium to pay respects to their town's beloved son. Joe, still recovering in hospital from his injuries, attended the funeral on a stretcher. Rumours circulated in the years that followed that Canadian musician Tom Cochrane wrote the 1988 hit song "Big League" about Pelawa's tragic passing, but that story has been refuted by Cochrane in several interviews, where he's admitted it's based on a different player's death.

"He was an animal in front of the other team's net," said Fletcher. "He was from Bemidji and he was a real animal.

I went down to Houston to see him play in the U.S. festival they used to have every summer, the top college players, and he was throwing guys around like they were paper dolls. We were visualizing him being in our lineup playing against the Oilers, the hated rival. Every time I think of George, even today, it makes me smile. It was an awful, awful tragic accident that took his life. It was very unfortunate. It was a real tragedy."

History very nearly repeated itself for the Flames in July 1999. Defensive prospect Robyn Regehr, acquired from the Colorado Avalanche as part of the blockbuster Theoren Fleury trade, was involved in a head-on-collision on a highway in rural Saskatchewan when the other vehicle veered into his vehicle's lane. Regehr, who was driving, broke both his legs but escaped life-threatening injuries, while two people in the other car passed away. (To make the parallels even odder, both Pelawa and Regehr were in Chevy Novas at the time of their accidents.) Despite gloomy initial predictions for Regehr's recovery, he miraculously ended up not only recovering in time for Flames training camp months later, but he ended up playing the majority of the season in the NHL aside from a short conditioning assignment to the minor leagues.

The Flames commemorated Pelawa by setting up a scholarship at Bemidji High School in his name: the George Pelawa–Calgary Flames Foundation Education Fund Scholarship. The Flames' original commitment was for a 20-year period, ending in 2007. After a handful of years where the scholarship was continued by Pelawa's parents, the Flames, the Pelawa family, and the local community fund-raised enough money to permanently endow the scholarship, providing a lasting opportunity for promising students from Bemidji to pursue higher education while providing a lasting commemoration for Pelawa in his community.

Like Pelawa, Mickey Renaud seemed born and bred to be a hometown hero. Born in Windsor and raised in the suburb of Tecumseh, Ontario, he was the son of former pro defenceman Mark Renaud, who played 152 NHL games with Hartford and Buffalo between 1979 and 1994. His uncle was Chris Renaud, who played in the minor leagues for three years in the early 1980s. But more than anything else, the young Renaud dreamed of playing for his hometown Spitfires and perhaps, someday, to play in the NHL.

For his part, Renaud took to hockey quite well. He played his minor hockey in the Sun County Panthers system—the same association that later produced Aaron Ekblad, selected first overall by the Florida Panthers in 2014—and he grew up tall, thick, and smart. What he may have lacked in high-end hockey talent he made up for in work ethic, attitude, and leadership, and he progressed through the various levels of minor hockey with success. He was a seventh-round selection by the Spitfires in the 2004 OHL Priority Selection draft.

After spending the 2004–05 season playing junior A hockey, Renaud earned a spot with the Spitfires in 2005–06, making the team about a month before his 17th birthday. He had 26 points in 68 games in his rookie season. In his second season he doubled his previous point totals, posting 54 points in 68 games. With his October birthday, he was one of the older first-time NHL draft–eligible prospects available, but his unique combination of size, skill, and intangibles earned him attention from scouts. He ended up being selected by the Flames in the fifth round, 143rd overall, in the 2007 NHL Draft.

After attending Flames training camp in September 2007, Renaud returned to the Spitfires where he was named the club's captain for the 2007–08 season. He got off to a strong start, posting 20 goals and 41 points in the club's first 56 games. Renaud played in Windsor's 4–1 win over Owen Sound on February 17, 2008. The following day, he collapsed at his family's home and was unable to be revived. He was pronounced dead at Windsor Regional Hospital at the age of 19. An autopsy later revealed the cause of death to be hypertrophic cardiomyopathy, a disorder that causes the heart muscle to be abnormally thick.

After having their games postponed for a week, the Spitfires proceeded with their season, ultimately losing in the first round of the playoffs. In the aftermath of the tragedy, there were several ripple effects. Junior clubs in Canada began conducting more rigorous medical screenings in an effort to potentially flag underlying medical issues such as Renaud's that could become serious. Four months after his passing, the Flames selected Spitfires forward Greg Nemisz, Renaud's teammate and friend, in the first round of the 2008 NHL Draft.

The Spitfires retired Renaud's jersey number, 18, and hung his jersey in their locker room for the entire 2008–09 season. The club rallied back from his tragic loss, capturing the Ontario Hockey League's championship in both 2008–09 and 2009–10, and also winning the Memorial Cup in both seasons as Canada's top major junior team. A scholarship was instituted in Renaud's name in the Windsor community, and the OHL established the Mickey Renaud Captain's Trophy in 2008–09, with the award going to "the OHL team captain that best exemplifies leadership on and off the ice, with a passion and dedication to the game of hockey and his community." Windsor captain Ryan Ellis, a rookie during Renaud's final season, received the award in 2010–11.

Both Pelawa and Renaud passed away well before their time, and never had the opportunity to pursue their dreams of hockey stardom to the fullest extent possible. However, their teams, friends, and families were able to band together after their deaths and ensure that their memories lived on and created a positive legacy in their two communities.

8

GOOD TIMES DON'T LAST FOREVER: DRAFTING IN THE LATE '80S

———

THE RULES THAT structured the 1972 expansion draft definitely handcuffed the Atlanta Flames—and their expansion cousins, the New York Islanders—and put an emphasis on drafting, development, and savvy maneuvering in the trade market in order for the Flames to at first ice a passable team, then eventually improve and move up in the standings.

The Flames improved rapidly during their time in Atlanta as a result of their ability to navigate player development and asset management; unfortunately, the team was never a strong enough on-ice attraction to survive in a competitive sports environment. The hockey club remained behind the city's baseball (Braves), football (Falcons), and basketball (Hawks) teams in terms of popularity, while the area's college teams also regularly out-drew the Flames. Unable to make the team financially viable in Atlanta, owner Tom Cousins sold to a group of Canadian businessmen led by Nelson Skalbania in 1980, and the team was moved to Calgary.

While Cliff Fletcher's team wasn't a big draw in Atlanta, they were immediately a hit at the box office in Calgary. Fletcher's scouting and hockey operations group kept up their wheeling and dealing. Seemingly every draft, the Flames were able to find a mixture of potential stars and useful depth players, or sometimes merely moveable assets. Between smart drafting and smart trading, the Flames slowly but surely became one of the top teams in the National Hockey League.

But eventually, the runaway success story that was the Flames' drafting record faced some diminishing returns. Taking a deep dive into some of their key early draft selections from 1985 through 1990 provides an illustration of the challenges that the Flames faced.

In 1985, first-round selection Chris Biotti was a high school defenceman from Massachusetts who drew comparisons to Dana Murzyn for his size and mobility. Biotti was labeled after his selection "the best defenceman in the draft" by Fletcher, who also told reporters that the club had rated Biotti highly—even ahead of first overall selection Wendel Clark. Biotti hit injury trouble shortly after being selected, initially suffering a knee injury at the U.S. National Sports Festival in Baton Rouge. He then endured a more significant ACL injury later during his freshman season at Harvard that resulted in surgery and a lengthy rehabilitation process. He also dealt with a shoulder injury that caused him to miss additional time. When he did play at Harvard, his offensive game stood out—to the point where the club's coaches used him as a centre at times—but the number of games he missed due to his injuries really impacted his defensive game, and his play in his own zone failed to progress as the club had hoped. Biotti signed a pro contract after seasons in college but failed to make much of an impact in the Flames' farm system. He never played an NHL game.

Second-round selection Joe Nieuwendyk (27th overall) of Cornell University (NCAA) was a home-run pick and turned into an excellent NHL player, scoring 616 points over nine seasons and becoming the club's all-time leading scorer at the time before departing via trade. The Flames' other second-rounder, Medicine Hat Tigers centre Jeff Wenaas (38th overall), and third-rounder, Harvard University winger Lane MacDonald (59th overall), never played NHL games. Wenaas was a solid Western Hockey League centre with size, whose playing style was compared to Doug Risebrough. He played three seasons in the Flames system but his strengths from junior simply didn't translate to minor league pro hockey. He played out his contract with Calgary's International Hockey League farm team in Salt Lake City and didn't play pro hockey after that. MacDonald, the son of long-time NHLer Lowell MacDonald, was a strong college winger who was a Hobey Baker Award finalist in 1986–87. He made the U.S. Olympic Team in 1987–88, but his rights were traded to Hartford in a five-player deal that resulted in the Flames landing Murzyn from the Whalers.

In 1986, first-round selection George Pelawa (16th overall),
a highly touted high school forward out of Edina, Minnesota,
who had committed to the University of North Dakota, passed
away in a car accident a few months after being selected.
Second-round selection Bryan Glynn (37th overall) had a
reputation as a defence-first, stay-at-home blueliner with the
WHL's Saskatoon Blades. He progressed well through junior
hockey and into the minor leagues, impressing enough at
Flames training camp in 1987 that he made the team. He spent
the entire 1987–88 season with the Flames as they captured
their first Presidents' Trophy as the league's top regular season
team, but Glynn was bumped to the sidelines near the end
of the season due to the return of Paul Reinhart from injury
and the acquisition of Rob Ramage from the St. Louis Blues.
Things went awry for Glynn with the Flames from there. A
disappointing training camp performance in 1988, combined
with him being the only holdover defender that could be sent
to the minors and avoid potential waiver complications, led
to him being sent to the IHL's Salt Lake Golden Eagles. He
spent the next two seasons in Salt Lake, getting called up for
just nine games, and he was traded to the Minnesota North
Stars in October 1990 in exchange for veteran Czech blueliner
Frank Musil—who was, oddly enough, selected by the North
Stars in 1983 with a draft pick they acquired from Calgary.
Glynn played more than 400 games in the NHL, but most of
them weren't with the Flames.

A uniquely challenging prospect from the 1986 draft crop
was fourth-round selection Tom Quinlan (79th overall), a talented winger selected out of high school hockey in Minnesota.
A two-sport athlete, Quinlan excelled at both baseball and

hockey, and he had been a 26th round selection of the Toronto Blue Jays in Major League Baseball's amateur draft a month prior to the NHL's own draft. Quinlan was slated to attend the University of Minnesota at the time, and the Flames were hoping that either he would attempt to split his time between the two sports, or he would become disillusioned with baseball's lengthy development path to the major leagues compared to the NHL's. But before Quinlan headed to college, the Blue Jays were able to get Quinlan to agree to a pro deal—bypassing college altogether—by including a reported $100,000 signing bonus with his contract. The Flames made repeated attempts to get Quinlan under contract, but not wanting to wear his body out attempting to play both sports, Quinlan opted to turn down the Flames' offers in order to focus on baseball.

"When we drafted him, we knew we were taking a very big risk, but we felt that the risk was worth it," said Fletcher. "By then you were in the fourth round. We didn't hesitate because we had such a wealth of good young players it was worth the gamble. Unfortunately, it didn't work out, but it was worth the gamble."

In 1987, the Flames' first-round selection was Bryan Deasley (19th overall), a freshman from the University of Michigan, who was touted as a winger with size and physicality and was compared by scouts to Pat Flatley and Al Secord. Deasley looked like a longer-term project and had mentioned in interviews his desire to finish out his college degree. He broke his ankle running down some stairs and landing wrong during the first month of the season and missed a couple months recovering, which derailed much of his sophomore season at Michigan. He left college early, signing following the 1987–88 season and spending the 1988–89 season playing with the Canadian Olympic Team. Deasley's experience with the Flames involved a pair of early training camp exits in 1989–90 and 1990–91. The Flames ended up trading away Deasley to the Quebec Nordiques, twice. He was originally traded to the Nordiques just prior to the 1991 trade deadline in exchange for depth forward Claude Loiselle. However, the trade was nullified by the league because the Nordiques had already placed Loiselle on waivers, making him ineligible to be traded at the time. So Deasley's rights reverted back to the Flames, only for him to be traded to the Nordiques—for real, this time—a year later for future considerations. Deasley never played an NHL game.

Second-round pick Stephane Matteau (25th overall) turned into a really reliable depth player and played more than 800 NHL games between six NHL clubs. But fellow second-rounder Kevin Grant (40th overall), a blueliner from the OHL's Kitchener Rangers, and third-rounder Scott Mahoney (61st overall), a winger from the Oshawa Generals, didn't fare nearly as well. Grant was a prototypical blueliner, listed at 6′4″ and 215 pounds in his draft year. He didn't boast much offensive skill or mobility, but he was considered a rock-solid, physical, stay-at-home defenceman. He had one strong season with Salt Lake in the IHL but then plateaued and left the organization early in the 1992–93 season. He never played an NHL game. Mahoney was ranked outside of Central Scouting's top 210 list at the time of his drafting. He was touted as a physical crash-and-bang forward with eye-popping penalty-minute totals. He also had fairly average offensive totals and didn't progress significantly after he was drafted. He didn't end up signing with the Flames and never played pro hockey.

In 1988, the good news was that both players the Flames selected in the first two rounds played NHL games, although the team had traded their third-round pick to the Philadelphia Flyers. The bad news is that neither of their selections became significant NHL players. The first-round selection in 1988, Jason Muzzatti (21st overall), was a freshman goaltender from Michigan State University. Born with a heart condition that included a murmur, Muzzatti had corrective surgery a couple months before the draft and posted a clear bill of health when the Flames selected him. He was a strong stand-up goaltender, and the Flames reportedly liked his competitive nature, which drew comparisons to Ron Hextall in terms of fiery on-ice demeanour. The challenge for Muzzatti in the Flames organization was two-fold: goaltending began to shift away from the stand-up style and toward the trendy butterfly style while Muzzatti played two years of college hockey following his selection in the draft, and the club took Trevor Kidd (a butterfly goalie) in the first round of the 1990 draft and Russian netminder Andrei Trefilov in the 12th round of the 1991 draft, which contributed to a logjam of goaltenders in the system.

Muzzatti seemed primed to grab hold of an NHL job early in the 1993–94 season, with the Flames carrying four goaltenders for a spell. Muzzatti gave up eight goals in his first NHL appearance, but he ended up catching a nasty viral infection and his projected second start instead went to Kidd, who grabbed the backup job and Muzzatti was assigned to the IHL. The following season, Muzzatti's attempt to cement himself as Kidd's backup following Mike Vernon's departure was derailed by an owner's lockout, and Muzzatti saw just 10 minutes of NHL action in relief during the shortened regular season before being sent to the minors in favour of Trefilov. After the arrival of veteran backup Rick Tabaracci in 1995, Muzzatti was claimed on waivers by Hartford. He bounced around the league a bit, including cups of coffee with the New York Rangers and San Jose Sharks, before finishing out his career in Europe—including a stint playing for Italy at the 2006 Winter Olympics.

The Flames' second-round selection was big-bodied two-way college centre Todd Harkins (42nd overall), a freshman from Miami (Ohio) University that was listed as 6'3" and 210 pounds in his draft year. The Flames had Harkins rated highly and were reportedly prepared to take him in the first round had Muzzatti been off the board by the time they went to the podium. Fletcher told reporters that the club's organizational depth on the blueline tilted their preferences toward accumulating forwards in the draft, which pushed them toward Harkins. Harkins progressed very nicely in college, but the Flames' forward depth at the NHL level—both at centre and on the wing—kept him in IHL Salt Lake for awhile. Harkins attempted to work his way into a niche as a physical enforcer type, even living with infamous Minnesota pugilist Link Gaetz for a summer, but the emergence of 21-year-old Sandy McCarthy beat Harkins out for a roster spot in 1993's training camp. Harkins was traded to Hartford midway through the 1993–94 season in exchange for depth forward Todd Morrow.

In 1989, the Flames had traded their first-round pick to Philadelphia for Brad McCrimmon—their third rounder from 1988 was part of this deal. They had a pair of second-round selections that had some NHL success, albeit not with the Flames, and a pair of third-round selections that didn't pan out as well.

College-bound Canadian centre Kent Manderville (24th overall) was drafted out of Saskatchewan Junior A hockey in the second round. An intriguing combination of size, strength, and on-ice smarts, Manderville was bound for Cornell University. He played two seasons at Cornell and showed well and represented Canada at a pair of World Junior tournaments. He left school following the 1990–91 season, with the idea that he would start 1991–92 with the Canadian National Team and then go pro and join the Flames following the Winter Olympics in Albertville, France. But he was instead traded to Toronto the month before the Olympics, part of the 10-player mega-trade that sent Doug Gilmour to the Maple Leafs. Fletcher, who had drafted Manderville in Calgary, had since moved onto the general manager's job in Toronto and still coveted the player. Manderville played more than 600 NHL games.

College-bound American centre Ted Drury (42nd overall) was drafted out of Connecticut prep school hockey in the second round. Considered a mature, well-rounded player— albeit perhaps one without a ton of offensive flair—Drury spent three seasons at Harvard and represented the United States at two World Juniors and the 1992 Winter Olympics. He finally signed with the Flames and went pro in 1993. He made the Flames roster out of training camp in 1993–94 but was traded to Hartford prior to that season's trade deadline in a five-player deal that saw Gary Suter become a Whaler (for a day) and the Flames receive Zarley Zalapski, James Patrick, and Michael Nylander. Nylander was thought to be the reason for Drury's inclusion in the transaction; Nylander had a bit more finesse and speed to his game, while Drury was a bit more low-key and, as a young player who grew up in New England, was a local product that appealed to Hartford. The two third-round selections just didn't pan out. Finnish blueliner Veli-Pekka Kautonen (50th overall) was listed at 6'2", 205 pounds and was considered a savvy puck-moving defender by scouts. He carved out a very effective pro career with stops in Finland, Sweden, Germany, and Italy, and simply never was lured over to North America. Calgary native Corey Lyons (63rd overall) was an offensive dynamo with the WHL's Lethbridge Hurricanes, posting 53 goals and 112 points in his draft year. While Flames brass noted to reporters that Lyons' skating needed to improve, they praised his scoring touch. Unfortunately, his skating didn't improve, and his scoring didn't translate to the pro level. He spent a season and a half in the IHL with Salt Lake before being demoted to the second-tier East Coast Hockey League mid-season. His Flames deal was terminated following the season.

There wasn't a single big factor that led to the diminishing draft returns for the Flames in the back half of the 1980s, but rather a bunch of smaller factors that compounded each other. If anything, you could point the finger to the Flames' prior successes as leading to their eventual challenges.

In the 1970s and the early chunk of the 1980s, the Flames simply weren't a great hockey team. They quickly got better, but it's much easier for a team that isn't challenging for a playoff berth or that doesn't have championship aspirations to integrate their draft choices immediately. The Flames' improving lineup in the '80s made it tougher and tougher for young players to grab hold of a spot, which in turn had the knock-on effect of keeping the players behind them on the depth chart from getting tougher assignments and in some cases may have slowed the development of players who had the potential to progress.

Professional sports is also full of copycats, in the sense that teams and individuals pay attention to what others are doing. If one team has success, other teams try to emulate those tactics or traits. In the case of the Flames' strong drafting early in their history, other clubs noticed their tendencies—investing in European and collegiate scouting—and adopted many of them, resulting in competition for players in those areas. Similarly, the success of the Flames in terms of drafting and development made several of their key hockey operations figures attractive commodities to other teams. Assistant GM David Poile went to the Washington Capitals in 1982. American college and high school scout Jack Ferreira joined the NY Rangers in 1986. Long-time assistant coach Pierre Page joined Minnesota in 1988. By the time Fletcher left the Flames to become general manager of the Leafs in 1991, a significant portion of the league had former Flames in their front offices—in fact, four of the other 21 league general managers at the time were former Flames brass.

Finally, in some cases the challenges the Flames' picks faced amounted to bad luck. Three consecutive first-round selections suffered significant injuries, with Pelawa's tragically resulting in his death, prompting a *Calgary Herald* columnist at the time to term the third injury as part of a "curse." In less significant situations, several players merely didn't develop as the Flames' scouts had projected. The Flames were still able to find hidden gems in their drafts, but overall, their draft results took a substantial step backward in terms of both frequency and on-ice impact.

9

THE LITTLE GUY WHO PLAYED BIG: THE EMERGENCE OF THEOREN FLEURY

FOR A CLUB to find success at the NHL draft, its strategies usually must involve consistently finding value by hitting on their high-value selections in the early rounds while finding unexpected value late in the draft by taking advantage of various factors—often fairly predictable biases and tendencies—that create market inefficiencies (and value) in the waning rounds.

One of the most significant examples of a late-round pick that produced tremendous value was when the Calgary Flames selected Theoren Fleury in the 1987 NHL Draft. An extremely talented player who arguably had everything but size, Fleury overcame some horrible off-ice circumstances to carve out a strong NHL career and became one of the most significant players in Flames franchise history.

Born in Oxbow, Saskatchewan, and raised in Russell, Manitoba, after his family relocated, Fleury quickly established himself as a passionate, albeit perennially undersized, hockey player in his local community. His on-ice talent soon emerged, and he opted to pursue major junior hockey, catching on with the Western Hockey League's Moose Jaw Warriors in 1984 as a 16-year-old. Playing in the WHL, the 5'6" Fleury was perpetually physically outmatched by the opposition players. But Fleury's combination of smooth puck-handling, elusive skating, and a surprising physicality and ferocity led him to tremendous success at the major junior level.

Fleury progressed quickly with the Warriors, posting 75 points in his rookie season in 1984–85 and scoring at higher than a point-per-game pace. He surpassed the 100-point level in his next two seasons, posting 108 points in 1985–86 and 129 points in his draft year of 1986–87. Fleury's strong play earned attention from Hockey Canada, and he earned a spot on Canada's World Junior Championship entry in 1987. That team ended up being involved in an infamous moment, with Fleury as a central figure—the Punch-up in Piestany. At the time the World Juniors were held under a round robin format, with the top three teams capturing medals. Canada was in a medal position and had a shot for gold, playing the final game of the tournament against a Soviet Union team that had been eliminated from medal contention, resulting in a game full of tension and physicality between the rivals. Following an early goal, Fleury celebrated with some theatrics toward the Soviet bench, drawing that team's ire. With just more than six minutes remaining in the second period and Canada leading the game, a line brawl erupted following a slash on Fleury by a Russian player. Unable to calm down the brawl, the officials turned off the arena lights, threw out the game, and both teams were disqualified from the tournament. The disqualification cost Canada at least the silver medal; had they defeated the Soviet Union they would have tied with Finland for first place in the tournament, with a goal differential tie-breaker determining which club received the gold medal.

Between his performance with the Warriors and at the World Juniors, there was some draft buzz around Fleury heading into the 1987 NHL Draft. But he was still a player generously listed as 5′5″ and 150 pounds in his draft year, which likely contributed to him being available when the Flames selected him in the eighth round.

"Quite frankly, my evaluation of him was, 'He'll sell a lot of tickets and be an exciting player for our farm team in Salt Lake City,'" said Cliff Fletcher, the Flames general manager at the time.

Former Flames executive Doug Risebrough, who at the time was sitting at the club's draft table learning the ropes of hockey operations following his retirement as a player, recalled an odd bit of buzz on the draft floor after Fleury's selection.

"There was a lot of conversation between tables, which is really unheard of," said Risebrough. "Once we made the selection, the Philadelphia guys are talking to the Flames guys, and the Flames guys are talking to somebody else on the other side. And I said, 'Well, who is this kid? Why is everybody talking about him?' And they said, 'He's a small player, he'll be really good in the minors.'"

Fletcher recalled some indecision on the part of his club's scouts as to whether to pull the trigger on Fleury's selection.

"They were debating among themselves as they always do," said Fletcher. "He was a small player. But I said, 'Guys, it's the eighth round, he's got a lot of skill, what have you got to lose?' So we drafted him."

Fleury seemed to understand the task in front of him, telling reporters during his first NHL training camp, "A lot of guys that are big have to prove they can't play. If you're small, you have to prove you can play." His impressive play became one of the bigger stories of 1987's training camp before he was returned to the Warriors.

"When they said he was a small player, I didn't know how small he was," said Risebrough. "When he came to camp, I thought, 'He is really small, this kid.' He might have been the best player in training camp. And he really caught everybody's eye. They sent him back to junior."

Fleury's season as a 19-year-old, his final junior campaign, was simply excellent. Serving as captain in Moose Jaw, he had a 160-point performance and tied with Swift Current Broncos forward Joe Sakic for the scoring lead in the WHL. He scored 68 goals in 65 games and accumulated 235 penalty minutes during the season. He returned to the World Juniors for Canada—one of a handful of holdovers from the team disqualified in Piestany—and captained the team to a gold medal. The Warriors missed the playoffs and the Flames, who had signed Fleury to a pro contract, brought him to the International Hockey League to join their farm team in Salt

Lake City for the remainder of their season. Fleury excelled in that setting.

"He got called up at the end of the year, [and] they put him in the minors, which was in Salt Lake City," said Risebrough. "But you could only play him 10 games. If you played him more than 10 games, it would count as a year of pro.... He was leading scoring in the playoffs. If you want to talk about luck, there's a piece of luck right there."

By the time the organization decided to shut down Fleury for the season to conserve the length of his contract—junior-aged players in his situation were allowed to play 10 combined regular season and playoff games before their contracts began to toll—he was leading the IHL's playoffs in scoring. Salt Lake ended up winning the IHL's Turner Cup Championship that season. Undoubtedly, Fleury's 1987–88 season served to raise expectations for his potential beyond him being strong minor league depth.

Expectations were raised for Fleury heading into 1988's Flames training camp after his strong performance in 1987's camp and the 1987–88 season as a whole. For the second year in a row, he was a training camp standout, but the Flames were coming off a Presidents' Trophy the previous season and were bringing back most of that team, which meant the numbers game dictated that Fleury began the season in the minors. When asked by Flames brass to work on his defensive game and avoid taking too many penalties, Fleury emerged as the Golden Eagles' leading scorer and most dynamic offensive player. With the Flames' offence sputtering a bit mid-season and the club mired in a win-one, lose-one lull, Fleury was called up in early January to provide a spark.

"We actually brought him up on New Year's Day in 1989," said Fletcher. "He played 40 games for us. Back then, we had a lot of real leaders on our hockey team, starting with Lanny McDonald and Brad McCrimmon, Jim Peplinski, Brian MacLellan. He had to toe the line and just play hockey for us, and he had a real good rookie year."

Fleury ended up sticking around for the rest of the season, posting 34 points in 36 games and being used by head coach Terry Crisp on effectively any line that required a spark. He added another 11 points in 22 playoff games as the Flames won the Stanley Cup.

Drafted as a centre, the Flames' depth at that position resulted in Fleury learning how to play the wing in order to get additional ice time. That added versatility allowed the Flames' coaching staff to use him in multiple game situations, contributing to him playing more often and progressing as a young player. As the Flames' established stars retired or moved onto other organizations—due to a combination of hockey and economic rationales—that versatility allowed Fleury to grow into a larger role in the club and emerge as one of the Flames' most important players. Over time, he established himself as one of the must-see players in the club, someone that could be counted upon to make a great play, score a great goal, or get into a scrap in order to spark his team.

For the Flames, Fleury was the defining player of the 1990s. He began the decade scoring 51 goals and 104 points in 1990–91, followed by a dramatic overtime goal in Game 6 in the 1991 playoffs against Edmonton—punctuated by a theatrical slide across the ice during his goal celebration that

Considered undersized at every level, Theoren Fleury was a key piece of the Flames' 1989 Stanley Cup team and the team's offensive leader throughout the 1990s.

became one of the most iconic moments in franchise history. (The Flames lost Game 7 to the Oilers and were subsequently eliminated from the playoffs.) He became the Flames' most consistent offensive weapon, reaching 100 points again in 1992–93 and just missing the mark in 1995–96. He served as alternate captain throughout the decade and served as captain for two seasons following Joe Nieuwendyk's contractual hold-out and eventual departure to Dallas. By the time the decade was nearing its end, Fleury was the franchise's all-time leader in points.

However, Fleury's time with the Flames came to an end in February 1999. Fleury was a pending unrestricted free agent at the end of the 1998–99 season and his camp and then general manager Al Coates were unable to come to terms on a new deal. The two sides were reportedly $1 million per season apart in their negotiations as the trade deadline approached. Near the end of February, several weeks before the trade deadline, the Flames made a move: Fleury and forward Chris Dingman were traded to the Colorado Avalanche in exchange for forward Rene Corbet, defenceman Wade Belak, a second-round pick in the 2000 NHL Draft, and a player to be named later, which the Flames would pick from the first five players the Avalanche selected in the 1998 NHL Draft. The Flames ended up selecting defenceman Robyn Regehr a month after the trade. Fleury left the Flames franchise as their all-time leading scorer at the time, with 830 points over 11 seasons— he passed the previous leading scorer, Al MacInnis, midway through the 1998–99 season.

Only one piece of the hefty trade return the Flames received for Fleury turned into an asset of note for the organization.

A reliable two-way forward, Corbet was with the Flames for just over a year (playing just 68 games) before he was traded to Pittsburgh. A physical depth defender, Belak was with the Flames for just less than two years (playing just 72 games) before he was claimed off waivers by Toronto. The Flames selected forward Jarret Stoll from the WHL's Kootenay Ice with the draft pick they received from Colorado but were unable to come to terms on a contract. The real gem of the Fleury trade was Regehr. While Regehr wasn't a high-end offensive talent, he was an incredibly reliable positional defender in his own end and one of the more effective hitters along the boards in franchise history—the left side of the Flames' defensive zone, which Regehr played on, was nicknamed "the tunnel of death" by fans. Regehr played more than 800 games for the Flames and ranked second in franchise history in games played at the time of his departure from the club via trade in 2012.

Fleury's career following his departure from Calgary was tumultuous, to say the least. He bounced between Colorado, the New York Rangers, and Chicago Blackhawks, and while he maintained a high level of play when he was in the lineup, he battled with drug and alcohol issues that saw him suspended multiple times and kept him off the ice for long stretches. Fleury briefly returned to the Flames in the fall of 2009, attempting a comeback in training camp and ultimately retiring as a member of the Flames. He released his autobiography in the weeks following his retirement, revealing not only the extent of his continued struggles with drugs and alcohol throughout his playing career, but also that he was sexually abused by junior coach Graham James during his time with Moose Jaw. Following the book's release, he became an outspoken advocate for victims of similar abuses.

"He was small in stature but big in heart and big in attitude," said Risebrough. "He could skate and [had] just a huge drive. And fearless, you know? He played like he was 6'3" and he was a talented player."

"To me he still had a Hall of Fame career even with the challenges he had two-thirds of the way through his career," said Fletcher.

Because of his size, Fleury was a gigantic long-shot to even play a single game in the NHL. But his perseverance, tenacity, and sheer ferocity—battling not only against the top players in the world, but also against off-ice challenges that didn't become fully apparent until his career had concluded—made him one of the top players in Flames franchise history, and one of the NHL's top drafting success stories regardless of round. Fleury was one of the smaller players in hockey throughout his career, but it's impossible to downplay his impact on the game.

10

BUILDING AND DISMANTLING THE 1986 AND 1989 STANLEY CUP RUNS

IT'S NO SMALL feat building a team that competes for championships, or even manages to win any. It often takes years of patience, prudent and measured moves, and a good amount of luck as well. The Calgary Flames made it to a pair of Stanley Cup Finals during the late 1980s—losing to the Montreal Canadiens in five games in 1986 and beating the Canadiens in six games in their rematch in 1989.

The Flames' two trips to the Cup Final were the culmination of the better part of two decades of hard work conducted by general manager Cliff Fletcher and many members of his hockey operations staff. Looking at the composition of those two teams provides a great deal of insight into the art and the science of team building, as well as how important it was to appropriately leverage draft selections during that era to maximize their value.

Twenty-eight players dressed for the Flames in the four rounds of the playoffs that culminated with the Final series loss to Montreal in 1986. Those players were goaltenders Mike Vernon and Reggie Lemelin; defencemen Al MacInnis, Paul Baxter, Neil Sheehy, Terry Johnson, Robin Bartel, Gary Suter, Paul Reinhart, and Jamie Macoun; and forwards Joe Mullen, Doug Risebrough, Lanny McDonald, Dan Quinn, Colin Patterson, Hakan Loob, Brian Bradley, Brett Hull, Mike Eaves, Tim Hunter, Perry Berezan, Nick Fotiu, Jim Peplinski, Yves Courteau, Steve Bozek, John Tonelli, Joel Otto, and Carey Wilson.

Of the 28 players on the playoff roster, 11 of them—a little shy of half the team—were homegrown Flames draft selections: Reinhart, Peplinski, and Hunter were 1979 picks, Loob was a 1980 pick, MacInnis and Vernon from 1981, Quinn, Bradley, and Berezan from 1983, and Hull and Suter from 1984. Seven players were signed as free agents. Another 10 players were acquired via trade, but half of those players were acquired in trades either directly for Flames draft choices or for players the Flames drafted. McDonald was the last piece of an intricate series of escalating trades that flipped draft-related assets that dated back to the Flames' second-ever draft in 1973—the club selected Tom Lysiak and Greg Fox in that draft, then made a sequence of swaps that resulted in McDonald's acquisition from the Colorado Rockies in November 1981.

The 1989 championship team had 23 players engraved on the Cup and 25 players who dressed in at least one post-season game. Those 25 players were goaltenders Vernon and Rick Wamsley; defencemen MacInnis, Brad McCrimmon, Dana Murzyn, Ric Nattress, Suter, Macoun, Rob Ramage, and Ken Sabourin; and forwards Mullen, McDonald, Gary Roberts, Patterson, Loob, Theoren Fleury, Jiri Hrdina, Tim Hunter, Mark Hunter, Peplinski, Joe Nieuwendyk, Brian MacLellan, Otto, Doug Gilmour, and Sergei Priakin. (Priakin and Sabourin didn't meet the games-played requirements to get their names etched onto the trophy.)

Gone from the 1986 team were Lemelin, Baxter, Sheehy, Johnson, Bartel, Reinhart, Risebrough, Quinn, Bradley, Hull, Eaves, Fotiu, Courteau, Bozek, Tonelli, and Wilson. New faces for the 1989 run were Wamsley, McCrimmon, Murzyn, Nattress, Ramage, Sabourin, Roberts, Fleury, Hrdina, Mark Hunter, Nieuwendyk, Gilmour, and Priakin. Much of the turnover between the two clubs was a concerted effort to build some veteran stability, physicality, and defensive zone structure to their blueline group, particularly through the additions of McCrimmon, Murzyn, Nattress, and Ramage.

Six of the 13 new faces for the playoff run were home-grown draft picks that moved onto the NHL roster: Roberts, Sabourin, and Hrdina (1984), Nieuwendyk (1985), Fleury (1987), and Priakin (1988). McCrimmon was acquired from the Philadelphia Flyers for a couple of draft picks, including their first-round pick in 1989, while Nattress was acquired from the St. Louis Blues for a pair of late-round picks. The remainder of the big pieces were obtained via swaps of existing assets from the 1986 team to other teams—most notably sending Hull and Bozek to St. Louis for Wamsley and Ramage.

It took the Flames the better part of two decades to put together a championship team. The disassembly of that team was more rapid. In the two years following the Cup victory, with Fletcher still at the helm, the Flames saw McDonald and Peplinski retire, and they consummated trades that sent several key players to other clubs. A surplus of defencemen, and a desire to open up a "light at the end of the tunnel" (as Fletcher told reporters at the time), led to Ramage's trade to the Toronto Maple Leafs a few weeks after the Stanley Cup win for a second-round pick. A year later, a disappointing season combined with a desire for more youth in the lineup saw Mullen sent to the Pittsburgh Penguins and McCrimmon to the Detroit Red Wings, netting a pair of second-round picks. Hrdina, Mark Hunter, and Murzyn were shipped off in-season in depth-for-depth moves of minor consequence.

The aging of the Flames' remaining championship players continued after Fletcher's departure to Toronto under his successor, Doug Risebrough, and the swap-out of players continued in an effort to stem the tide and extend the club's window of championship contention. A contract dispute, culminating with a bitter arbitration process where the player and club were very far apart on salary expectations, led to the Flames deciding to trade Gilmour. Solving the Gilmour problem soon combined with a desire to inject some new faces into the lineup, leading to a massive 10-player swap with the Maple Leafs on January 2, 1992, that saw Gilmour, Wamsley, Nattress, Macoun, and prospect Kent Manderville head to Toronto in January 1992 in exchange for goaltender

Jeff Reese, defencemen Alexander Godynyuk and Michel Petit, and forwards Craig Berube and Gary Leeman. The five players the Flames acquired failed to really flourish in Calgary. Reese was a solid backup goaltender for a few seasons and Berube was an effective physical depth forward, but Godynyuk and Petit didn't gel with the rest of the club's defensive group, and Leeman failed to recapture his past scoring touch. The Flames ended up being weakened across their lineup through the Gilmour trade.

By the mid-1990s, a pair of economic considerations led to additional trades. First, player salaries began to rise significantly. In 1990, the estimated average salary was around $250,000 U.S. By 1995, that had risen to nearly $900,000 U.S. At the same time, the Flames—and the other Canadian clubs— were facing the challenge of a Canadian dollar that was diminishing in value relative to its American counterpart, with the Canadian dollar falling to around 70 cents per American dollar by 1995 after peaking at 89 cents in 1991. (The Canadian dollar reached its all-time low in value in 2002, trading at 62 cents per American dollar.) This situation meant that the Flames were taking in revenue in Canadian funds and paying the ever-escalating player salaries in American currency.

These economic challenges created problems for the Flames, as they often couldn't afford to pay their established veteran players the same salaries as their American counterparts. This contributed to a succession of often contentious contract negotiations with several prominent players and led to a series of Flames general managers opting to move their best players to other teams via trade rather than potentially lose them in free agency and receive nothing back.

Under Risebrough, the Flames had three more 1989 alumni follow Gilmour's path and be sent to other teams. At the March 1994 trade deadline, the Flames sent Suter and forwards Paul Ranheim and Ted Drury to the Hartford Whalers in exchange for defencemen James Patrick and Zarley Zalapski, and forward Michael Nylander. The Flames received reliable depth for the blueline and Nylander's offensive flair added an element to their attack, but Suter was easily the best player to change zip codes in the transaction.

Three months later, in June 1994, the Flames sent Vernon to Detroit for veteran defenceman Steve Chiasson. At the time, the Flames had young Trevor Kidd, Vernon's backup, looking like a promising alternative in net who happened to make significantly less money than Vernon did at the time. Adding Chiasson was also an appealing proposition as an offensive defenceman who could be physical, productive, and a leader for a team that was becoming younger— Chiasson had been an alternate captain in Detroit and was a year removed from scoring 12 goals and 62 points. But replacing an established goaltender in Vernon with a less polished up-and-comer in Kidd led to some occasional challenging nights in net, particularly with the Flames utilizing an increasingly youthful blueline group that was prone to occasional mistakes.

The following month, MacInnis, then a restricted free agent, signed an offer sheet with the Blues for a hefty raise. As part of the compensation system for restricted free agents at the time, the Flames and Blues were permitted to work out a trade for MacInnis' rights. Eventually, MacInnis and a fourth-round pick in 1997 were sent to St. Louis in exchange for veteran blueliner Phil Housley and second-round picks in 1996 and 1997. Housley was a highly regarded offensive force from the back end, just a year removed from posting 97 points with the Winnipeg Jets, but his game wasn't as well-rounded as MacInnis', and he was seen at times as being one-dimensional. He helped the Flames generate offence, but his play away from the puck wasn't spectacular.

Under Risebrough's successor, Al Coates, the prominent departures of 1989 alumni concluded with Nieuwendyk and Fleury. Nieuwendyk was embroiled in a contract dispute with the Flames, with an arbitration award leading to protracted negotiations over a longer-term extension that dragged on into the season. Nieuwendyk held out until December 19, 1995, when Coates pulled the trigger on a trade with the Dallas Stars that sent Nieuwendyk to Texas in exchange for checking winger Corey Millen and junior prospect Jarome Iginla. Nieuwendyk made Dallas better immediately and was part of a progressing group that won the Stanley Cup in 1999. Millen was useful depth for the Flames, but the star of the swap for their side was Iginla—eventually. After taking a few seasons to mature at the NHL level, Iginla became one of the top power forwards in the NHL during the 2000s. This turned into a rare case of the Flames trading a future Hall of Fame player for another future Hall of Fame player, but in the short term the Flames lost a significant piece who played in every game situation and was good enough to cover up a lot of the team's shortcomings in all areas of the ice.

Fleury was the final piece of the 1989 team to depart, heading to Colorado via trade in February 1999. He was on an expiring contract and was a pending unrestricted free agent. The Flames and Fleury's camp negotiated but couldn't find enough common ground to hash out a contract. The Flames traded Fleury and checking winger Chris Dingman to the Colorado Avalanche in exchange for forward Rene Corbet, defenceman Wade Belak, a second-round pick in 2001, and a player to be named later, which ended up being defensive prospect Robyn Regehr. The Flames weren't going to be getting back a player who was as impactful as Fleury, so the strategy appeared to be getting a bunch of assets in return. Corbet and Belak were solid players but weren't difference-makers for the club, while the player selected with the 2001 pick, Jarret Stoll, never signed with the Flames. Regehr ended up being the hidden gem in this trade, emerging as a top-flight shutdown defender, but not until the mid-2000s. In the immediate aftermath of the trade, the Flames' roster got weaker.

In the years following their championship win, the Flames lost several key players from that roster via trade and didn't get any players back that could plug the holes in their lineup in the immediate aftermath—the players they got in return through these trades were, generally speaking, a mix of forgettable depth players and prospects that were years away from becoming impactful NHL contributors. As the remaining members of the Flames' championship roster disappeared, increasing pressure was put on the club's drafting and development to find players who could step in to make up the difference. Unfortunately, the Flames' drafting results during this period were mixed and contributed to a challenging period for the hockey club both on and off the ice. Fan support diminished as the Flames dropped in the standings.

To put it more simply, the Flames benefitted from smart decision-making and some favourable draft luck over several years as their roster was built up to championship contention. Their fortunes then swung the opposite direction as that contending team was gradually dismantled over time due to economic circumstances and accelerated somewhat by a few trades that didn't provide the Flames with the returns on their assets that they had desired. Eventually players acquired during the tear-down of the 1989 club—Iginla and Regehr— became core pieces on another strong Flames playoff run in 2004. The hockey club would need to persist through a challenging period before that would happen.

11

TREVOR KIDD AND THE CHALLENGE OF DRAFTING A STAR GOALTENDER

THERE'S PROBABLY NO position more important to a hockey club's success than the goaltender. As such, it's the position that teams take the most care to get right when it comes to drafting and development, and often teams will do what they can to hedge their bets. Goaltending is so important that clubs often draft their prospective "goalie of the future" while their "goalie of the present" is still with the club and often still in their prime. Sometimes teams hedge their bets further by drafting multiple prospective future starting netminders. When you take into account the history of the Flames franchise in terms of drafting goaltenders, and their low levels of success, multiple options seem prudent.

Dating back to Atlanta, the Flames began their existence with a tandem of Dan Bouchard and Phil Myre thanks to the expansion draft. Bouchard had been in the Boston Bruins system, while Myre had been the Montreal Canadiens' third-string goalie. The Flames utilized that pairing in different configurations for their first five seasons before swapping Myre out for Yves Belanger as part of a trade with the St. Louis Blues during the 1977–78 season. Belanger was swapped out for free agent signing Reggie Lemelin during the 1978–79 season.

Lemelin eventually became the primary goaltender for the Flames, but they tried 1979 draft choice Pat Riggin for a couple seasons as the other tandem goaltender, followed by Don Edwards, who was acquired in a draft day trade in 1982 with the Buffalo Sabres that involved two players and six draft picks, for three seasons. The first homegrown goaltender to really make an NHL impact was Mike Vernon, taken in the third round of the 1981 draft. Vernon emerged as the Flames' undisputed top goaltender when he backstopped them to an appearance in the 1986 Stanley Cup Final, a five-game loss to the Montreal Canadiens. The nine goaltenders selected by the Flames prior to drafting Vernon had failed to pan out in the NHL—even Team USA "Miracle on Ice" backstop Jim Craig, taken in the 1977 draft—and the club selected another three before Vernon made his NHL debut. Vernon was arguably the first netminder in franchise history who was their definitive, reliable, everyday goaltender, while previously they operated in a split-duties situation.

Vernon remained their undisputed starter for the balance of the decade, leading them to a Stanley Cup win in 1989. In 1988, the Flames selected college goaltender Jason Muzzatti in the first round. In 1990, with Muzzatti seen as a bit of a longer-term project and Vernon having recently turned 27, the Flames felt that based upon where their organization was sitting in terms of their depth in net, and how the upcoming draft class looked, it was the right time to find another goaltender.

There were three highly touted netminders in the 1990 draft class. The top-ranked goaltender, according to Central Scouting, was Trevor Kidd of the Western Hockey League's Brandon Wheat Kings. The second-ranked goaltender was Felix Potvin of the Quebec Major Junior Hockey League's Chicoutimi Sagueneens. And the third-ranked goaltender was Martin Brodeur of the QMJHL's Saint-Hyacinthe Laser. Of the three, Kidd played the most in his draft year, had the strongest save percentage of the three goaltenders, and represented Canada at the World Juniors as Stephane Fiset's backup. He was the youngest player on the team and, while he didn't play, he got to soak in the experience and was seemingly being groomed to be Canada's starter in future tournaments. Kidd was named the top goaltender in not just the WHL, but all of Canadian major junior hockey. While Kidd didn't get any playoff experience that season—his Wheat Kings lost a playoff tiebreaker game to Swift Current in overtime—he had a very strong draft eligible season.

The Flames, based in western Canada, heavily scouted and relied upon the WHL throughout their drafting history—as you would expect them to based on proximity—and when all else failed and a decision between players seemed to be a toss-up, they seemed to lean toward the familiarity of the WHL. In the first round of the 1990 NHL Draft, after Kidd slipped past the Minnesota North Stars at eighth overall, general manager Cliff Fletcher began working the phones. After a pair of tense picks, the Flames pulled the trigger on a trade with the New Jersey Devils, who held the 11th overall pick.

The Flames had two additional second-round picks in addition to their own—the Detroit Red Wings' (24th overall) from trading Brad McCrimmon and Minnesota's (29th overall) from trading minor leaguer Peter Lappin—and had no hesitation in using those picks to move up to get the goaltender they wanted. They sent the 20th, 24th, and 29th overall picks to New Jersey in exchange for 11th and 32nd overall. They selected Kidd with the 11th overall pick. (They soon recouped one of their second-round selections via a trade with Pittsburgh for Joe Mullen.)

"We had people who had done a lot of goaltending, both in the NHL and the American League, who thought that Kidd was going to be an absolute top goaler in the NHL, so I made the trade," said Fletcher.

At the time, Kidd was an astute gamble as far as both goaltenders and draft picks go, and the decision to leverage the team's surplus of second-round picks to add depth in a key position was a savvy move. But, as the saying goes, hindsight is 20/20. While the Flames made the goaltender many scouts—including their own—felt was the best available in the 1990 class the first goaltender chosen in that draft, he ended up being the third best of the prominent goaltending prospects taken in that draft. To add a bit of salt to the wound, the Devils used the Flames' pick at 20th overall to select a player who ended up becoming arguably the best goaltender in NHL history: Martin Brodeur. (The Toronto Maple Leafs took Potvin in the second round at 31st overall.)

"I've never professed to be an expert on goaltenders," said Fletcher. "I just watch them and say, 'Stop the goddamn puck.' But I had people who were experts on it, and they wanted Kidd, so we took him."

The Flames were high on Kidd after his selection. He was a tall, aggressive, butterfly-style goalie who seemed to be built for the modern game. His temperament drew comparisons to Ron Hextall, one of Kidd's personal heroes. His playing style drew comparisons to Sean Burke. Fletcher told reporters Kidd was "the best goaler that's been available in the draft since Grant Fuhr" at the time, while Brandon general manager Kelly McCrimmon called him "a good goalie with the potential to be a great goalie." With Vernon and veteran backup Rick Wamsley in the NHL, Steve Guenette and Warren Sharples with the International Hockey League's Salt Lake Golden Eagles, and Muzzatti and Kidd waiting in the wings, goaltending was an organizational strength. (The position was strengthened further when the Flames selected Russian netminder Andrei Trefilov late in the 1991 draft.)

The two seasons following Kidd's draft selection went about as well as they possibly could go for a player in his position. He had a strong start to the 1990–91 season with Brandon and was the starter for Canada at the World Juniors tournament, winning a gold medal. Shortly after the tournament, the Wheat Kings traded him to the playoff-bound

Spokane Chiefs. He led them to a WHL playoff championship and a Memorial Cup tournament win. The following season, he joined the Canadian National Team as they prepared for the 1992 Winter Olympics in Albertville. He returned to the World Juniors again, capturing gold for the second time, then was part of a Canadian team that captured silver at the Olympics. He finished the season making his NHL debut for the Flames, starting twice for a team that had fallen just out of the playoff picture.

While Kidd's two strong post-draft seasons positioned him well for his first pro season in 1992–93, he was in an organization with an established top-tier starter in Vernon and a reliable backup in Jeff Reese. Despite a strong training camp, the numbers game dictated that Kidd begin his pro career in Salt Lake playing behind Trefilov. After a slow start, playing infrequently, and adjusting to the nuances of the pro game, Kidd adapted well and built momentum, but his season was cut short when he suffered a broken right leg when one of his defencemen crashed into him while trying to take down an opponent.

Flames management pledged to give their young netminders a chance in 1993–94, leading to the bizarre circumstances of breaking camp at the beginning of the season with four goaltenders on their roster: Vernon, Kidd, Reese, and Muzzatti. That odd situation lasted for the first month of the season, but soon Reese injured his shoulder and Muzzatti caught a virus that briefly hospitalized him. After the two injured goalies recuperated, Muzzatti was sent to the minors and Reese was traded to the Hartford Whalers, leaving the full-time tandem as Vernon and Kidd.

The Flames saw enough from Kidd's body of work as Vernon's understudy that they traded the veteran to Detroit in the 1994 off-season, making Kidd the club's undisputed number one. He became Calgary's starter a season after Brodeur did in New Jersey and two seasons after Potvin did in Toronto.

When Kidd was given the reins by the Flames, he emerged as a good but not great starting netminder. He was a consistent regular season performer who usually gave the Flames a chance to win but rarely stole games. His big challenge was finding consistency, especially in the postseason, to the point where Theoren Fleury openly pondered in interviews following the 1996–97 season when the team would get some goaltending.

Fleury's comments seemed to spell the beginning of the end for Kidd in Calgary. He was traded to the Carolina Hurricanes, the relocated Hartford Whalers, in August 1997 with Gary Roberts in exchange for two-way forward Andrew Cassels and goaltending prospect Jean-Sebastian Giguere, ironically someone who scouts were touting as the next Martin Brodeur. The Flames' search for a franchise netminder would continue until Miikka Kiprusoff's arrival via trade from the San Jose Sharks in November 2003.

Kidd ended up playing 387 NHL games between his time with the Flames, Carolina, the Florida Panthers, and Toronto. Potvin played 635 NHL games and also bounced around quite a bit, spending time with Toronto, the Los Angeles Kings, New York Islanders, Vancouver Canucks, and Boston Bruins in his career. Brodeur played 1,266 NHL games, primarily with New Jersey but briefly with the St. Louis Blues, and between three

Stanley Cups and four Vezina Trophies, Brodeur established himself as the best goaltender of all time.

Drafting and development is not an exact science. Sometimes you can select the player who seems to perfectly fit your club's needs, nurture their drafting and development properly, and they still might not turn out precisely as imagined. The Flames trading up in 1990 to select Kidd instead of taking Brodeur isn't necessarily a cautionary tale about taking the wrong player, but rather an illustration of how much variability exists in player development, especially with goaltenders. Kidd turned into a productive, reliable goaltender at the NHL level.

His main fault was that he didn't turn into Martin Brodeur.

12

THE 1990S: A DECADE OF TRANSITION AND CHALLENGES

THE 1970S AND 1980s were a period of remarkable stability for the Flames franchise. Sure, they moved from Atlanta, Georgia, to Calgary, Alberta, but the relocation was the primary disruptor. They maintained the same general manager, Cliff Fletcher, throughout both decades, and aside from swapping out head scout Don Graham for Gerry Blair when the club moved to Canada, much of the major pieces of drafting infrastructure remained constant.

"There was a philosophy here," said Al Coates, who served in several hockey operations roles for the Flames, including as general manager between 1995 and 2000. "When the team was always drafting late in the first round, like 24, 25, 23 kind of thing, there was a solid emphasis on making sure that we got high-end skill in the first round, and it didn't always work. And then it was a bit of a change of philosophy to make sure they got a guy that's going to play in the second round."

The same stability of the 1980s would not follow the Flames very far into the 1990s. The Flames would experience significant changeovers with their general managers and head scouts, and they would also experience the most persistent challenges at converting draft picks into reliable NHL players in their franchise's history.

The 1990 draft was the final one with Fletcher at the helm. After selecting junior standout goaltender Trevor Kidd in the first round (11th overall), the club focused on defencemen with the remainder of their early selections: Nicolas Perreault (26th overall) from the Ontario junior A Hawkesbury Hawks in the second round; Etienne Belzile (41st overall), a freshman at Cornell University, in the second round; and Glen Mears (62nd overall), an American junior player committed to Bowling Green, in the third round. Second-round selection Vesa Viitakoski (32nd overall), a big-bodied forward from Finland, was arguably the player with the most offensive upside. Kidd had a good NHL career, playing 178 games over five seasons with the Flames (and 387 games overall in the NHL). Viitakoski was a fairly productive pro (both in Finland and the North American minors) who had a few short NHL stints, spending 23 games with the Flames. But aside from fourth-round pick Paul Kruse (83rd overall)—who played more than 200 games with the Flames and 400 overall in the NHL—few of the team's picks that season turned into impactful NHL players.

In an odd bit of trivia, the 1990 draft also featured the only rejected draft selection in Flames franchise history.

In the 11th round, 230th overall, the Flames selected 23-year-old Swedish right winger Thomas Bjuhr, playing with AIK of the Swedish Elitserien. However, Bjuhr's rights were already held by the Detroit Red Wings, who had selected the player back in the seventh round of the 1985 NHL Draft and, as reported by the *Detroit Free Press* and other local outlets but not widely publicized to the NHL's member clubs, had signed him to a three-year contract in May 1987. Bjuhr spent one season with Detroit's farm team before returning to Sweden to continue his playing career, which may have added to confusion about the status of his NHL rights. The initially attempted selection was deemed invalid by the league and the Flames weren't permitted to select another player with the pick.

Fletcher left the Flames organization in 1991, joining the Toronto Maple Leafs later that year as general manager and team president. Head coach Doug Risebrough, who had previously worked as assistant general manager following his retirement as a player in 1987, succeeded Fletcher as general manager. In Risebrough's first draft, the club selected Swedish forward Niklas Sundblad in the first round after an attempt to trade up from 19th overall to sixth overall to select Peter Forsberg didn't materialize. Sundblad was described by *The Hockey News* as a "Swedish Wendel Clark," and his playing style was characterized as aggressive and fearless. He made the transition to North America from Sweden but only spent three seasons in the Flames' system, playing just two NHL games, before returning to Sweden.

The two best value picks by the Flames in the 1991 crop were physical Laval winger Sandy McCarthy, a third-round selection (52nd overall), and Russian goaltender Andrei Trefilov, a 12th round gamble at 261st overall. McCarthy played more than 700 NHL games, including parts of five seasons with the Flames, while Trefilov spent a decade in North America and made a few appearances for Calgary, the Buffalo Sabres, and Chicago Blackhawks, accumulating 54 NHL games. Puck-moving Shawinigan blueliner Francois Groleau, a second-rounder (41st overall), impressed in junior but got caught in a minor league defender logjam in the Flames' system and played just eight NHL games, all with the Montreal Canadiens. Third-rounder Brian Caruso (63rd overall), a freshman winger from the University of Minnesota–Duluth, had a brief pro career and only played a single game in the Flames system.

The 1992 class was full of players who spent time in the NHL, though most of the NHL games they played were with other organizations. Sixth overall pick Cory Stillman of the Windsor Spitfires was considered the best playmaker in the draft. Stillman didn't turn into another Doug Gilmour, as was originally hoped, but he was a smart, reliable centre who played 393 games over parts of seven seasons for the Flames and won two Stanley Cups during a 1,025-game NHL career. He was traded to the St. Louis Blues in 2001 for forward Craig Conroy, who became an important player for the Flames, and a seventh-round pick in 2001.

Beyond Stillman, several players had decent enough showings, including NHL stints.

American high school defenceman Chris O'Sullivan (second round, 30th overall) played a few short stints with the Flames before being traded to the New York Rangers for minor league defender Lee Sorochan. O'Sullivan played 49 games with Calgary and 62 NHL games overall.

Swedish centre Mathias Johansson (third round, 54th over-all) stayed in Europe until 2002, played half a season with the Flames before being traded to the Pittsburgh Penguins for Shean Donovan. Johansson spent 46 games with the Flames and played 58 total NHL games.

Czech blueliner Robert Svehla (fourth round, 78th overall) had his rights traded to the Florida Panthers in exchange for a third-round pick in 1996 before he played a single game with Calgary. He then had a nine-year NHL career, playing 655 games.

Finnish blueliner Sami Helenius (fifth round, 102nd over-all) played in seven games for the Flames before being traded to the Tampa Bay Lightning for future considerations. He played 155 NHL games overall.

Verdun blueliner Joel Bouchard (sixth round, 129th over-all) spent parts of four seasons with the Flames before being claimed by Nashville in the 1998 expansion draft. He played 126 games for the Flames and 364 games in the NHL over 11 seasons.

Swedish winger Jonas Hoglund (10th round, 222nd overall) played two seasons with the Flames, seeing 118 games before being traded to Montreal for Valeri Bure. Hoglund played seven seasons in the NHL, suiting up in 545 games.

Risebrough's third draft, the 1993 class, had lean results. The Flames traded forward Craig Berube to the Washington Capitals so they wouldn't select Swedish forward Jesper Mattsson with the pick before Calgary. The Flames had 18th overall, while the Capitals took forward Jason Allison at the 17th spot. An offensive-minded forward, Mattsson's game didn't translate well to North America. He played three seasons in the Flames' minor league system, played zero NHL games, then returned to Europe when his deal expired.

Second-round pick Jamie Allison (44th overall)—no relation to Jason—was a mobile blueliner playing junior hockey in the Ontario league with the Detroit Junior Red Wings and played parts of four seasons in the Flames system but couldn't cement himself in the lineup. He played 64 games for the Flames, was traded to Chicago, then was claimed back on waivers by the Flames three years later, and traded again, that time to the Columbus Blue Jackets. He played 101 games for the Flames overall and 372 games in the NHL over his career. American junior winger Dan Tompkins, a third-round pick (70th overall), played in college at Wisconsin and then played Canadian junior in Seattle, but never played in the Flames system.

Outside of the first three rounds, fourth-round forward Marty Murray (96th overall) played 26 games with the Flames and 261 overall in an eight-year NHL career. Forward John Emmons, taken in the fifth round (122nd overall) never played in the Flames system, but played 85 NHL games between the Ottawa Senators, Tampa Bay, and Boston. Sixth-round forward Andreas Karlsson (148th overall) was traded to the Atlanta Thrashers for future considerations in 1999 and ended up playing 264 NHL games between the Thrashers and Lightning.

The best value pick for the Flames in 1993 may have been Russian winger German Titov, drafted as a mature 27-year-old European pro out of the Finnish elite league in the 10th round (252nd overall). He came over immediately, playing five seasons and 345 games with the Flames, and nine seasons and 624 games in the NHL. He was traded to the Penguins with depth forward Todd Hlushko in a swap that netted the Flames forward Dave Roche and goaltender Ken Wregget.

The Flames replaced Blair with Tom Thompson as head scout for the 1994 draft, with Blair taking a position with the NHL's Central Scouting Service. Looking for some size to help the club's small, skilled forwards, the Flames opted for Brandon forward Chris Dingman at 19th overall. He spent one full season with the Flames as a physical forward but failed to stick in their lineup in his second season and was sent to the Colorado Avalanche in the Theoren Fleury trade after playing 72 games with the big club. (He played 385 games in his entire NHL career.)

Russian defenceman Dmitri Riabykin, their second-round pick (45th overall), never left Russia. Third-round pick Chris Clark (77th overall), a defensive-minded forward from Clarkson University, provided good value at that part of the draft. He spent parts of five seasons with the Flames (and 11 in the NHL overall with Calgary, Washington, and Columbus), playing 278 games with Calgary and 607 games overall.

The Flames' late-round picks in 1994 provided some decent value. Fifth-round pick Nils Ekman (107th overall) was a Swedish forward the Flames traded to Tampa Bay for Andreas Johansson. Ekman played 264 NHL games in his career. Czech forward Ladislav Kohn was a seventh-round pick (175th overall) playing as an import with the WHL's Swift Current Broncos. He played nine games for Calgary before a trade to Toronto for minor league forward David Cooper. Kohn played 186 NHL games in his career. Ninth-round pick Jorgen Jonsson (227th overall) was a Swedish winger they traded to the NY Islanders for Czech forward

Jan Hlavac. Jonsson played 81 games over a one-season NHL run. Tenth-round pick Mike Peluso (253rd overall) stayed in college and never signed with the Flames, eventually playing 38 NHL games—his cousin, also named Mike Peluso, ended up playing 23 games for the Flames in 1997–98. And 11th-round pick Pavel Torgaev (279th overall) was a Russian forward playing in Finland. He played 50 games for the Flames, was claimed off waivers by Tampa Bay, then played five more NHL games.

Looking for another physical player, this time a blue-liner, the Flames hit paydirt in the first round of the 1995 NHL Draft with Denis Gauthier. Selected at 20th overall from Drummondville of the Quebec Major Junior Hockey League, Gauthier spent seven seasons with the Flames. While he wasn't a tremendous scoring threat, he became known for his punishing open-ice hits. He played 384 games for the Flames and later got to 554 NHL games after a trade to the Phoenix Coyotes.

Beyond Gauthier, Russian winger Pavel Smirnov, taken in the second round (46th overall), played just a single game in the Flames' minor league system, while Medicine Hat's Rocky Thompson, a third-round pick (72nd overall) as a physical defender, played three seasons in the Flames system but failed to gain a toehold in the NHL lineup with just 15 games. He was traded to Florida and played 10 more NHL games. The best value pick was sixth-rounder Clarke Wilm (150th overall), a checking forward from Saskatoon of the Western Hockey League, who spent four seasons with the Flames and served as a strong penalty killer for the club before leaving in free agency. He played 303 games for Calgary and 455 in his career.

After Risebrough's departure from the club in late 1995, assistant general manager Coates took over as general manager, and he and Thompson were at the helm of the 1996 draft. At 13th overall, Regina Pats blueliner Derek Morris was the Flames' first-round selection. Morris was a well-regarded puck-moving blueliner with a complimentary skill set to Gauthier's more smash-mouth style.

"We stepped up and it was a bit of a surprise quite frankly that we took Derek Morris," said Coates. "I don't think anybody else in the league had him in the first round. And it turned out to be a really good pick."

Morris made the Flames' roster in 1997–98 as a 19-year-old and played five seasons and 343 games with the club, as part of a 1,107-game NHL career. He went to Colorado in 2002 in a trade that brought forwards Stephane Yelle and Chris Drury to Calgary.

Beyond Morris, though, the draft crop leaned out. Second-rounder Travis Brigley (39th overall), a winger from the Lethbridge Hurricanes, spent three years in Calgary's system and played 19 games but could never cement himself in the NHL roster. He played another 36 NHL games with Colorado after changing organizations a few times. Val-d'Or Foreurs centre Steve Begin, taken one pick after Brigley (40th overall), played more than 500 NHL games—including parts of five seasons (159 games over two stints) in the Flames' system—but did so as a journeyman who bounced between the big league and the minors. Russian winger Dmitri Vlasenkov, selected in the third round (73rd overall), spent one season in North America but otherwise remained in Russia following his selection.

Aside from Morris, the two best value selections by the Flames in 1996 were likely puck-moving Finnish defence-man Toni Lydman, from the fourth round (89th overall), and rugged Slovakian winger Ronald Petrovicky, from the ninth round (228th overall). Lydman spent a few seasons after his selection playing in Finland, but when he came over to North America in 2000, he was able to make the Flames roster and remained a productive player for four seasons and 289 games before a trade to Buffalo. He ended up playing 11 seasons and 847 games in the NHL overall. Petrovicky was playing as an import in the Western Hockey League and spent a few seasons in the Flames' system, including a season and a half in the NHL where he played 107 games, before bouncing around the league for the rest of his career. He made 342 NHL appearances across four teams.

The Flames' first selection in the 1997 NHL Draft was the subject of a good deal of internal debate within the club's hockey operations staff.

"That was Joe Thornton's draft. Patrick Marleau went second, and we had the sixth pick in the draft," said Coates. "We actually tried to move that pick to another team with a player on the current roster to move up in the draft, which almost worked but didn't materialize. And we drafted based on the needs of the team. The biggest need of the team that particular year was to get an up-and-coming, promising cen-treman for the team for the next X amount of years."

The two most likely players available to the Flames at sixth overall that suited their needs were Russian winger Sergei Samsonov, who was playing pro hockey in North America with the Detroit Vipers of the International Hockey League, and Ontario junior star centre Daniel Tkaczuk, who was playing with the Barrie Colts. Which player to select was the subject of debate, with Samsonov perceived as a more mature player who could step into the NHL immediately and contribute offensively, but Tkaczuk playing a more important position (centre) and being seen as having more developmental upside over the long term.

"There was a big debate about that," said Coates. "Samsonov, if I remember correctly, was playing in the IHL at the time. We had a bit of a split camp on that, quite frankly. And obviously he stepped in. He went eighth to Boston and played in the league right away."

The decision was made to select Tkaczuk, which allowed Samsonov to slide to Boston.

"As it turns out, based on what Samsonov did, maybe that's the decision we should've come up with," said Coates. "But we were really in need of a centreman for the future. I know because I surveyed a bunch of NHL teams myself thereafter, and there wasn't an NHL team in the league that didn't have Daniel Tkaczuk in the top 10."

While Samsonov joined the NHL ranks in the next season, 1997–98, Tkaczuk took a little longer to mature, eventually going pro in 1999–2000 after playing two more OHL seasons with Barrie and playing in two World Junior tournaments for Canada, winning silver in 1999. Tkaczuk seemed on-track in his development, making the team out of camp in 2000–01. But Tkaczuk suffered a concussion in a game against Phoenix 19 games into the season, falling down while tangled up with an opponent and face-planting on the ice. He suffered a second concussion later that season, and his play tailed off after his recovery. He was eventually traded to St. Louis and never played a game in the NHL again. Incidentally, Thompson left the Flames organization following the 1997 draft to pursue other scouting opportunities, soon landing in a scouting position with the Edmonton Oilers.

Beyond Tkaczuk, the draft class had very sparse pro success. Prince Albert goaltender Evan Lindsay (second round, 32nd overall) re-entered the draft and was selected by Montreal in 1999. Oshawa winger John Tripp (second round, 42nd overall) went pro right away but spent his three years in the Flames system bouncing around in the minors. He ended up playing in 43 NHL games with other clubs. Russian defenceman Dmitri Kokorev (second round, 51st overall) stayed in his homeland and never signed with the Flames. Spokane centre Derek Schutz (third round, 60th overall) never signed with the Flames and re-entered the draft. University of Denver centre Erik Andersson (third round, 70th overall) ended up signing with the Flames, but he only played 12 games with big clubs as he bounced up and down from the minors. He was eventually traded to Chicago. The entire 1997 draft class played just 81 NHL games, with only 31 of those being for the Flames.

By the 1998 NHL Draft, Coates had senior scout Nick Polano running the draft board. With the sixth overall pick—for the second draft in a row—the club opted for another offensive-minded Ontario junior product, winger Rico Fata. Fata was a very productive, dynamic offensive forward in junior. He made the Flames roster out of camp the fall after his selection, but he mustered just one point in his first 20 games. After playing for Canada at the World Juniors, he was returned to his junior team in London. He played two more seasons in the Flames organization, primarily in the minors, getting called up for just seven games. He was claimed off waivers by the NY Rangers early in the 2001–02 season. He appeared 27 times for the Flames and played 230 NHL games in an eight-year NHL run.

Beyond Fata, Prince George centre Blair Betts, a second-round selection (33rd overall), was an astute pick. A savvy defensive forward, Betts played 35 games over parts of three seasons for the Flames before being traded to the Rangers. He had a 477-game career as a depth player in the NHL. Third-round selection Paul Manning (62nd overall), a blueliner at Colorado College, had his rights traded to Columbus before he went pro, eventually making eight NHL appearances. Fourth-rounder Dany Sabourin (108th overall), a goaltender from Sherbrooke in the Quebec Major Junior Hockey League, played just four games for the Flames but developed into a reliable minor league goaltender for several organizations. He worked his way into 57 NHL contests.

The 1999 draft was again run by Coates and Polano, the final one under their stewardship. At 11th overall, the Flames went with aspiring power forward Oleg Saprykin, a Russian import playing for Seattle of the Western League. The club reportedly considered trading that pick to the NY Islanders for veteran forward Brad Isbister but opted against it when Saprykin was still available for selection. Saprykin played 187 games over parts of five seasons for the Flames and was a strong role player during their 2004 Stanley Cup Final appearance. He was traded to Phoenix for Daymond Langkow and played 325 NHL games overall. Behind Saprykin, the most prominent picks were Boston University centre Dan

Cavanaugh, a second-round pick (38th overall) whose rights were traded to the expansion Minnesota Wild the following year, and third-rounder Craig Anderson (77th overall), an impressive goaltender for Guelph in the Ontario League whose rights the Flames lost when he wasn't qualified following a management changeover after the 1999–2000 season. Anderson played more than 700 games in the NHL over 20 seasons with six different NHL clubs, remaining active into the 2022–23 season.

The Flames had a lot of draft choices throughout the 1990s and drafted a lot of players. Through three different GMs and three different head scouts running their drafting, they made some good picks and some bad picks. Unfortunately for the club's developmental system, very few of the picks they made turned into bankable NHL stars, or even significant assets that the club could use to upgrade their roster. In fact, few of their selections even turned into significant figures in the club's minor league system, which only served to make existing organizational depth challenges even worse.

The '90s were a decade of transition for the Flames, as they experienced their first management changeovers and departures of head scouts, but the majority of their new faces were individuals promoted from within their own organization. The Flames would undergo a much more extensive transition before the 2000 NHL Draft.

13

DRAFTING A MEMBER OF QUEBEC PRO WRESTLING AND HOCKEY ROYALTY

IN MANY SPORTS, growing up in a family that has a background in that particular sport is seen as a huge benefit. In addition to having experience and expertise that could help with a young player's skills development, the knowledge of the rigours of pursuing a sport professionally—and the sacrifices necessary to be a high-level athlete—are often big difference-makers.

The two major sports that Calgary is best known for, aside from perhaps rodeo, are hockey and professional wrestling. The Flames are the latest in a line of several prominent professional and junior hockey teams to play in the city, and

Calgary gained worldwide fame as the home of Stampede Wrestling for several decades. The Flames even played their first three seasons in the Stampede Corral, where Stampede Wrestling held their major events during the same period in the early '80s. Heck, beloved local broadcaster Ed Whalen was arguably more famous for announcing Stampede Wrestling matches than he was for Flames games, with several of his iconic turns of phrase debuting during wrestling broadcasts before being used to describe hockey.

In 1995, the Flames selected 18-year-old Drummondville Voltigeurs defenceman Denis Gauthier in the first round with the 20th overall pick. Despite being a French Canadian who was drafted by a team in Canada's province known far more for cowboys than bilingualism, Gauthier's personal background made him an ideal fit for the Flames and for the city. He had deep family roots not just within the game of hockey, but also within the realm of professional wrestling. Gauthier is a member of the Rougeau family, essentially Montreal's answer to Calgary's Hart family of wrestlers and promoters.

"I don't think Denis had the will to go into the family business," said wrestling historian Pat Laprade. "He was training in hockey since he was a little kid."

Tracing Gauthier's lineage back to the beginning of his family's time in pro wrestling, his great-uncle, Jean Rougeau, and his grandfather, Jacques Rougeau Sr., were extremely prominent sporting figures in the Montreal area between the 1950s and 1980s. Both men began wrestling in the 1950s, following in the footsteps of their uncle by marriage, Eduoard (Eddie) Auger. While Auger wrestled throughout the eastern portion of Canada and the United States, his nephews focused on Canada, and more precisely the province of Quebec. In addition to wrestling, Jean began promoting shows and also branched out into hockey. He was one of the founders of the Quebec Major Junior Hockey League, and he owned the Laval Nationals for several years, and briefly coached the club during a period where a young Mike Bossy became a star. He also served as the second president of the QMJHL between 1981 and 1983, having the role until just prior to his death due to cancer in May 1983. The QMJHL's Jean Rougeau Trophy, awarded to the team with the most regular season points, is named in his honour.

Jacques Sr. had five children, three sons and two daughters. All three of his sons—Jacques Jr., Raymond, and Armand—became professional wrestlers. Jacques and Raymond formed a tag team that rose to international stardom in the World Wrestling Federation as the Fabulous Rougeau Brothers, a pair of over-the-top caricatures of French-Canadian stereotypes. (They also went through a period where they claimed to be Americans and entered the ring to a song that satirically proclaimed them "All-American Boys.") Following Raymond's retirement due to injuries, Jacques also wrestled as the villainous Mountie and teamed with fellow Quebecois wrestler Pierre-Carl Ouellet as The Quebecers, a tag team along the same lines as the Fabulous Rougeau Brothers. One of Jacques Sr.'s daughters, Joanne, became a wrestling show promoter, even serving as the local promoter for the WWF in eastern Canada during the late 1990s, and ended up marrying a professional wrestler named Denis Gauthier. Their son, Denis Jr., was born in 1976.

Growing up, the younger Denis didn't display much interest in pro wrestling and instead gravitated toward hockey, where he excelled. But in his teens, he was briefly enlisted to help his uncle, Jacques Jr., in the ring.

"He was pretty much used as a crash test wrestler, in a sense. Just before Pierre-Carl Ouellet and Jacques Rougeau Jr. started teaming together for WWF, Jacques had a big ring in his backyard and they wanted to practice some tag team maneuvers, so they actually used Denis Jr. to practice moves," Laprade said. "So they were actually doing moves on him to make sure the timing was right."

Joanne, Denis' mother and Jacques' sister, was nervous about her son helping out due to his promising hockey career.

"She was panicking saying, 'Be careful with my son, he's going to play in the NHL one day!'" said Laprade. "There was no harm, Denis was alright, he didn't get injured. But I do believe that was the only time he ever stepped foot in a ring and did any actual wrestling, but he wasn't really wrestling. He was just there to take the shots or take the moves."

If there's one benefit to being part of a family of wrestlers and bodybuilders, it's likely that you learn how to train and diet properly. As a result, Gauthier grew up strong, which probably contributed to his physical, bruising playing style. He was drafted into the QMJHL in 1992 and began playing in that league with Drummondville full-time as a 16-year-old. Gauthier played three seasons in the QMJHL before he was drafted by the Flames with the 20th pick in the 1995 NHL Draft. He was the 14th-ranked North American skater according to the Central Scouting Service.

At the time, Flames scouting coordinator Tom Thompson described him to reporters as such: "He is an enthusiastic open-ice hitter. Sometimes, a little overly enthusiastic." General manager Doug Risebrough praised his physicality, noting, "We have been looking for this type of defenceman for a long time." Gauthier played one more season with Drummondville—also representing Canada at the World Juniors tournament—then he began playing pro hockey late in the 1995–96 season, finishing the season and playing in the playoffs for the Flames' farm team in Saint John.

How quickly Gauthier was going to get to the National Hockey League was always going to depend on how rapidly he could find the balancing act between playing physical and playing too physical. In hockey, bodychecking can be a big benefit for a team: a good check can separate a player from the puck and make the puck-carrier a little nervous whenever they hold onto the puck for too long, especially around a player known for their punishing checks. As a result, having physical players can lead to a team having the puck more than it normally would without them.

That said, when a player is thinking about throwing a big body check all the time, they can lose sight of other aspects of the game—the hockey equivalent of, "If the only tool you have is a hammer, all problems start to look like nails." At his worst, Gauthier would follow the puck carrier and then plow into them without regard for whether that player still had the puck. Sometimes that resulted in a boarding or inter-ference penalty. Sometimes that resulted in an odd-man rush, as his defence partner would be left to defend against multiple opposition players because Gauthier pulled himself out of position going for a hit.

It took Gauthier the better part of two seasons to find the right balance, but he proved to be an effective enough defensive player to earn call-ups during the 1997–98 season and to spend most of the 1998–99 season with the big club. He became a full-time NHLer in 1999–2000, though a pair of injury-related absences limited him to playing about half the season. With the Flames, Gauthier found a niche. He wobbled between the second and third defensive pairing during much of his time with the club, playing a stay-at-home game and also working on the club's penalty kill. The only thing that seemed to hamper his run with Calgary was bad injury luck. Most notably, he suffered a knee injury in the sixth game of the 2004 playoffs and was sidelined for the remainder of the club's run to the Stanley Cup Final.

Following the 2004 postseason, Gauthier and Oleg Saprykin were traded to the Phoenix Coyotes in exchange for two-way centre Daymond Langkow. Gauthier played three NHL seasons after leaving Calgary, split between Phoenix, the Philadelphia Flyers, and Los Angeles Kings, before his retirement in 2009.

All three of Jacques Rougeau Jr.'s sons wrestled, but only briefly—his final match in 2017 saw him team up with his sons, mirroring his own father's retirement match decades prior. The impact of the extended Rougeau–Gauthier clan continues in the hockey world, though. Denis Gauthier's nephew, Julien, was a first-round selection of the Carolina Hurricanes in 2016—selected one spot later than his uncle, 21st overall. Denis' son Kaylen played four seasons in the

QMJHL and captained the Sherbrooke Phoenix in the 2022–23 season. Younger son Ethan was selected by Tampa Bay in the second round of the 2023 NHL Draft and was teammates with his brother for two seasons in Sherbrooke.

The focus of the extended family has swung from the ring to the rink for the current generation.

"When you look at the Rougeau-Gauthier family, it's all about hockey, no doubt about that," said Laprade.

Calgary is, at its core, a city that loves rough-and-tumble sports and its most beloved sports figures have been the rough-and-tumble athletes. Jarome Iginla, the greatest Flames player of all time, came from the same 1995 draft class as Gauthier and was a higher-end skill player. But Gauthier was a quietly important player for the franchise and fit the Flames' style, needs, and culture, on and off the ice, like a glove.

14

CRAIG BUTTON'S FIRST TWO, VERY DIFFERENT DRAFTS AS FLAMES GENERAL MANAGER

THE 1980S WERE a fantastic decade for the Calgary Flames as a franchise. The club relocated to Canada, found a fervent local fanbase, and enjoyed tremendous on-ice success. Between the 1980–81 and 1989–90 seasons, the team had the sixth-most regular season wins in the NHL, made the playoffs every single season, reached the league semi-finals in 1981 and the Stanley Cup Final in 1986, and won a Stanley Cup in 1989. Simply put, the 1980s set a very high standard for the franchise.

The 1990s did not live up to that lofty standard. Between the 1990–91 and 1999–2000 seasons, the Flames had the 15th-most regular season wins in the NHL and made the playoffs five times, never advancing past the first round.

In 1996, the Flames named Ron Bremner as their new team president. Following the 1999–2000 season, with the Flames finishing outside of the playoff picture for the fourth consecutive season, Bremner decided that changes were necessary. Big changes. On April 11, three days after the club's final game and about two months before Calgary was set to host the 2000 NHL Draft at the Saddledome, Bremner fired general manager Al Coates and player personnel director Nick Polano and announced that the expiring contracts of head coach Brian Sutter and assistant coach Rich Preston would not be renewed.

The sweeping changes resulted in long-time amateur scouting coordinator Ian McKenzie becoming (by default) the highest-ranking person in hockey operations for several weeks, as well as the person responsible for handling the final preparations for the upcoming draft. In early June, Bremner cemented the hiring of a new general manager: Dallas Stars director of player personnel Craig Button. Button was part of a family with an extensive background in hockey—and scouting in particular. His father, Jack, was a long-time front office fixture with Pittsburgh and Washington and helped create the NHL's Central Scouting Service, serving as its first director. Craig had worked in scouting and the Stars' front office for more than a decade, helping to construct the 1999 Stanley Cup championship team. Taking the reins of the Flames seemed like the logical next step for his career progression. Button was the first general manager in franchise history who wasn't promoted from within.

But there were some strings attached regarding Button and his first draft with the Flames. Because Button was intimately involved in the direction of Dallas' amateur scouting and the construction of their draft list and overall drafting strategy, the Stars didn't want him involved in Calgary's drafting in 2000. As a matter of fact, restricting Button's involvement in the draft was brought up very early in the interview process. Flames brass was sufficiently convinced that Button was the right man to chart their club's future that they were completely fine with the restrictions. So it came about that when the Flames hosted the NHL draft for the first time, their new general manager was not allowed to make picks, and their drafting was handled by the most senior scout left in the organization: McKenzie.

"My work had been done in the scouting arena with Dallas, and they didn't feel that Calgary should benefit from that at their expense," said Button. "I had information and knowledge that could impact them. That's what Calgary agreed upon...I even removed myself from the table."

Because he wasn't allowed to be involved in picks, and to avoid the appearance of impropriety—it wouldn't look great if he was sitting at the table for the entire draft while the Flames were making picks, even if he wasn't involved in deciding which players were selected—Button set up shop in the owners' suite at the Saddledome for the draft.

"With papers flying all around, I didn't even want to give any type of spectre that I may know about players and that I may be influencing their picks," said Button. "The deal was straightforward and you know what, you abide by it, and I thought that was the best way to do it. I could make trades, I could do things surrounding the draft with respect to moving picks or whatnot, but in terms of working the draft list and guiding the scouts, [I was] not part of it."

Button was allowed to make trades, so he was armed with a phone and stayed in constant communication with McKenzie at the Flames' table, armed with questions about whether a proposed pick would be worth it but not allowed to ask about players the Flames were considering taking at those picks. Button ended up pulling the trigger on two trades during the two days of the draft. On the first day, he sent the 43rd overall pick—previously acquired earlier in June when Button traded young goalie Jean-Sebastien Giguere to the Mighty Ducks of Anaheim so he could protect veteran Fred Brathwaite in the upcoming expansion draft—to the Washington Capitals for minor league forward Miika Elomo and a fourth-round pick. On the second day, he traded an eighth-round pick—a compensatory pick the club received after Tom Chorske left as a free agent—to the Buffalo Sabres for an eighth-round pick in the following year's draft.

At the draft table, McKenzie made nine selections: two goaltenders, four defencemen, and three forwards. Their top pick was junior goaltender Brent Krahn, starter for the local Calgary Hitmen junior team, at ninth overall. Krahn was a 6'4" goaltender who had a strong performance in his draft year. While the selection was met with a few chuckles—of course they took the kid from the local junior team in the draft they hosted—within scouting circles, Krahn was seen as one of the top netminders in his age group. While Krahn was a promising pick, he had some extremely bad injury luck in the years following his selection. He played three WHL seasons after being drafted and missed significant chunks of time with recurring knee injuries, which resulted in a pair of surgeries. He failed to progress in the minor leagues and, aside from one period played for Dallas in relief, he never made a splash in the NHL.

"I know from our group in Dallas, we held Brent Krahn in high regard," said Button. "There [are] things that happen development-wise, injury-wise, that impact a player, and that's what makes it such an inexact exercise. Brent was a competitor, he was talented, but he got derailed by injuries. And when a goaltender starts to have injuries in his knees or his hips, that's a real problem."

Their two second-round picks were blueliner Kurtis Foster from the Peterborough Petes at 40th overall and centre Jarret Stoll of the Kootenay Ice at 46th overall. A highly touted defenceman in his draft year, the 6'5", 205-pound Foster slid down the rankings in the back half of the season. Stoll was touted as a dynamic offensive forward who could score key goals at key times. Neither played a game of pro hockey in the Flames organization. Foster's rights were traded to the Atlanta Thrashers midway through the 2001–02 season in exchange for veteran defenceman Petr Buzek. Stoll and the Flames couldn't come to terms on an entry-level contract, and a trade involving his NHL rights wasn't consummated before the signing deadline, so he re-entered the draft in 2002 and was selected by the Edmonton Oilers in the second round.

Among the later picks were Hungarian import goaltender Levente Szuper from the Ottawa 67's in the fourth round,

6'5" defenceman Wade Davis from the Hitmen and winger Travis Moen from the Kelowna Rockets in the fifth round, 26-year-old Finnish winger Jukka Hentunen from HPK Helsinki in the sixth round, big Czech defenceman David Hajek from KLH Chomutov in the eighth round, and 5'8" offensive blueliner Micki DuPont from Kamloops in the ninth round. McKenzie insisted on selecting DuPont, who served as Blazers team captain and led all WHL defencemen in scoring in 1999–2000, his 19-year-old season. The Flames declined to offer contracts to Davis and Moen. Hentunen signed and played part of the 2001–02 season with the Flames, but he suffered a knee injury mid-season and was traded to the Nashville Predators at the trade deadline. DuPont went pro with the Flames organization right after the draft and became a productive minor leaguer who played a handful of games between Calgary, the Pittsburgh Penguins, and St. Louis Blues.

The results of the 2000 draft, nominally Button's first, were fairly unimpressive. But one could argue that Button's first "real" draft at the helm was the 2001 edition, and it was a weekend where he definitively put his stamp on the organization with a few big trades and savvy draft selections. The busy weekend was the end result of earlier trade talks, dating back to before the trade deadline.

"A lot of seeds are planted at a trade deadline," said Button. "Most things that are talked about leading into a trade deadline don't come to fruition. The bigger ones do, and certainly those become known, but when you go forward and you start to look at the period around the draft, those things didn't just start at the draft. Those were the continuations of discussions that had happened previously. You've got a pretty good handle on your team, you're trying to understand what you want to do differently, what types of positions you're trying to address and whatnot."

On the first day of the draft, Button made three trades. Looking to upgrade the club's goaltending, the Flames sent incumbent goalie Fred Brathwaite, prospects Daniel Tkaczuk and Sergei Varlamov, and a ninth-round pick to the Blues in exchange for goalie Roman Turek and a fourth-round pick. Turek was a reliable netminder and eventually served as the team's backup during the 2004 run to the Stanley Cup Final. Looking to change up the forward group, the Flames sent forwards Valeri Bure and Jason Wiemer to the Florida Panthers for forward Rob Niedermayer and a second-round pick. Niedermayer didn't have a big long-term impact, but he provided the Flames with centre depth before a subsequent trade to Anaheim.

During the first round, the Flames accepted an offer from the Phoenix Coyotes for their pick; the Flames ended up moving down from 11th to 14th, getting their own previously traded second-round pick in the swap. At 14th overall, the Flames took Boston College freshman winger Chuck Kobasew, an offensive-minded player who scored the goal that won his team the NCAA national championship in his draft year. Kobasew went pro in 2002 and played four seasons with the Flames as a checking forward, including playing every game during the Flames' run to the 2004 Stanley Cup Final, before being traded to the Boston Bruins in 2007.

The club selected a pair of Russians in the second round with a pair of picks that they didn't have prior to the weekend's

trades: centre Andrei Taratukhin from Avangard Omsk at
41st overall and goaltender Andrei Medvedev from Spartak
Moscow at 56th overall. Taratukhin was seen as a solid all-
around forward—a jack-of-all trades but master of none—but
played just a single season in the Flames system. Medvedev
was a goaltender praised for his raw potential but criticized
for his lack of fitness, listed at 6'1" and 249 pounds—the
news reports after his selection flat-out referred to him as
"chubby"—and his reputation didn't improve over time, with
him later termed the "roly-poly goalie." He never migrated
to North America.

On the second day of the draft, Button acquired veteran
winger Dean McAmmond from the Philadelphia Flyers in
exchange for a fourth-round pick. McAmmond was a versatile addition to the team and formed a strong forward trio
alongside Jarome Iginla and Craig Conroy. The Flames also
made eight draft selections on the second day. Very few of
them amounted to much in North American pro hockey,
unfortunately. Finnish winger Tomi Maki, selected from
Jokerit in the fourth round, signed an entry-level deal and
played in the Flames system for three seasons. He earned a
call-up, played a single game on the fourth line, and didn't get
a second opportunity. He returned to Finland at the end of his
contract. A more successful late-round selection was winger
David Moss, a seventh-round pick out of Cedar Rapids in the
United States Hockey League junior circuit and committed to
the University of Michigan. Moss took his time developing,
spending four seasons at college before going pro. He was a
productive minor leaguer and earned a mid-season call-up
in 2006–07 due to a few injuries on the NHL club's roster.

He scored goals in each of his first three NHL games and never went back to the minors. Moss ended up playing nine seasons in the NHL, including six with Calgary.

While Button was theoretically in charge of the 2000 draft for Calgary, it was his draft in name only. The scouting work had been completed by the time he was hired, and he didn't have the authority, given the conditions surrounding his hiring, to really sink his teeth into things. The draft, on many levels, ended up being a bust. But his 2001 performance, the product of a year of familiarizing himself with his team's needs, his scouting staff's skill, and the other general managers' tendencies, was much more productive.

Button noted that some advice from Ken Holland, then the GM of the Detroit Red Wings, helped shape how he approached managing his staff during the drafting process given his own experiences running the show for the Stars.

"He told me, your instincts are going to be to want to do something that you know really well," said Button. "Resist those temptations. You know what, let the scouts do it. Think about your own self. Bob Gainey let you do it. People let me do it. You've got to let the group do it. It was great advice. It was something I already believed in. But it was just a really good reminder from Kenny: [talk to the] scouts, set out the parameters, [explain] what you're looking for, and then let them go."

The Flames didn't enjoy a lot of on-ice success during Button's tenure as GM. They made zero playoff appearances during his three seasons at the club's helm. But Button's wheeling and dealing during his time with the club did a lot to set the team up with assets. Some of them played for the Flames, while some of them were able to be swapped into other assets. Much of the construction of the team that went to the 2004 Stanley Cup Final was done after Button's departure, but he acquired several key pieces and helped set the table for the team's future success.

15

A FAMILY AFFAIR: THE SUTTERS, THE FLAMES, AND THE DRAFT

IN THE FIVE decades of Flames franchise history, members of many different hockey families have made their mark on the franchise. Off the ice, the clan that had the largest impact is likely the Seaman family, as brothers Byron and Daryl were among the original ownership group that purchased the Atlanta Flames and moved them north to Calgary. But from an on-ice perspective, in terms of drafting, developing, coaching, and otherwise shaping the team that hit the ice over the years, no family has had the same impact as the Sutters.

Louis and Grace Sutter put down roots on a farm just outside of Viking, Alberta, a farming community located east of Edmonton. They had seven children, all sons. All seven of their sons played hockey growing up and showed a lot of promise. Their eldest son elected to stay on the farm and not pursue hockey further, but his six younger siblings all chased their dreams on the ice and achieved success to various degrees—for a 24-season period between 1976–77 and 2000–01, at least one of the six brothers was on a National Hockey League roster. Five of those six Sutter siblings went on to have a significant impact on the course of the Flames franchise.

The eldest Sutter sibling was Gary, born in 1954. He was reportedly a defenceman, though he never played high-end organized hockey, so details about his hockey prowess remain sparse and often veer into the realm of urban legend. His brothers maintain that he was the most talented member of the family, but that his heart wasn't into pursuing hockey as a career.

The six Sutter siblings that pursued hockey were Brian (born 1956, left wing), Darryl (1958, left wing), Duane (1960, right wing), Brent (1962, centre), and twins Rich (1963, right wing) and Ron (centre). Gary and Brian were offered try-outs by the Alberta Junior Hockey League's Red Deer Rustlers in 1972; Gary declined, but from then on, every Sutter played for the Rustlers. From 1972–80, the Rustlers had at least one Sutter on their team every season. They peaked at three simultaneously, with Brent, Rich and Ron during the 1979–80 season.

The Sutter boys all moved on from the Rustlers to the Western Hockey League's Lethbridge Broncos. From 1974–83, the Broncos had at least one Sutter on their team every season. Like the Rustlers, the Broncos juggled Brent, Rich, and Ron, though they did so for two seasons: 1980–81 and 1981–82.

All six brothers were drafted by NHL clubs. Brian was taken in the second round (20th overall) by the St. Louis Blues in 1976. Darryl was an 11th-round selection by the Chicago Black Hawks (179th overall) in 1978. Duane went 17th overall, in the first round, to the New York Islanders in 1979. The following season, the Islanders nabbed Brent 17th overall in the first round—reportedly, Flames scout Ian McKenzie begged general manager Cliff Fletcher to select Brent Sutter over Denis Cyr at 13th overall, but Fletcher opted for Cyr instead. In 1982, the twins were separated, but both were selected by Pennsylvania teams in the first round: the Philadelphia Flyers took Ron at fourth overall, while Rich went 10th overall to the Pittsburgh Penguins.

All six brothers played in the NHL. Darryl played the fewest games, limited to 406 due to a slew of injuries that ultimately contributed to his playing career ending prematurely. Brent played the longest, reaching 1,111 games, with Ron's 1,093 just behind him. Between 1976 and 2001, there was always at least one Sutter brother playing in the NHL. Between 1982 and 1987, when Darryl retired, all six Sutters were playing in hockey's top league. Two brothers won Stanley Cups as players, with Duane playing on four consecutive championship teams with the Islanders (from 1980–83) and Brent joining him for two of them (1982 and 1983).

Following the end of their playing days, all six brothers stayed involved in the game. Brian, Darryl, and Brent went into coaching, all spending time as NHL head coaches. Ron, Rich, and Duane went into scouting and player development. Five of the six brothers worked for the Flames organization in some capacity, with at least one Sutter brother being employed by the organization—as a player or staffer—between 1997 and 2023. Rich was the only brother to never work or play for the Flames, though he worked as an intermission analyst on Sportsnet's television coverage of the team for several seasons.

The six Sutter brothers all held positions of significance within the Flames' hockey operations and development side. Brian coached the Flames for three seasons, from 1997–2000. While he was head coach, the Flames drafted his son, Shaun, in the fourth round (102nd overall) of the 1998 draft—Brian told reporters at the time he was unaware that the club had planned on selecting him—with Shaun playing a handful of seasons in the Flames system before departing to play pro hockey in Europe. Ron played with the Flames during his final NHL season, 2000–01, then retired and joined the front office. He served as a pro scout for several seasons, then moved in a series of roles in player development, ultimately working for the Flames for roughly 20 seasons. Duane worked as Calgary's director of player personnel for three seasons between 2008 and 2011. Brent was head coach for three seasons from 2009 to 2012. Needless to say, Brian, Ron, Duane, and Brent all held positions of influence when it came to the club's direction and personnel decision-making.

But the Sutter brother who was most influential in shaping the Flames was definitely Darryl. Darryl had two tenures with the Flames, with his job description changing a few times during his first go-around. He was hired mid-season in 2002–03 as head coach to replace Greg Gilbert—Gilbert had been feuding with forward Marc Savard and, in an attempt to solve the issue, then-general manager Craig Button traded Savard to the Atlanta Thrashers, then ended up firing Gilbert as head coach anyway. After Button's departure following that season, Sutter assumed the dual role as head coach and GM, which he juggled for two seasons straddling the 2004–05 lockout. He decided to focus on his GM position after the 2005–06 season, replacing himself as coach with assistant Jim Playfair, and remained in the GM position until he resigned in December 2010. He rejoined the Flames organization, resuming his old post as head coach midway through the 2020–21 season, though his arrival behind the bench was delayed for a week after the announcement due to the league's COVID-19 protocols and assistant coach Ryan Huska coached two games on an interim basis. Sutter was fired as head coach following the 2022–23 season, leaving as the franchise's all-time leader in games and wins by a coach.

During his tenure as Flames GM, Sutter had a tremendous impact on the club's drafting and development trajectory. His particular impact was felt in two ways: picks the Flames didn't make (because Sutter traded them away) and the varying levels of success from remaining picks that the Flames did make.

Sutter's first season as GM was the 2003–04 campaign, where the Flames returned to the postseason for the first time since 1995–96 and went on a run to the Stanley Cup Final. Wearing the dual title of GM and head coach, Sutter was in the unique position to have a hands-on analysis of what his hockey club was missing, in his mind, and the ability to go out and make trades to fix those roster issues. During that season, he developed a preference for sending out future draft selections in order to solve immediate issues.

One case in point was the Miikka Kiprusoff trade. The Flames needed goaltending help and Sutter, who had previously coached with the San Jose Sharks before joining the Flames, had a familiarity with Kiprusoff and the knowledge that San Jose was juggling three goaltenders and would probably be willing to move the Finn for the right price. So the Flames sent a second-round selection in 2005 to the Sharks for his services. The Flames solved an immediate roster issue but did so at the expense of future draft choices.

This deficit spending became a trademark of Sutter's tenure as GM. He frequently attempted to solve roster con-struction issues by throwing draft picks at the problem via trade. While that tendency was successful—albeit to varying degrees—it only served to hollow out a farm system that was already beginning to feel the pinch from some sub-par draft day performances during the late portion of the 1990s and early portion of the 2000s.

The perceived cycle appeared to work like this. The Flames experienced a roster construction challenge, often related to lacking NHL-ready depth in their system. So to address that immediate issue, which was often a symptom of those diminished recent draft performances leaving the farm system thin of players who could contribute on the NHL roster, they traded future picks to acquire them from other clubs. This served to remove draft capital from future drafts, exacerbating the challenges the Flames faced with their farm system and leading to future trades sending picks to other clubs in order to plug holes, creating a vicious cycle.

Couple that with the introduction of the salary cap following the 2004–05 lockout, which placed additional importance on clubs drafting and developing homegrown players to fill roster gaps in an inexpensive manner—in terms of both salaries and acquisition costs—and challenges gradually mounted for the Flames during Sutter's tenure. One such instance occurred late in the 2008–09 season. The Flames were tight against the salary cap and, after a spate of short-term injuries, didn't have sufficient cap space to call up any replacement players. So for the final five games of the season, they dressed fewer than the standard 18 skaters. (The fewest they played with was 15 skaters, which they did twice.) The Flames weren't the only team that experienced this roster challenge due to the salary cap, but it led to an emergency recall rule being negotiated into the next collective bargaining agreement in 2013.

Over his tenure, Sutter traded away 37 picks with an average value of 91st overall and acquired 33 picks with an average value of 101st overall. Sutter tended to move draft capital from particular rounds:

- Five first-round picks traded and four acquired, for a net loss of one.
- 11 second-round picks traded and three acquired, for a net loss of eight.
- Six third-round picks traded and 10 acquired, for a net gain of four.
- Four fourth-round picks traded and six acquired, for a net gain of two.
- Four fifth-round picks traded and four acquired, for a net gain of zero.
- Four sixth-round picks traded and two acquired, for a net loss of two.

- Two seventh-round picks traded and four acquired, for a net gain of two.
- One eighth-round pick traded and zero acquired, for a net loss of one.

It must be stated that the Flames often received established NHL assets when they traded these selections, so the trades themselves served a purpose. However, the net loss of nine selections in the first two rounds of the draft had a big ripple effect because it was more challenging for the Flames to draft strong prospects with a better chance of becoming impact NHL players. There are definitely good players who are selected in the later rounds, but selections earlier in the draft tend to have higher expected value because of higher historical success rates. Fewer early picks translated into the club needing to get lucky in the later rounds to keep the farm system stocked.

Additionally, Sutter was GM for eight drafts and traded away 11 second-round picks. Before his departure from the position, and well in advance of the 2011 NHL Draft, he traded away the club's second-round (23 months before the draft) and third-round picks (15 months before the draft). After his departure, his successor, Jay Feaster, inherited a depleted farm system and significant cap commitments and faced an impending draft with only a single pick in the first three rounds. This situation led Feaster to attempt to find solutions while staring down the choice of using draft choices as an incentive for other teams to take on bad contracts or trying to address the club's expended draft capital.

With the selections that Sutter didn't trade to other teams, the Flames had very mixed results during the drafts he helmed.

The Sutter brothers' network came in handy in 2003. With Sutter's first selection as a GM, he selected defenceman Dion Phaneuf at ninth overall from the WHL's Red Deer Rebels—the team owned, operated, managed, and coached by brother Brent. Darryl was reportedly sold on Phaneuf when he saw how Brent used him with the Rebels: all the time, in every game situation. Phaneuf was a prototypical "Sutter player," a rough-and-tumble, big-bodied kid hailing from western Canada. Phaneuf wasn't considered a high-end finesse player by any stretch, but he played a distinctly north-south game full of simple elements executed very well, often punctuated by a bruising bodycheck. Given where the Flames' farm system was—the cupboards were bare enough that they needed everything—selecting Phaneuf with the first pick made complete sense given that he could do a lot well and was physically developed enough that he wouldn't need to percolate in junior or the AHL for very long to be NHL-ready. Reportedly, the Flames were aiming to get one of three young blueliners: Phaneuf, Ryan Suter, or Braydon Coburn; Phaneuf was the only player remaining of the trio when the Flames went up to pick.

Phaneuf went pro in 2005, jumping straight onto the Flames' roster following the owners' lockout, and ended up having a strong NHL career, playing more than 1,000 games between stops in Calgary, Toronto, Ottawa, and Los Angeles. Phaneuf's time in Calgary was a bit uneven, with early promise—and a brief flirtation with bonafide Norris Trophy contention a few seasons into his tenure—devolving to the point where Sutter traded him to Toronto in a seven-player trade in January 2010 that some analysts and fans compared to the Doug Gilmour trade from decades prior in how uneven the yield was for the Flames. They received four players, headlined by reliable two-way centre Matt Stajan, and filled out with depth pieces such as blueliner Ian White and forwards Niklas Hagman and Jamal Mayers. While the Flames' asset management regarding Phaneuf might not have been ideal, he was still a valuable draft selection and contributed on their roster, playing 378 games.

Following Phaneuf, though, the Flames drafted a series of tall, large young men. The *Calgary Herald*'s Scott Cruickshank summarized the nine picks: "Not a single one of them was under six feet tall. Seven were more than 190 pounds." He also noted that the Flames were "going long on size, not scrimping on grit." The eight players the Flames selected after Phaneuf combined for just 13 NHL games, with just one of those appearances—second-rounder (39th overall) Tim Ramholt's brief cameo in 2007–08—coming with the Flames. A Swiss-born defenceman, Ramholt was the only selection to become a productive player in the Flames' farm system. Two forwards combined for 12 NHL games elsewhere: fourth-rounder Jamie Tardif (112th overall) played two games for Boston, while fifth-rounder Greg Moore (143rd overall) played 10 games with the NY Rangers and Columbus.

For the next several seasons, the Flames under Sutter continued drafting an abundance of large, physical, often western Canadian players. Often, though, this tendency didn't produce minor league depth or players with NHL upside.

In 2004, the Flames stayed on-brand, selecting burly winger Kris Chucko at 24th overall. Described as a power forward by scouts, Chucko drew some stylistic comparisons with then-Flames captain Jarome Iginla and Toronto Maple Leafs forward Darcy Tucker for how he was able to hit, battle for pucks, and score goals around the net. A product of the Junior A British Columbia Hockey League, Chucko was committed to the University of Minnesota. He spent two seasons in college and then played in the Flames' system for parts of five seasons—playing two games in the NHL in 2008–09 after being called up during his best AHL season. Chucko appeared to be a solid pick late in the first round who was developing well, but bad injury luck halted things. A series of concussions and related neck injuries ended his career by 2011.

Beyond Chucko, the Flames made nine selections in 2004, with four players selected having respectable NHL careers of more than 200 games apiece. Third-rounder Brandon Prust, selected 70th overall, was touted as a physical, energy player from the Ontario Hockey League's London Knights who was projected as a fourth-line checker. He turned into precisely that, playing 486 NHL games (78 with Calgary) over nine seasons and memorably being traded away by the Flames twice in consecutive seasons, both times in mid-season trades involving Finnish forward Olli Jokinen.

Third-rounder Dustin Boyd, selected 98th overall, was a speedy, versatile forward from the WHL's Moose Jaw Warriors. Boyd progressed well offensively following his draft, but he projected as a complimentary forward—he might not be the "star" of a line, but he could play with the team's stars and contribute. He played 200 NHL games (192 with Calgary) over five seasons before pursuing a career in Europe. He ended up playing extensively in Kazakhstan and represented that country internationally in the World Championships and Olympic qualification tournaments.

A physical, defensive-minded blueliner from the QMJHL's Cape Breton Screaming Eagles, Adam Pardy was a sixth-round pick (173rd overall). He played a simple defensive game that translated well to the pro ranks and made him a reliable depth player, and he played 342 NHL games (147 with Calgary) over nine seasons. Ninth-round selection Adam Cracknell, selected 279th overall from the WHL's Kootenay Ice, was a big-bodied utility player whose main skill—hockey sense—made him extremely adaptable. He played 210 NHL games (none with Calgary) over nine seasons and remains active in the AHL as of this writing.

The Flames' 2005 draft class saw the club select eight players who combined for 74 NHL appearances, led by Sutter's son, Brett, who accounted for 60 of them. First-round selection Matt Pelech, taken 26th overall, was a big-bodied defensive defenceman from the OHL's Sarnia Sting. Pelech battled a slew of injuries that slowed his development, though he established himself as a reliable depth player in the minors and Europe. He played 13 NHL games (five with Calgary). The fifth-round selection, goaltender Matt Keetley, was taken 158th overall from the WHL's Medicine Hat Tigers. He played nine minutes in relief in the NHL in 2007–08 but eventually got lost in the shuffle as the Flames drafted other goaltenders.

Arguably the star of the Flames' 2005 class was Brett Sutter, a sixth-round selection appropriately enough taken at 179th overall, the exact same pick his father was taken with in 1978.

"We had talked to a number of teams, but Calgary actually wasn't really one of them," said Brett Sutter. "I knew I was probably projected right in that fifth, sixth, seventh round, and luckily enough when my name was called by Calgary, it was pretty exciting."

Brett Sutter grew into a reliable checking forward and played 18 games for the Flames over three seasons, emerging as a possible option as a checking forward on the fourth line. However, an altercation outside of a bar in Phoenix during a road trip early in the 2010–11 season spelled the end of his time with the club, and he was traded by his father to the Carolina Hurricanes shortly after. Sutter developed into a really strong minor league forward and mentor for young players, serving as captain in both Charlotte and Ontario of the AHL, the farm teams of Carolina, and the Los Angeles Kings, respectively.

Brett returned to the Flames organization in 2022–23, signing a minor league contract to serve as captain of the Flames' farm team. The former Stockton Heat had relocated to Calgary to become the second iteration of the Wranglers, and the Flames organization—likely with some nudging from Darryl—had been able to lure Brett to Alberta to continue his career close to home. Brett conceded that the conversation to rejoin the Flames system might have gone differently had he had to choose between Stockton and Ontario rather than Calgary and Ontario, noting the Kings organization had treated him very well during his time there.

The return to the organization that drafted him gave Brett the unique opportunity to be a mentor to young players in the same city where his career got its start.

"Getting to be a fly on the wall, so to speak, to watch these guys chase their dreams and accomplish their dreams, is awesome," said Sutter. "You want to be there to support them, help them any way you can. And when they get there, it's an amazing feeling."

Despite modest NHL success, Brett ended up carving out an exceptional career at the AHL level, becoming one of just eight players to play 1,000 games at that level.

One of the more bizarre footnotes of the 2005 draft was third-round pick Daniel Ryder, a Peterborough Petes standout and younger brother of Michael Ryder, who at the time was a young Montreal Canadiens player on his way to a lengthy NHL career. The younger Ryder was an impressive offensive player in the OHL and signed a pro deal with the Flames organization, but he struggled to make the transition to the pro ranks, even returning home early in the 2007–08 season to contemplate his future.

He was eventually released by the Flames and, aside from a brief stint with Providence, the Boston Bruins' farm team, didn't play pro hockey again. His name resurfaced in early 2010, though, after he faced several criminal charges—robbery, being disguised with the intent of committing a crime, using an imitation firearm to carry out a crime, and theft under $5,000—related to a convenience store robbery in Newfoundland, though he was later deemed mentally unfit to stand trial after a psychiatric assessment.

The Flames chose a goaltender in the first round in 2006, selecting Everett Silvertips standout Leland Irving with the 26th overall pick. Irving developed into a very solid goaltender in the AHL, but through 13 appearances with the

Flames across the 2011–12 and 2012–13 seasons wasn't able to carve out a spot as the heir apparent to aging incumbent Miikka Kiprusoff. Irving went on to play in Europe for almost a decade after leaving the Flames organization but never got another shot at playing in the NHL. None of the other seven players selected in 2006 became players of note in the Flames system.

The 2007 draft was much better for the Flames. Swedish centre Mikael Backlund was their first-round pick, taken at 24th overall after trading down from 18th overall and gaining a third-round selection in the process from the Blues. Backlund developed slowly but became a stalwart of the Flames' lineup and one of their longest-serving players. The third-round selection was used to pick blueliner John Negrin (70th overall), who played three games with the Flames after finishing his tenure in the WHL, but otherwise turned into a reliable minor league defender. Fourth-round selection Keith Aulie (116th overall) translated his 6′6″ frame and stay-at-home style into a really nice career, playing 167 NHL games (zero with Calgary).

The Flames' 2008 first-round pick, aspiring power forward Greg Nemisz from the OHL's Windsor Spitfires at 25th overall, couldn't quite translate what made him a strong junior scorer into the pro ranks—playing against men, he wasn't able to as consistently battle to the front of the net.

"Some guys just can't put on weight for whatever reason," said Flames director of scouting Tod Button, who selected Nemisz. "They can work all they want. Greg Nemisz is a perfect example. He could never get his lower body strong enough. He worked at it, but he just couldn't do it, then he had the knee injury."

Nemisz played just 15 NHL games, all with the Flames. But third-round selection Lance Bouma (78th overall), a checker in the Prust mould from the WHL's Vancouver Giants, carved out a solid career with 357 NHL games (304 with Calgary) and was able to play the same general style in the pros that had made him successful in junior. OHL blueliner TJ Brodie, taken in the fourth round (114th overall), had to adapt his defensive game to the nuances of the pro level, but his superb skating allowed him to have a strong pro career with long stints in Calgary and Toronto.

The 2009 draft class featured a promising pick that created a post-draft challenge, and a depth selection that turned into a promising young goaltender. First-round selection, Swedish blueliner Tim Erixon, was selected at 23rd overall amidst excitement about his skill, poise, and NHL bloodlines—his father, Jan, had played 10 seasons with the New York Rangers between 1983 and 1993. However, Erixon's desire to play in the NHL immediately, doubts it would happen in Calgary, and lingering affection for his father's old team soon became evident, creating a saga that the Flames had to navigate. Sixth-round pick Joni Ortio, a raw but promising Finnish goaltender taken at 171st overall, was a pleasant surprise. He came over to North America and impressed in the AHL, resulting in parts of three seasons spent with the Flames in the NHL. However, he wasn't able to cement himself as a permanent NHL goaltender, and eventually he returned to Europe. But 37 NHL games from a late-round goaltender was a very solid late-round find.

Sutter's final draft in Calgary, the 2010 edition, saw the Flames make no selections in the first two rounds after they were utilized by the GM in trades—the first-round pick was part of a package sent to the Phoenix Coyotes in exchange for Olli Jokinen, while the second-round pick was sent to Chicago for Rene Bourque. Fifth-round selection Micheal Ferland, another physical forward in the Prust or Bouma template, translated well to the pro ranks and played 335 NHL games before his career was cut short by concussion issues. Four of the other five players the Flames drafted in 2010 played NHL games: third-rounder Max Reinhart, son of Flames' 1979 first-rounder Paul, played 23 games; seventh-round pick Patrick Holland (five games); fourth-rounder John Ramage, son of former Flame blueliner Rob, who played two games; and fourth-round pick Bill Arnold, who played once.

A few of Sutter's draft picks translated quite well to the professional ranks, often because their playing styles didn't need to change significantly to be effective at higher levels of hockey. But the combination of the club trading away high draft selections during his tenure and a reliance on the same player archetype—usually a variation of big, physical, and/or western Canadian—led to the Flames' draft portfolio becoming very homogeneous and vulnerable to shifts in how the game was being played. As the NHL adapted to a post-lockout world, the league embarked on a crackdown on so-called "obstruction" penalties like hooking or holding, which allowed smaller, faster, skilled players to flourish— and exposed the types of players Sutter was often stockpiling through the draft to be irrelevant assets in the new NHL.

At the time, Sutter's roster moves made tremendous sense for the short term. In his first season as head coach and GM, the Flames went to the Stanley Cup Final and came within a goal of winning the championship. In his second season, following the lockout, the Flames won their division and seemed poised for a lengthy playoff run. Given that Iginla and Kiprusoff, the Flames' best players, were in their prime years, it made sense to leverage assets to maximize the club's playoff contention window. But those decisions came with a cost, and Sutter's deficit spending when it came to draft picks and the club's poor performance at converting remaining picks into useful players—either on the NHL roster or their farm system—put the organization behind the developmental eight-ball at a time where finding effective young players with favourable salary cap impacts was rapidly becoming incredibly important to every club's success.

Several of the Sutter brothers have sons that remain active in the hockey world. Shaun, Brian's son, serves as assistant general manager for Red Deer in the WHL, while Lukas, Rich's son, serves as an amateur scout, covering the WHL for the Buffalo Sabres. Brett, Darryl's son, remains active as a player with the Flames' AHL affiliate.

16

THE MAN BEHIND
THE CURTAIN:
TOD BUTTON

IN THE SPORTING world, the half-joking notion is that staffers are hired to be fired. The lifespan of a general manager or head coach isn't particularly lengthy; coaches usually last between three and five seasons with a club, and the person who hires them, the GM, usually only gets a hiring or two before they, too, are shown the door after about a decade in their position. Regime changes for general managers are often followed by wholesale changes to other staff, often scouts, as the new boss frequently likes to bring in their own people rather than rely on staff from the old regime. While rank-and-file scouts often stick around, one of the most common occurrences is a changeover of the head scout, the individual running a club's drafting, to reflect the philosophies and desires of a new GM.

Since the 2005–06 season, the man in charge of the Calgary Flames' amateur drafting, the guy running the show at the table besides the GM, has been Tod Button. Despite the tendencies of pro sports teams to reset the club's org chart like a toddler shaking an Etch-A-Sketch when a new GM is installed, Button has been retained through multiple changeovers in Calgary. The 2023–24 campaign was Button's 27th season with the Flames organization in a scouting capacity and 19th season significantly contributing to, under various titles and organizational schemes, the club's selections at the NHL draft. He spent the 2023–24 season working under Craig Conroy, his sixth different GM as a scout.

Tod's family has been involved in hockey for decades. His mother, Bridget, worked for the Toronto Maple Leafs as secretary for long-time coach and GM Punch Imlach. His father, Jack, is a legendary figure in scouting circles. He worked as assistant general manager for the Pittsburgh Penguins from 1969–74, then as GM in 1974–75. After the Penguins went bankrupt, Button left the club and founded the NHL's Central Scouting Service, the league's central repository for draft-related information, and served as its director from 1975–79. He then joined the Washington Capitals in various scouting capacities from 1979 until his passing in 1996. The elder Button was credited for finding several key players who helped the Capitals rise to prominence in the late '90s, such as Sergei Gonchar, Olaf Kolzig, and Peter Bondra.

Tod's older brother, Craig, was a scout for the Minnesota North Stars and Dallas Stars organizations for more than a decade, eventually working his way up to running their amateur scouting and drafting. He was an important behind-the-scenes piece in the Stars winning the Stanley Cup in 1999 and had his name engraved on the Cup that year. A year later, Button was lured away from Dallas for the GM's position in Calgary, a position he held for three seasons. Aside from a brief tenure as a scout with the Toronto Maple Leafs, Button has largely left hockey operations for the media side of the business, where he's been a fixture on TSN's programming, especially regarding their World Junior Championship tournament and the NHL draft coverage, as that network's director of scouting.

Tod broke into the league in 1989, working as a hockey operations departmental assistant for the Washington Capitals. He was pursuing a potential coaching career with the Capitals, eventually working up to being assistant coach under head coach Jim Schoenfeld, before a staff overhaul in Washington saw him become a free agent in 1997. Flames GM Al Coates brought him on, convincing him to give scouting a try. He worked for three seasons under Coates until his departure, at which point he worked with Craig, then recently hired as Calgary's GM.

During a tumultuous 2000–01 transition year that saw Craig figure out the Flames' staffing and organizational dynamics, Tod and incumbent scout Mike Sands were leaned on heavily during the drafting process. They both received new titles the following season, with Tod being named director of scouting and Sands director of amateur scouting, nominally working under Tod but functionally running the club's amateur scouting efforts. Tod's duties, which had previously straddled amateur and pro scouting responsibilities depending on the club's needs at the time, remained broad and involved him primarily working as a pro scout and assisting the amateur staff late in the season, following the trade deadline. When Darryl Sutter was hired in April 2003 as GM, succeeding Tod's brother, the younger Button grew anxious that his time with Calgary was coming to an end.

"I got hired because of my name...but I thought it'd be much worse to be fired because of my name," Tod remarked to the *Calgary Herald* at the time. At the time of Sutter's ascension to the GM position—a title he held in addition to head coach—the Flames were in the midst of their final preparations for the NHL draft. Sutter retained Sands and Button in their previous roles, with Sands continuing to run the team's drafting. But Sutter adding to the club's pro scouting staff gave Button the opportunity to start shifting his workload toward the amateur side.

"When Darryl got hired, he added to the staff significantly," said Button. "He wanted a couple pro scouts for two reasons. In San Jose, their model was for pro scouts to also do development, so they spent a lot of time with the farm team."

By 2005–06, Button's efforts moved primarily to the amateur side of Flames scouting. When Sands' contract wasn't renewed and he left the organization in the 2010 off-season, Button began running the show for the team's drafting. In 2010, the Flames changed over their hockey operations boss once again, with Sutter resigning as GM and being replaced by assistant GM Jay Feaster. The transition happened in December, literally the middle of the scouting season, and so a wholesale changeover of the club's amateur scouting apparatus simply wasn't prudent.

The Flames had a fairly successful 2011 draft—they selected five players, including WHL standout Sven Baertschi and promising American junior forward Johnny Gaudreau—and Feaster came away impressed with Button's staff. New assistant GM John Weisbrod was brought on after the 2011 draft and assisted with some tweaks to setting draft criteria, but aside from Feaster and Weisbrod's focus on "working the list"—using the club's criteria to create a clear and concise order of preference for players, and then sticking to that list when selecting—Feaster's regime largely just provided Button's crew with marching orders and let them execute those orders.

Similar circumstances prevailed when Brian Burke dismissed Feaster in December 2013 and hired Brad Treliving in April 2014. When Burke took over as interim GM, it wasn't necessary to make a changeover—especially given that Burke was planning on hiring a new manager soon—so he used the remainder of the season as an evaluation period for the existing staff and helped oversee the draft preparation process himself. When Treliving took over, he too wasn't hellbent about making changes right away, preferring an approach similar to Burke's of observation before making any staff alterations. After spending a season evaluating his group's needs, Treliving ended up consulting with Button and then hiring additional scouts and adding resources in strategic areas.

"I think he works hard, he really knows players, and he's fearless," said Burke. "So you get into a meeting and someone says, 'I don't like this guy,' and Tod says, 'Well, I'm leaving him right where he is, 'cause I do.' That's the GM breathing down his neck, me, or the president of hockey operations saying, 'I don't like this, I don't like that,' and Tod was fearless. He says, 'I have the conviction of my beliefs and I'm sticking to my guns.' It's a good combination of being knowledgeable, bending when you should bend and not bending when you shouldn't. And that's a tightrope. It's a new GM and a president of hockey operations a couple months apart. Not an easy job for a scout to walk that tightrope."

Even relative to his scouting peers, Button's longevity with one organization is remarkable. The secret to his success may be twofold. First, he's shown the ability to be extremely malleable and able to adapt his scouting staff's approach to their jobs to what their GM desires. For his part, Button's approach to scouting and player evaluation seems quite holistic, with a clear view of the challenges involved in the process.

"Hockey's hockey," said Button. "People watch hockey, especially in Canada, [so] you can tell when it's a good player and who the bad player is. The difficulty in scouting is you have to project them at 17, and you have to break down the individual skill sets and what that looks like at the next stage. Is a guy going to get strong enough to be a good player at the next stage? Or when he's 25? That's the biggest challenge. As far as GMs coming in, the hockey talk is always the same. We want compete, competitors, we want skill, we want hockey sense."

Some managers view the draft through the lens of player archetypes. Some managers view the draft through specific attributes. And from year to year, as a club's prospect base grows, ages, and shifts in composition, managers often focus on different things. While leading his staff, Button has shown the ability to shift gears and navigate the draft's ever-changing dynamics and turn his bosses' desires into a tangible scouting and drafting strategy that the scouts can execute and the development staff can support.

Some of Button's success in helping his scouting staff adapt to management changes may be related to the surprising smallness of the hockey world and his knowledge and awareness of the various figures within its orbit. When everybody in hockey seems to know everybody else, it aids in smooth transitions for new management groups.

"There's never been a GM, except for Jay Feaster, that I didn't know ahead of time before," said Button. "I'm not saying I had a relationship with them, but I knew who they were. I used to see Tree [Brad Treliving] at the rinks all the time, he did a lot of scouting in Arizona. I knew Darryl [Sutter] from way back in my days in Washington when he was in Chicago. There was nobody I didn't know. I'm not saying it's seamless, you still need direction from management, but if they make a little switch, it's not like you haven't been watching that part of the game. We want more speed, or whatever, you know who those guys are. It's not like you have to start over. The draft is in four months, [we've] got to start over? You've already done that basic part of it."

But above all else, Button has stuck around through the years, and through multiple management transitions, because he's been good at his job. Ignoring first-round selections, as GMs are often a bit more hands on early in the draft, his group has been able to identify, scout, and select many players who ended up having notable NHL careers. Picks with significant value relative to where they were selected, defined as players who played 200 or more NHL games, include second-rounders Markus Granlund (2011), Rasmus Andersson (2015), and Dillon Dube (2016); third-rounders Lance Bouma (2008) and Adam Fox (2016); fourth-rounders TJ Brodie (2008), Johnny

Gaudreau (2011), and Brett Kulak (2012); fifth-rounder Micheal Ferland (2010); and sixth-rounder Andrew Mangiapane (2015).

Clubs increasingly utilize the expertise of their area scouts as they get deeper into the draft, and the notable thing about the Flames' success of finding players outside the first round under Button is that they came from many different areas of hockey. Multiple notable players have been selected after the first round from all three Canadian major junior leagues— the Western, Ontario, and Quebec Major Junior Hockey Leagues—and the United States' collegiate and junior leagues. This reflects that the Flames had multiple area scouts under Button that they could rely on to find players with upside in the later rounds. Ontario area scout Fred Parker and western area scout Rob Sumner were both promoted to assistant directors of scouting in 2017, working under Button, likely due to the strong work they did as area scouts.

It's pretty rare for a head scout to be retained after a general manager changeover. It's virtually unheard of for a head scout to be retained through several of them. Button has not only proven to be an adaptable scouting point person for his many different bosses over the years, but he's also assembled a scouting staff that has been able to find value throughout the hockey world and the many rounds of the draft. When somebody's good at their job, they tend to stick around, and that may be the key to Button's longevity.

17

BUILDING AND DISMANTLING THE 2004 STANLEY CUP RUN

THE CALGARY FLAMES of the 1980s were a powerhouse built over nearly two decades of strong drafting, prudent trades, and signings under the watchful eye of general manager Cliff Fletcher. The two teams that went to the Stanley Cup Final in 1986 and 1989 were largely built through the entry draft. The Flames improbably made the return to the Stanley Cup Final in 2004 with a roster built in fits and starts over several years by several different general managers.

The 2004 edition of the Flames had 26 players eligible for engraving on the Stanley Cup, had they managed to defeat the Tampa Bay Lightning in the seven-game Cup Final series:

goaltenders Roman Turek and Miikka Kiprusoff; defence-
men Mike Commodore, Denis Gauthier, Jordan Leopold,
Steve Montador, Andrew Ference, Robyn Regehr, Toni
Lydman, and Rhett Warrener; and forwards Chuck Kobasew,
Dave Lowry, Stephane Yelle, Jarome Iginla, Chris Simon,
Shean Donovan, Chris Clark, Matthew Lombardi, Oleg
Saprykin, Craig Conroy, Martin Gelinas, Ville Nieminen,
Marcus Nilson, Steven Reinprecht, Krzysztof Oliwa, and
Dean McAmmond.

Uniquely, the 2004 Flames only had six homegrown
draft selections on their roster. Instead, the club was built by
leveraging picks by trading them, or by trading away players
who were initially drafted by the Flames. The homegrown
players were Clark (1994), Gauthier (1995), Lydman (1996),
Saprykin (1999), Kobasew (2001), and Lombardi (2002). Clark
and Gauthier were drafted under Doug Risebrough, Lydman
and Saprykin under Al Coates, and Kobasew and Lombardi
under Craig Button. At the time, coach and GM Darryl Sutter
had only overseen one draft.

Now, six homegrown players out of 26 players on the
team is a fairly low proportion. But the Flames' managers
leveraged their picks well as trade chips. Under Button,
McAmmond was traded to the Colorado Avalanche in a
five-player deal prior to the 2002–03 waiver draft, then
traded back to Calgary at that season's trade deadline for
a third-round pick—McAmmond was deemed ineligible
to play, though, with the league citing an obscure roster regulation related to waiver draft rules. Under Sutter,
Kiprusoff (from the San Jose Sharks) and Nilson (from the
Florida Panthers) were acquired for second-round picks.

Ference was acquired from the Pittsburgh Penguins for a third-round pick. Nieminen was acquired from the Chicago Blackhawks for a sixth-round pick and minor leaguer Jason Morgan.

In addition to trading picks, the Flames became adept at trading players who were prior draft choices in order to upgrade the team. This was also a process that spanned multiple management regimes.

Iginla was acquired in the Joe Nieuwendyk trade with the Dallas Stars in 1995. Nieuwendyk was a second-round pick in 1985, selected with a pick acquired from the Minnesota North Stars for Kent Nilsson, who himself was a fourth-round pick in 1976.

Regehr was part of the Theoren Fleury trade with the Avalanche in 1999. Fleury was an eighth-round pick in 1987.

Conroy was acquired from the St. Louis Blues for Cory Stillman in 2001. Stillman was a first-round pick in 1993.

Virtually every player on the 2004 roster was a product of asset-flipping, often in convoluted chains of trades that began with a draft pick or a drafted player.

The acquisitions of three players in particular were products of extensive chains of traded assets that would make Fletcher, a GM whose Flames tenure was defined by lengthy trade chains, proud.

Leopold was acquired from the Mighty Ducks for a 2001 second-round pick and Andrei Nazarov. Nazarov was originally acquired from the Tampa Bay Lightning in a trade for Michael Nylander. Nylander came to Calgary with James Patrick and Zarley Zalapski in a trade with the Hartford Whalers for 1984 ninth-round pick Gary Suter,

1984 second-round pick Paul Ranheim, and 1989 second-round pick Ted Drury.

Warrener and Reinprecht were acquired from the Buffalo Sabres for 1996 second-round pick Steve Begin and Chris Drury (Ted's brother). Drury was acquired (along with Yelle) from Colorado for 1996 first-rounder Derek Morris, Jeff Shantz, and Dean McAmmond. McAmmond was acquired from the Philadelphia Flyers for a 2002 fourth-round pick. Shantz was acquired (with Steve Dubinsky) from the Chicago Blackhawks for 1993 second-rounder Jamie Allison, 1997 third-round pick Erik Andersson and Marty McInnis. McInnis was acquired (along with Tyrone Garner and a 1997 sixth-rounder) from the New York Islanders for Robert Reichel, who was a 1989 fourth-round selection of the Flames.

Only four players—Montador, Lowry, Gelinas, and Oliwa—joined the small-market Flames via free agency. Everybody else was either drafted directly or acquired via the wheeling and dealing of the club's GMs.

The Flames' miraculous run to the 2004 Cup Final was followed immediately by the last thing a team that finally had some on-ice momentum needed: a prolonged owners' lockout that wiped out the entirety of the 2004–05 season. When hockey returned in 2005–06, a salary cap had been instituted—the cap's introduction was the last part of a multi-part plan from the league's owners to protect smaller market teams, which had previously seen a Canadian currency equalization plan and small-scale revenue sharing utilized. An emphasis from the league office on calling "obstruction" penalties—hooking and holding—led to games being imbued with more speed, creating a distinct change in overall playing style. It took a few years for Sutter to adjust as general manager.

The Flames made some savvy trades to leverage the value of some of their 2004 roster players, enabling the team to maintain their window of playoff contention for a few seasons after the lockout. Commodore and Lydman were traded to the Carolina Hurricanes and Buffalo, respectively, for third-round picks. Gauthier and Saprykin were sent to the Phoenix Coyotes for highly touted two-way centre Daymond Langkow, who was able to combine a goal-scoring touch with great defensive play during his time with the club. Jordan Leopold was packaged with a pair of second-round selections to Colorado in exchange for winger Alex Tanguay, who brought speed and offensive creativity to the Flames. Matthew Lombardi was part of a package (also involving forward Brandon Prust and a first-rounder) sent to Phoenix for offensive forward Olli Jokinen and a third-round pick. Jokinen wasn't a great fit with the Flames and didn't quite click offensively, leading to a trade the following season to the Rangers. (Jokinen was subsequently added back to the team via free agency several months later.)

But the challenge for the Flames was that they did not get a ton of value back for their most attractive assets, often holding on too long and missing the window to maximize their returns. Gelinas and Conroy each left the Flames to pursue free agency, though Conroy's departure from the club only lasted a season and a half before Sutter expended additional assets—prospect Jamie Lundmark plus second- and fourth-round picks—to re-acquire him from the Los Angeles Kings.

The process continued under Sutter's successor, Jay Feaster. Regehr was sent to Buffalo in 2011 with a second-round pick and forward Ales Kotalik in a trade that landed the Flames depth players Paul Byron and Chris Butler—Regehr's departure was influenced heavily by salary cap considerations, as the Flames had a desire to re-sign Tanguay to an extension before he became a free agent but had to free up cap space to do so. (The second-round pick was added to entice Buffalo to take Kotalik's contract and get it off the Flames' books.) Moving Regehr and his contract opened up the space the team needed, and Tanguay's new deal was announced the same day Regehr became a Sabre. Byron was later lost on waivers and Butler left the Flames as a free agent. When the club's rebuild began in 2013, the club began sending out veteran assets to other clubs to open up some salary cap flexibility. They ended up packaging Tanguay with blueliner Cory Sarich to Colorado for Shane O'Brien and David Jones. O'Brien's contract was eventually bought out, while Jones was traded to the Minnesota Wild.

The last assets remaining from the 2004 club were Iginla and Kiprusoff. Iginla remained a productive scorer with the Flames for many seasons. But with free agency looming and the club wanting to give Iginla a chance to win a Stanley Cup (and get some assets back for him), Iginla was sent to Pittsburgh in 2013 in exchange for a late first-round pick and college forwards Kenny Agostino and Ben Hanowski. Iginla was a pending unrestricted free agent and had a no-move clause within his contract, which served to limit the number of teams able to bid on Iginla's services to only the handful of teams that he would consider going to. Neither Agostino or Hanowski became significant NHL prospects, while the first-round selection was used to get Morgan Klimchuk, a promising WHL forward who failed to blossom in pro hockey.

Kiprusoff remained a high-level goaltender for several seasons, with his play only dipping slightly as he aged into his mid-thirties. As the team eyed its rebuild, Kiprusoff ultimately declined a trade to the Toronto Maple Leafs prior to 2013's trade deadline, preferring to remain with the Flames, eventually deciding to retire following the end of the season a few months later.

It took a lot of hard work and fortunate luck for the Flames to assemble the team that went to the Stanley Cup Final in 2004, with players on the club spanning three different general manager regimes. However, the quick shift in playing style after the lockout, combined with the Flames not getting tremendous value from the players they were losing from the 2004 team, conspired to create some distinct challenges on the ice for the hockey club as the 2010s neared.

18

PATIENCE PAYS OFF: THE RISE OF MIKAEL BACKLUND

THE CALGARY FLAMES franchise has had a lot of great players, and they've drafted many great players during their history. But some of their longest-tenured and most impactful players weren't originally selected by the club.

Jarome Iginla was drafted by the Dallas Stars and acquired via trade. Robyn Regehr was drafted by the Colorado Avalanche and acquired via trade. Miikka Kiprusoff was drafted by the San Jose Sharks and acquired via trade. Mark Giordano was an undrafted free agent that the Flames signed to play within their farm system. Lanny McDonald was drafted by the Toronto Maple Leafs and acquired via trade with the Colorado Rockies.

The record for most games played for the Flames by a homegrown draft pick is held by a somewhat surprising player. Rather than Al MacInnis, Theoren Fleury, or Joe Nieuwendyk, it's Swedish centre Mikael Backlund. A 2007 selection taken during the often-challenging draft tenure of general manager Darryl Sutter, Backlund was a late pick in 2007's first round that turned into one of the organization's best drafting and development success stories.

A product of local hockey in Vasteras, Sweden—a city in central Sweden, about an hour's drive west of Stockholm— Backlund first landed on the North American scouting radar as a 16-year-old, leading Team Sweden to a championship and being named most valuable player at the 2005–06 edition of the Mac's AAA Midget Tournament held in, coincidentally enough, Calgary. He worked his way up through his youth in the VIK Vasteras HK organization, playing his first pro games in the second tier HockeyAllsvenskan during his 16-year-old season.

A 17-year-old Backlund bounced around a bit during his 2006–07 season—the season leading up to the 2007 NHL Draft—playing for VIK Vasteras HK in Sweden's under-18 league, under-20 league, and HockeyAllsvenskan, as well as representing Sweden in the Ivan Hlinka Memorial Tournament and Under-18 World Championships. Backlund led the Under-18 Worlds in goals and helped Sweden capture a bronze medal, which helped elevate his draft stock. He ended the season as the second-ranked European skater, according to the NHL's Central Scouting Service, behind only Alexei Cherepanov. But there was some concern in the scouting community regarding how he was recovering from a mid-season knee injury.

According to Backlund, former Flames player Kent Nilsson, at the time a European scout with the Edmonton

Oilers, told him that he would likely be selected by the Oilers. That season the Oilers had three first-round picks and entered the 2007 draft with the sixth, 15th, and 30th overall selections. However, Backlund had multiple chats with the Flames before the draft and met with Sutter and then head coach Mike Keenan the morning of the draft in Columbus to discuss his injury recovery, which made Backlund believe the Flames had significant interest in selecting him.

The Oilers didn't end up selecting Backlund. They selected Sam Gagner at sixth overall and Alex Plante at 15th overall. They traded up from 30th to 21st overall to select Riley Nash, with Backlund still on the board. The Flames traded down six spots from 18th overall, gaining a third-round pick in the swap, and selected Backlund at 24th. Backlund noted that he suspected the Flames were drafting him when he saw Swedish regional scout Anders Steen walk onto the stage with Flames brass to make the pick.

"I knew when Anders Steen went up on stage," said Backlund. "I didn't know it was going to be me, but my Swedish agent told me it's going to be a Swede now, because they're bringing the Swedish scout on stage."

Backlund returned to Sweden after being drafted and played 2007–08 with Vasteras. He also represented Sweden at the World Junior tournament, scoring the game-winning goal in overtime to help Sweden advance to the gold medal game. (They lost to Canada and earned a silver medal.) Hoping to earn an NHL job, Backlund signed his entry-level deal with the Flames in May 2009 and attended their training camp prior to the 2008–09 season, but he didn't make the team and was assigned back to Vasteras via a loan agreement. Vasteras had high hopes for the season, aiming for promotion from the second-tier Allsvenskan to the top-flight Elitserien.

After a tough start to the season for Vasteras and the 2009 World Junior tournament looming, Vasteras general manager Leif Rohlin publicly called out Backlund's performance in an interview with a local Swedish newspaper, VLT. "We think Mickis should absolutely dominate in VIK, and he hasn't done that.... He must make a good [World Juniors], then we will see what happens. We are not at all satisfied. We have to think about what is best." The comments fuelled speculation that Backlund could be headed to another Swedish team—as a first-round NHL pick he was in demand—or that he could be sent to either the Flames' American Hockey League farm team in Quad City or the Western Hockey League's Kelowna Rockets, who owned his Canadian junior rights via the import draft, following the upcoming tournament. Speaking to the *Calgary Herald*, Sutter mused, "There's not only one place in the universe where he can play hockey."

The proverbial "other shoe" dropped after Sweden won their second consecutive silver medal at the World Juniors. The day after the tournament concluded, it was announced that Backlund was leaving Vasteras and heading to North America—the Flames terminated his loan agreement with the club. He briefly joined the NHL club, filling in for a game against the New York Islanders due to an injury to Todd Bertuzzi before joining Kelowna for the remainder of the season. (Over a nine-day span, he played in the gold medal game at the World Juniors, his first NHL game, and his first WHL game.) He impressed, posting 30 points in 28 games, helping the Rockets capture a WHL league championship, and representing that league in the Memorial Cup tournament.

Making the jump to North America was a key part of Backlund's development as a player.

"I think it definitely helped my career and it's one of the reasons why I'm here today," said Backlund on Sportsnet radio in early 2023. "Going back, I kind of wish I would have made a decision to go earlier that year. Playing a full season in Kelowna would've been great for me because I had so much fun playing in that second half. I wish I would've gone earlier, but you can't go back in time. Looking back on it, that's how I feel."

Backlund made the jump to the AHL in 2009–10, posting 32 points in 54 games with the Abbotsford Heat and earning a call-up to the NHL, where he spent much of the last two months of the regular season. He spent almost all of 2010–11 in the NHL, carving out a niche for himself in the club's bottom six (and penalty kill units) as a tough-minutes centre under head coach Brent Sutter and, aside from not posting eye-popping offensive totals, thriving in the role.

Backlund was penciled in for a promotion to the top six for 2011–12, likely to serve as centre to Jarome Iginla, but he broke his hand in the final practice before the season began and missed the first month of the season. He worked himself back into top form and cemented himself as the team's second-line centre, but he then suffered a shoulder injury and missed the final six weeks of the season.

The 2012–13 lockout, as odd as it sounds, might have served to rejuvenate Backlund's career. With the NHL not playing games, Backlund jumped at an opportunity to return home. He played for VIK Vasteras HK for the first time in three and a half seasons—whatever lingering bad feelings existed in Sweden after Backlund's earlier dramatic departure had become water under the bridge. Backlund played big minutes for Vasteras, and the level of play in the Allsvenskan was upped as several locked-out NHL players—such as Anze Kopitar, Marcus Johansson, and Gabriel Landeskog, among others—headed there. Playing against some of the top players in the world, Backlund's two-way game thrived, and he also managed to score at a higher clip than in previous seasons. At the time of the lockout's resolution, he was among the Allsvenskan's scoring leaders.

"He was a first-round selection. Usually those guys, for the most part, are high-end offensive players as amateurs," said Brad Treliving, general manager of the Flames later in Backlund's tenure. "And they've probably been high offensive players and the best player on their team throughout their careers [as] you go through minor hockey and into junior, college, or in Europe, whatever it is you're playing. When you're drafted that high, usually there's a high offensive ceiling. Well, when you get to the league, not everybody's going to be a high offensive player. And now as you make the league and you try to establish yourself in the league, [it's about] finding a role where you can have an impact."

"I felt better after the lockout, for sure," said Backlund. "It definitely helped my career. The year before was really tough for me, with a couple injuries. That lockout was huge for me, but I remember the '13–'14 season, as the season moved on, I started playing better and better. I got more minutes and more responsibilities. I went 10 or 15 games without being on the ice for a goal against, [and I] got to be on the ice more against the top players on the team. That's more when [head coach] Bob [Hartley] started to trust me against top lines, [and] that's when I started feeling like I was going to be a really good two-way player and a top player in this league."

Backlund's confidence came back with him from Sweden. In a campaign shortened by the lockout and a knee injury that kept him sidelined for a month, he managed 16 points in 32 games. As the NHL experienced its data revolution, and fans and media gradually got access to more sophisticated performance metrics, Backlund's on-ice impacts became more and more pronounced. He continued to excel as a shutdown centre, but as his offensive numbers remained consistent—he averaged between 0.48 and 0.65 points-per-game each season between 2013–14 and 2021–22—he began to build a reputation throughout the league as one of the top two-way players in hockey.

"There are a lot of players who come into the league, and all sorts of young guys, who equate success with points," said Treliving. "And there's certain players who you rely on, that they need to be offensive producers, no question. And Mikael's always been [what] you would call a productive player, but he's never been a huge point guy. He's not a guy who's a point-per-game guy or that sort of stuff. He learned the value and the impact he has on team success by him being a real premier 200-foot player, playing against the other team's best players. First of all, producing on his own, but also his ability to check the other team's players, to be a top-end penalty-killer, to play in a shutdown role. Maybe he doesn't come out with two goals, but he's playing against the other team's best, and they've gotten nothing tonight."

There was a shift in how Backlund was used during this period. Initially, he was used to help prop up the Flames' weakest players or lines as a sort of line-fixer—Backlund's ability to boost the underlying numbers and offensive performances of his linemates became known in the online analytics community as the "Backlund Bump." Notably, Lance Bouma and Joe Colborne both experienced career offensive years playing with Backlund. Bouma scored 16 goals in 2014–15 playing primarily with Backlund, triple his prior career-high, and Colborne scored 19 goals in 2015–16 playing partially with Backlund, nearly double his prior career-high. As his sample size against the league's top players increased, and his performances stayed strong, Backlund was used more extensively in that role, to the point where by 2016 his line was the default match-up against the other teams' top lines.

Backlund experienced a slight offensive breakout in 2016–17 with 53 points in 81 games, playing on a line alongside veteran Michael Frolik and rookie Matthew Tkachuk that emerged as one of the top puck possession lines in hockey. For the first time in his career, he received Selke Trophy consideration, ultimately finishing fourth in balloting. Following that season, he became a fixture on Selke Trophy ballots, receiving a few votes from Professional Hockey Writers Association members in most seasons.

Backlund's emergence as an elite shutdown forward had some ripple effects within the lineup. Typically, offensive-oriented players aren't the best defensive players—outside of truly elite players, nobody's great at every part of the game—but

Backlund's strong two-way up the middle allowed the Flames' coaches to place him with offensive-minded wingers whose defensive games weren't fully fledged, allowing them to marry Backlund's shutdown savvy and puck possession prowess with players who could score with regularity. This circumstance led players like Tkachuk and Andrew Mangiapane to experience strong offensive seasons alongside the Swede.

But having the puck possession line also become an offensive threat really complicated matters for the opposing coaches. Typically, Backlund's line was the Flames' second line, and the club's pure scorers were on the first line—usually comprised of some or all of Elias Lindholm, Sean Monahan, and Johnny Gaudreau—and were countered against the other team's top lines. But when Backlund's line was scoring, it put opposing coaches in the tough predicament of deciding which forward line they would try to shut down in a given game. This particular ripple effect is what helped Backlund become the backbone of some of the Flames' strongest editions, because his emergence led to a lot of complications for the other sides.

In the 2022–23 season, Backlund passed Regehr for third on the Flames franchise's all-time games played leaderboard. The previous season, he surpassed MacInnis for the top spot in franchise games played among Flames draft selections. He serves as an alternate captain, a post he's held since 2018–19, and as of 2022–23 was the longest-serving active member of the club.

Backlund's development path was not smooth sailing. Undoubtedly, he or the organization had thoughts about moving him to another organization when things weren't

Mikael Backlund's development into a top-flight NHL centre was gradual, but he emerged as one of the most reliable shutdown forwards in the NHL.

completely clicking at various junctures throughout his development. He had to navigate challenges with his Swedish club team, a slew of ill-timed early injuries, labour stoppages, along with the usual bumps in the road that are part and parcel in developing as a young man and hockey player. But he has emerged as a role model for the Flames' young players, on and off the ice, a fixture in his local community, and a very important hockey player for his organization.

"We have the puck more than the opposition when Mikael's on the ice," said Treliving. "He touches every part of the game. When you first come into the league, everybody wants to be a power play guy, right? The hardest part is those guys that get drafted high and all of a sudden, usually when they come into the NHL, they're not on the power play, 'cause they haven't been on the power play their whole life. Well, all of a sudden you see value when you become a solid penalty-killer, or when you're playing on a five-on-three. Or when the other team's top player is out there, and your job is to shut him down. In my time here, he's learned to really value that part of the game, not just an offensive part of the game. He's really, really valuable to us."

When it comes to player development, progression is never a steady path. There are bumps along the way. But Backlund's emergence as a top-flight player within the Flames system shows that patience often pays off. All it takes is some time, a lot of perseverance, and a little bit of luck along the way.

19

THE NUMBERS GAME: HOW VIDEO AND ANALYTICS CHANGED HOW THE FLAMES DRAFT

IN A LOT of important ways, player scouting, drafting, recruitment, and development within hockey have always been part of a numbers game that includes elements of art and science within the limitations of business. With an influx of additional teams that has swelled the National Hockey League to 32 clubs, along with rising player salaries and the introduction of a salary cap, drafting and player development has become a realm where mistakes can be costly and efficiencies crucial to finding an edge in a very competitive environment.

In the days before the amateur draft, teams had domain over their local areas but had to find ways to balance the recruitment of key players from outside their territories with the needs of the players currently in their systems. They could promise outside prospects heaven and earth, but if they didn't have the ability to deliver it because of the composition of their NHL or farm team rosters, it might not work out.

The amateur draft added an additional wrinkle. Gone were the exclusive local territories for clubs, replaced by what amounted to a veritable gold rush for draft eligible prospects—structured by the selections in the amateur draft itself. Since the prior regime had focused exclusively on North America, with much of that focus drilled down into Canadian junior leagues, that practice continued, with clubs throwing a lot of scouting bodies at particular teams and leagues to try to find an edge. This scouting frenzy only got crazier with teams beginning to compete for high-end players in American colleges and Europe. The emergence of American major junior leagues, the United States Hockey League and the North American Hockey League in the 2010s, only served to complicate scouting and swell NHL clubs' scouting staffs. These days, the full-time members of an amateur scouting staff often exceed a dozen dedicated area scouts.

Even with large staffs of experienced, skilled scouts, scouting can be challenging, chaotic, and random. At its core, scouting involves sending someone who is trained to look for the right things to look at the right players. The randomness factors in via player performance, which, especially at young ages, can vary significantly from game to game. So teams often hope to send the right scout to look for the right things from the right players and hoping that they're watching on the right night. If the player performs well at the right time, it can be life changing. If not, that player could fall between the cracks—or potentially get selected by a rival team that's there on a different evening.

In this context, in a competitive scouting environment where teams probably prefer not to expand their scouting legions more than they already have—paying 12–15 scouts and having them travel throughout the world isn't inexpensive—finding any edge or additional efficiency can be a massive boost. Rather than hiring additional personnel to focus on particular leagues or regions, increasingly clubs are using technology to become cleverer and more efficient with how they expand their limited personnel, time, and resources. The ability to arm a scouting staff with useful, accurate player information has become essential to success in drafting.

"When you're drafting 18-year-olds, you're making projections on their size, you're making projections on their skating to some degree," said Doug Risebrough, general manager for the Flames from 1991–95. "And some people who are decent skaters at 18 can't find that final gear that NHL players play at. Or they don't get as strong as you thought they would get. That's just part of it. You try to hedge your bets by finding out more history on them. You try and find your medical people to get involved with making some element of a prediction, and yet it's not a complete science."

"The difficulty in scouting is you have to project them at 17," said long-time Flames director of scouting Tod Button. "And you have to break down the individual skill sets and what that looks like at the next stage. Is a guy going to get strong enough to be a good player at the next stage? Or when he's 25?"

In this context, it's logical that clubs have latched onto any system that provides additional information that could assist in projecting player development. Fitness testing became more commonplace during the 1980s and 1990s, to the point where the NHL began organizing the Draft Combine in 1994 to provide centralized information—and to remove the need for prospects to do the same fitness testing for clubs multiple times. Teams have also utilized personality tests and psychological evaluations over the years, often incorporating them into their pre-draft interview processes with prospective draft selections.

As computers became more commonplace throughout the 1990s, many teams experimented with integrating technology into some aspects of their scouting. This tended to take the form of databases to make scouting reports more accessible. The Flames briefly used what was termed an "athletic tracking system" under Risebrough in the mid-1990s. The program was designed by University of Alberta researcher Ralph Renger— expanding upon work Renger did during his doctoral studies at the University of Calgary—and aggregated 10 years of past scouting reports from the NHL's Central Scouting Service into a computerized predictive model of what traits led to success, then produced a draft ranking based on those traits. The system was reportedly only used for the 1994 draft.

As early as the 1990s, while looking for more information on upcoming opponents, NHL coaches began creating their own metrics that they tracked while doing video pre-scouting.

The idea was to provide their team with additional context regarding opposition tendencies, tactics, and performance. It was a very small step toward the league's clubs delving into the analytical revolution that had already grabbed hold of high-level baseball, as coaches, scouts, and managers in that sport had developed tools that went beyond the standard box score to assist in player evaluation.

"I tell people this—when I was an assistant coach under Jim Schoenfeld, we did analytics," said Button. "We did blueline entries and exits, and which side. We had all these forms we filled out and video. The difference now is we didn't have it across the league. We had it for our team, [and] we used to do our two upcoming opponents, sometimes three. But you didn't have it across the league. You didn't have it for every team, every player, American League. That's what you didn't have."

At the time, due to technological and time limitations, a club's analytics attempts were often very small scale—perhaps two or three games at a time, and perhaps in the vicinity of 500 data points. While this provided additional information, it wasn't sufficient to conduct any substantive regressions or other statistical analysis.

However, as publicly available data from several leagues became more readily available to hobbyists in the 2000s and 2010s, the hockey world experienced a data revolution similar to what had already been seen in baseball, basketball, and soccer. When publicly available data wasn't extensive enough for analysis, particularly regarding specific player traits and specific leagues or game situations, the growing availability of game video from throughout the world was used by hobbyists to produce data via manual tracking. As computers became more sophisticated, some aspects of manual tracking soon became automated, which helped make data production less labour intensive and increased the quality and quantity of data available in the public and private realms. Not coincidentally, countless hobbyists who showed proficiency in manual tracking, computer programming, or both began to be hired by NHL clubs eager to find an edge.

But even before delving fully into analytics in the 2010s, the Flames were continuing to look at computational and technological approaches to finding a drafting edge. A few of those early attempts occurred under GM Darryl Sutter.

"[Under] Darryl Sutter, we had guys doing [computer analytics] since 2003 in different ways," said Button. "We were always trying to have an advantage. We had this company in the Maritimes do regression analysis for us, seeing if they could go back and project the draft. They did that for three years."

The Flames later contracted a company from Virginia to assist with the streamlining of draft-related decision-making by centralizing much of the relevant information utilizing software known as Decision Lens.

"Then we hired this company called Decision Lens that takes scouts' biases, so to speak, out of it with mathematical analytics," said Button. "Before that, we hired Chris Snow to run our analytics department. Now, Chris overlapped with Decision Lens, so he saw a lot of what they did and he tried to incorporate some of that into the analytics."

After dipping their toe into computer analytics a little bit in previous years, the Flames began delving into player analytics more thoroughly under GM Jay Feaster in the early 2010s. The important entry point into this revolution for the

Flames was PUCKS. Created by American software developer Sydex Sports, PUCKS was the hockey cousin to their primary sports software system, BATS, which had been used by baseball clubs throughout North America—including Major League Baseball—to integrate their video and statistical analysis into a combined system.

PUCKS was initially released by Sydex Sports in 2007 and came on the radar of Snow, a former sportswriter who covered baseball's Boston Red Sox for *The Boston Globe* and hockey's Minnesota Wild for the *Minneapolis Star Tribune*. After a tenure working for the Wild in hockey operations under Risebrough, Snow pitched Feaster on the PUCKS system. Feaster hired on Snow, initially as a consultant and later as director of statistical and video analysis, to build out the system and run the data and analytics side of the Flames' hockey operations.

"We see applications of great value, and we saw them in Calgary," said Brian Burke, president of hockey operations for the Flames between 2013 and 2018. "Chris Snow really led that revolution for the Flames. That goes back 10 years, when I first got there."

Rather than engage in the proverbial wild goose chases that pro and amateur scouting often turned into, the goal of introducing PUCKS was to modernize the operations a bit. Utilizing PUCKS, a database of video could be built focusing on specific leagues, teams, and players, and part of the database development was turning what the Flames valued in players into specific snippets of games or player performances that could be targeted, clipped, and compared. For example, if they needed a player who was good at face-offs, they had to define what that meant, but they could also pull video from specific game situations to compare. The idea was to give the club the ability to be more targeted with their scouting, especially on the amateur side when scouting coverage could be more challenging.

Button attributes the success the Flames have had integrating information from data and video into their scouting apparatus to the buy-in throughout the organization, starting with GM Brad Treliving, who embraced the idea of the club having more tools at their disposal upon his hiring in 2014.

"The biggest thing for me is analytics wasn't accepted across the board by a lot of people when it first started, when you had these people coming up, and we've tried to mesh it really, really quickly," said Button. "And the reason I think we were successful in doing it is number one, Tree was on board, he wanted to do it.... But if you don't believe in something as a scout, as a manager, you're never going to get the best use of it, right? It's just not going to work because you're not going to believe in it."

The existence of the PUCKS system didn't make the build-out of the Flames' data and video apparatus a walk in the park. Undoubtedly, they faced challenges. There were database construction and integration challenges, data and video availability challenges. Heck, there were even data operationalization challenges—once you define what a quality, concept, or attribute is within your organization's scouting, what does it look like and how do you ensure irrelevant items aren't included? (If you're trying to compare horses and define a horse as broadly being a four-legged equine creature, your data will also include donkeys and zebras.)

"The two biggest challenges are entering proper accurate data and then being able to retrieve it on demand for your scouting staff," said Burke. "All those challenges, Chris Snow is the lead guy on it, and he provided us with some thoughtful analysis, and we relied on him a lot for draft preparation and for trades."

While more than a decade after starting its construction, the Flames are still refining their data and video systems as they relate to scouting, but what they have now is a significant improvement over what came before. Rather than sending scouts across the world relatively unarmed in terms of detailed player information, they can flag certain players with certain attributes for more targeted scouting. They can follow up one night of in-person scouting snapshots with video that can span multiple seasons or target specific attributes or shifts. They can compare and contrast players from throughout the world in ways they couldn't do before, and they can do so in a much more efficient manner. Integrating data and video into the scouting system doesn't completely minimize all of the elements that have always made drafting teenagers a risky proposition, but with these added tools, scouts and general managers have much more information that they had a decade ago to make more calculated gambles on players.

Button explained some of the ways that having access to additional player analytics can assist and enhance the Flames' scouting and draft preparation process.

"One part is we can see if what the analytics says matches up to what the scout says," said Button. "And if not, we go back both analytically and scouting-wise and watch more or analyze differently or in a different way.

"The other part is the analytics has their own list. And what they say is, 'These are the seven guys that aren't in our top 50 that we want you guys to go back and watch, and this is why. He has high hockey sense or he's very competitive or he shows more skill than our scouts have rated.' Then the scouts can say, 'Here are some guys that you don't have on your list. Can you check these guys out analytically?'"

The addition of prospect data to the scouting picture provides the Flames with an additional angle of analysis and invites comparisons that likely make their decision-making more robust when they build out their player profiles and their draft list.

The data piece can also be integrated with some of the other resources the Flames have put in place to provide more context on a player's development on and off the ice. The ability to look at data points over different time periods in a player's season can perhaps provide a more holistic picture of their potential growth.

"We had our meetings, and the data came back really average on this player," said Button. "The scouts like him, but there were some concerns. An event happened in this guy's life; we asked if we had the data from before this event and after, and they broke it down and showed us and, lo and behold, this guy had [taken] off after this event in his life had happened. Now we're like, okay, that makes sense. So when I talk about things like that, and I talk about Matt Brown and mental profiles, 17-year-old kids, maybe their parents go through divorces, maybe it's a job, the pandemic didn't help a lot of people—forget 17-year-olds and teenagers, it didn't help a lot of people overall. Those are the things we try to tie in with the analytics."

NHL clubs do extensive research on players, often interviewing a prospect's family, teachers, friends, and coaches to get an insight into their character, maturity, and potential. The mental development side of the game remains a challenge for clubs, as they utilize resources such as Brown, the Flames' mental performance coach, in order to evaluate potential draft selections and assist them in dealing with the rigours of becoming a high-level professional athlete.

"We do a lot of work on the psychological part of the game," said Button. "But you've got to understand, 17-year-old kids, I think in reality their brains are only 70 per cent developed. There's lots of development left mentally and physically for these kids when we draft them. Those are the things we keep trying to put in place."

Decades ago, success in drafting was seemingly the product of many elements of chance: the right scout being in the right arena on the right night, and often of players being selected out of sequence by the teams drafting ahead of your club. The human element of scouting remains crucially important, and the randomness and luck involved in drafting and projecting the development of teenagers can never be engineered or removed by data or analytics. But now the expertise of scouts can be more targeted, which likely gives clubs a better opportunity at success.

Drafting used to be the product of long hours, hard work, and quite a bit of luck. Now, more than ever, it's the product of information and preparation, as the influx of video and statistical analysis have given scouting teams more useful information to make informed projections on which players to look at, which to select, and how they may turn out.

And scouting is only going to get smarter as data becomes more robust, video more widely available, and processes more refined.

"It's more information, right?" said Treliving. "To me, you need everything. It's not just an add-on, it's a critical piece of your evaluation now. You can't just trust your eyes to see everything. And so it's incorporated in. It's just part of the meal, right? It's just how you do things. The difference is there's so much more information now that you can break down all facets of a player versus, back in the day, you went in and watched him. That's still a very critical piece of scouting, the viewings and live viewings, but there wasn't the availability of that stuff. It didn't seem that long ago that you were really using a lot of video, right? Now video's tied into everything and as much as you've got live viewings, you're watching a lot of video, and it's tied into all your data analysis. It's night and day from the amount of information that you have available now to what you had even 10 years ago."

"Now you have vast amounts of information," said Button. "And with kids, you're still trying to predict the future, even with analytics."

Button noted that the number of tools at scouts' disposal has rapidly increased in recent years as clubs attempt to find an edge in their drafting. Given the fierce competition in the league to find young stars, he expects that trend to continue as teams try new things in an effort to gain an advantage.

"We have to be ever-learning in our business, because we'll never know it all," said Button. "Something will come along in two years that will add to the scouting process or derail it a little bit more."

The hockey business is a small world where everyone knows and talks to each other, and teams are fairly guarded regarding the specifics of much of what they do from a scouting perspective. When teams hear about a new concept, idea, or tool that another team is utilizing, they usually try it out themselves in an effort to gain an edge (or just to negate the possible advantage another team might have). Button joked that he was surprised that the baseball teams revealed as much as they did to Michael Lewis when he wrote *Moneyball*, given how much of a competitive edge analytics gave the clubs that had integrated them well.

"It's a copycat league," said Button. "But there are always guys trying to get an advantage. Hockey managers, coaches, scouts, even players—they're ever-learning. They're going to keep trying to improve in every way they can."

20

HOW THE FLAMES DRAFTED JOHNNY GAUDREAU

THE **2011 NHL** Draft was the culmination of many months
of transition for the Flames franchise. After nearly seven
years at his post, Darryl Sutter resigned as general manager just prior to Christmas in 2010. His replacement was
his newly hired assistant Jay Feaster, ironically enough one
of the architects of the Tampa Bay Lightning club that beat
Sutter's Flames for the Stanley Cup in 2004, who had joined
the Flames organization in July 2010. Initially an interim
replacement, Feaster was hired permanently following the
2010–11 season.

Feaster took over the Flames in challenging times. After
reaching the Stanley Cup Final in the 2003–04 campaign, his
first season as GM, Sutter spent the remainder of his tenure

trying to get his team back to that elusive promised land and attempt to maximize the window of contention during the prime years for stars Jarome Iginla and Miikka Kiprusoff. This approach meant regularly trading draft selections for players who could immediately provide a boost to the NHL roster.

This deficit spending removed the potential for future stars from the Flames' developmental system. The remaining draft selections were often in the later rounds, where it's much harder to select future stars, and a string of challenging performances at drafts under Sutter added few significant players to the developmental system. Add those challenges to a developmental pipeline that was already lean when Sutter began as GM, and Feaster had some work to do to restock the cupboards.

He also inherited a fairly major and immediate problem: 2009 first-round selection Tim Erixon.

The son of long-time NHLer Jan Erixon, a forward who played 556 games for the New York Rangers between 1983 and 1993, the younger Erixon was a highly touted defensive prospect in the 2009 NHL Draft class. He was the fifth-ranked European skater by the Central Scouting Service in that class, and the Flames selected him in the first round, 23rd overall.

But as Feaster settled into his new job as GM in late 2010, Erixon had still not signed an entry-level deal with the Flames, and the June 1 deadline for signing him was looming closer. Despite the Flames' best efforts, Erixon was not interested in signing with the club. Prior to Feaster's arrival, the Flames had engaged in lengthy negotiations with Erixon's camp. Player personnel director Duane Sutter, a family friend who had known Erixon's father from their time in the NHL together, visited the family. Pro scouts Ron Sutter and Michel Goulet reached out to his camp. Sutter and scouting director Tod Button had discussions as well. But Erixon remained hesitant.

Among the reasons related by Feaster at the time for Erixon's reluctance was due to his desire to play in the NHL immediately and his lack of confidence that would happen in Calgary (based on how few young players had been integrated recently). Erixon's camp also reportedly told the Flames that he was feeling ignored by the organization at times, something the club disputed. When Feaster came into the GM position, he requested the scouting team document all the points of contact in an effort to illustrate how valued Erixon had been to the club.

From there, Feaster attempted to assuage Erixon's concerns and convince him that being a Flame would be the best bet for his future. Former Flames player Hakan Loob, a popular figure in Sweden who was utilized at times as a scouting consultant for the club following his retirement, was even engaged to help with the situation, but to no avail.

"We worked it hard and used as many of our human assets and resources as we could to try to get him to sign," said Feaster. "Constant conversations with the agent, trying to speak regularly with the player and his family. I recall that Hakan Loob was speaking with the Erixon family all the time, practically visiting the house multiple days every week, trying to convince Tim there was, in fact, a legitimate opportunity for him to play in Calgary, but we could never get any traction."

The Flames reportedly offered to include a European assignment clause in his deal, so if Erixon didn't make the

NHL roster he could go play in Sweden rather than the Flames' farm team in the American Hockey League, but to no avail. It was looking like the deadline would pass and Erixon would re-enter the draft in 2011.

Faced with losing Erixon's rights and only receiving a compensatory second-round pick out of the situation, Feaster got to work. He eventually negotiated a trade involving Erixon's rights at the eleventh hour. Erixon and a fifth-round pick went to the Rangers, a team Erixon made it known that he would sign with throughout the saga, in exchange for forward prospect Roman Horak and a pair of second-round picks. The Rangers received a player they coveted, Erixon ended up signing a contract with his father's old team, and the Flames received three assets.

Since Erixon's departure from the organization, and the dramatic situation surrounding it, the Flames have made discussions about a potential draft selection's desire to play for Calgary a standard part of their draft interview process.

"This is part of learning from stuff you're always trying to find out," said Button. "Calgary's a faraway place from the East Coast. So we do take the time, spend the time with the East Coast kids and say, 'You going to come? You going to come? Would you come if we drafted you?' We have the final say. We don't have to draft the kids. We've had a few kids say, 'No, I don't want to play in Calgary.'

"We have absolutely put stuff in place to try to vet these guys out as much as possible. We ask them the question in more than one interview. There's not a questionnaire we send out, there's not an interview we do with the area scouts or at the end of the year at the combine or pre-draft with

Matt Brown where we don't ask that question. We don't ask that of a Calgary kid, because we don't have to, but we ask them, 'No problem playing with the hometown Flames?' 'No problem at all. Love to. Can't wait.'"

The Flames ended up stick-handling a difficult situation and getting a lot of value from the trade.

"All things considered, it worked for us as we acquired three assets including a player who played for us right away in Roman Horak," said Feaster. "It really was a difficult situation and one I believe to this day had nothing to do with Calgary or the Flames, meaning there was nothing more the organization could have done or anything we could have or should have done differently to make it happen."

In Horak, the Flames received a versatile young Czech forward. A fifth-round selection of the Rangers in the 2009 NHL Draft, the Flames had a familiarity with Horak due to him being junior teammates with Ryan Howse of the WHL's Chilliwack Bruins, a third-round pick of the Flames from the same draft. While Horak wasn't necessarily considered to have the same high developmental ceiling as Howse, he was seen as a solid prospect who could be a productive pro player.

The compensatory selection the Flames would have received from the NHL as a result of Erixon re-entering the draft would have been the 23rd pick in 2011's second round, or 53rd overall. The selections they received from the Rangers were 45th and 57th overall, which provided the Flames with a fair deal of value in the trade and saved the Rangers a few nervous hours at their draft table hoping that Erixon might fall to them.

Despite seeming like a very promising prospect, and the dramatics involving his move to the Rangers organization,

Erixon never really panned out in North American hockey. He spent just a season with the Rangers before bouncing around the NHL, spending time with the Columbus Blue Jackets, Chicago Blackhawks, and Toronto Maple Leafs, then two seasons in the Pittsburgh Penguins minor league system. After two more seasons in the American Hockey League on minor league deals, he returned to Europe in 2019. His NHL career comprised just 93 games. (Horak played 84 NHL games, all but two with the Flames.)

Meanwhile, the 2011 draft class ended up becoming one of the Flames' stronger crops of talent in the salary cap era.

The Flames entered the event with five selections. Aside from the two second-round picks, they had picks in the first, fourth, and sixth rounds. Other than Feaster sending their fifth-round pick to the Rangers in the Erixon shuffle, Sutter had previously traded away their second, third, and seventh-round spots—their third-round pick had been traded to Edmonton in the first-ever trade between the two Alberta rivals.

In the first round, at 13th overall, the Flames selected Swiss import Sven Baertschi, a left wing playing with the WHL's Portland Winterhawks. A strong finesse player who could skate and distribute the puck well, Baertschi was seen as a smart, relatively safe selection at the time based on his all-around skill set—with the thought that perhaps he could even develop into a power forward over time.

In the second round, the Flames selected Finnish centre Markus Granlund at 45th overall and Baertschi's Winterhawks teammate, blueliner Tyler Wotherspoon, at 57th overall. Granlund was the younger brother of Minnesota Wild prospect Mikael Granlund, the ninth overall pick in 2010, and was seen as a good but not elite prospect—the Valeri Bure to Mikael's Pavel Bure, if you will—who could become a solid two-way centre with some offensive upside. Wotherspoon projected as a steady, reliable, stay-at-home defender.

In the sixth round, the Flames opted for a goaltender, going for Edmonton Oil Kings backup netminder Laurent Brossoit at 164th overall. Brossoit had developed well over his rookie season in the WHL, even out-performing veteran teammate Jon Groenheyde in the Oil Kings' short playoff run. With Edmonton considered an up-and-coming team in the WHL, the hope was Brossoit could get some development out of some potentially lengthy playoff runs.

Finally, the Flames selected American junior forward Johnny Gaudreau in the fourth round at 104th overall. In his draft year, Gaudreau had some eye-popping numbers working for him and against him: he posted 36 goals and 72 points with the Dubuque Fighting Saints of the United States Hockey League, and he was listed by Central Scouting by his early season measurement of 5'6" and 137 pounds. His offensive stats made jaws drop. But even by small player standards, he was small, which was one of the few reasons he was available in the fourth round of the draft to begin with.

Gaudreau easily turned into the best of the Flames' 2011 picks, and his selection stands out as some of the strongest late-round gambling the club has embarked upon since perhaps Theoren Fleury in 1987. How they pulled it off is a fairly unique story.

A product of Carney's Point, New Jersey, a suburb just across the Delaware River from Philadelphia on the New Jersey side, Gaudreau was two things growing up: really good at hockey, and undersized relative to kids his age. His father, Guy, ran the local rink, and Gaudreau was constantly on the ice tooling around with the puck. As Gaudreau got older, he became more and more entrenched in local hockey, where he excelled. Every season, onlookers and scouts acknowledged his prowess but expressed doubts that he could do it at higher levels of hockey against bigger, faster opposition. Every season, Gaudreau did just that. He landed on the Flames' radar from his performance at USA Hockey's selection camp for the 2010 Ivan Hlinka Memorial Tournament—Gaudreau ended up making the team.

After impressing in high school hockey and committing to play at Northeastern University, Gaudreau made a bet on himself and left home for the first time, moving to Iowa to play for coach Jim Montgomery in Dubuque. Playing in an up-and-coming league that was just starting to be seen as a proving ground for future NHLers but had already established itself as a main feeder system for college teams, Gaudreau excelled. He finished fifth in scoring in his draft year, was named the USHL's Rookie of the Year, and helped the club capture the Clark Cup as the USHL's playoff tournament champions.

When Northeastern head coach Greg Cronin departed his school for a position with the Toronto Maple Leafs and assistant coach Albie O'Connell, who recruited Gaudreau, left for a job with Harvard, Gaudreau was given his release from his letter of intent. Gaudreau was still weighing his college options with his brother, Matt, who he had pledged to attend college with, as the 2011 NHL Draft approached.

Because there are other teams selecting in the NHL draft, and they're vying for the same pool of coveted young players, some NHL organizations try to be sneaky during the later rounds of the draft. When it comes to the projected first-round talents, there are no secrets; every team likes them and even if the various draft lists are a bit different from each other, in most years the projected first-round mix for each team is the same group of players in slightly different orders.

The later rounds are where scouting teams, especially area scouts, make their hay and provide their value. The later rounds are when it does sometimes pay for teams to be sneaky, and Gaudreau's particularly situation lent itself to some minor subterfuge. The Fighting Saints were co-owned by Peter Chiarelli, at the time the GM of the Boston Bruins, so if the Flames were seen at too many games or talked to Gaudreau or his advisors or his coaches, it could tip their hand and reveal their growing interest in the young forward.

Button downplayed the notion that the Flames engaged in any special shenanigans to disguise their interest in Gaudreau. If nothing else, they were merely being cognizant of the various connections within the hockey world and doing what they could to enhance their chances to land the young forward at the draft.

"I don't think it was as cloak and dagger as the stories have made it out to be," said Button. "The thing is you don't want people to know what you're doing. Chiarelli was part-owner of that team in Dubuque. And we didn't want it getting back to them that we were digging around on Johnny. We just didn't. We'd done it in Sweden, too. When you're in this business, you know who's connected to who.

"It was cloak and dagger in that we didn't interview him, which at the end of the day could've turned out the other way, right, if you don't interview a guy. We've done it in the past. No, stay away from the guy when we have interest. It doesn't happen at the top of the draft, but it does happen in the bottom of the draft."

So the Flames kept their distance and did their best to camouflage their attendance at Dubuque's games. They built their draft profile on Gaudreau slowly, usually through conversations with opposition coaches.

"You're always trying to hide stuff, that's for sure," said Button. "And at the same time you're trying to hide it, you're trying to get information, too. You're listening, you're trying to figure out where these guys are going. Cloak and dagger's good. It makes it sound more exciting than it really is."

Meanwhile, the Flames' U.S.-based scout Bob Pulford advocated for Gaudreau internally, and Button also became a fan.

The 2011 NHL Draft was the first under Feaster's guidance, and he had a very specific instruction to Button and his staff: work the list. By that, Feaster meant that the club should rely on an ordered list of best players in the draft class, based upon the criteria the club identified for what they valued in prospects. This would help simplify decision-making at the draft. For selections, they would go with the top remaining player on their list, and when deciding to make any in-draft trades, they would have a clear idea of the opportunity cost of any such moves.

"In both organizations [Tampa Bay and Calgary], we spent a lot of hours and went through a lot of discussion and debate, ordering our list and ensuring it was in the order we would draft the players," said Feaster. "To then move off that order for purposes of 'need' or whatever the case may be did not make sense to me. I found in Tampa that while we were try-ing to draft that 6′5″ or 6′6″ D-man, for example, we were skipping over players who became regular NHL players and contributors for their teams. I wanted to get away from mak-ing that mistake. If that meant drafting another centre when we already had four good young centre ice prospects in the minors, so be it, because if we were correct and we ended up with five or six or seven quality centre icemen in the organi-zation, we could always use them as assets in making trades."

Feaster hoped that a focus on clear drafting criteria would help the Flames hit a reset button on any other biases that had crept into their drafting habits, such as a tendency to shy away from selecting smaller or collegiate players.

"In effect, I told Tod we wanted to draft hockey players who fit the criteria we had established for being a Calgary Flame, period," said Feaster. "No biases, no pre-conceived notions. Let's identify hockey players who fit our mold based on our criteria. Let's get them in the proper rank order and draft our list."

While Button's team embraced the list approach, the head scout and Feaster agreed to two exceptions—they "boxed" Gaudreau and Russian prospect Nikita Kucherov outside the main draft list and kept them aside as wild card picks to take if either player was available past a certain point in the draft. The question wasn't if they wanted Gaudreau; rather it was if he would somehow be available when they felt it was a good time to draft him.

The Flames went through the first two rounds, selecting Baertschi, Granlund, and Wotherspoon, then decided that their next selection would be Gaudreau.

"Tod would make the point that if we really want this player or that one, we would have to take him by the X round to ensure we would get him," said Feaster. "That analysis was based on what was happening on the floor of the draft and on when/where our next picks were. Sometimes you would take that information and go fishing for a trade to try to move up and barring any luck doing so we would have to decide if this particular player was worth stepping up for and going off the list."

The Flames waited nervously for the entire third round before selecting Gaudreau.

Button told the Flames' website years later, "We thought we had a good chance at still getting him but from 57 to 104 we sweated a little bit." The Flames pulled the trigger, selecting Gaudreau at 104th overall. At the time, Gaudreau was at a hockey tournament organized by his father and found out that he was drafted during a stoppage in play.

From there, Gaudreau experienced a stepwise progression. He committed to Boston College with his younger brother. He impressed onlookers and fans at the Flames' development camp, with murmurs about his diminutive size soon being replaced by oohs and aahs at his speed and puck-handling.

He adapted quickly to the college game, playing on a strong Boston College team coached by the legendary Jerry York. Gaudreau grasped the college fundamentals quickly, and by mid-season he was one of the top offensive players in the nation. He was named his conference playoff tournament's most valuable player and was part of an Eagles team that won the NCAA national championship.

Gaudreau went back to college as a sophomore, wanting to round out his game. He continued his strong play from the prior season and was named a finalist for the Hobey Baker Award, given to the top player in college hockey. He also played a starring role for the United States at the World Juniors, where he led the tournament in goals and helped his nation win a gold medal.

Despite conversations with the Flames about going pro, Gaudreau opted to return to school for his junior season— primarily, he told reporters, because he wanted to play with his brother for a season as they had planned years earlier. Gaudreau continued to torment opposition defenders with his skill and finesse.

Boston College qualified for the 2014 Frozen Four, the NCAA's national semi-final and final round, located that year in Philadelphia, near Gaudreau's hometown. With Feaster having departed the Flames organization by then, interim GM Brian Burke dispatched special assistant Craig Conroy to Philadelphia with a mission: get Gaudreau signed to a contract.

The Eagles were eliminated from the tournament on a Thursday night. Gaudreau attended the NCAA's year-end awards banquet and was named the winner of the Hobey Baker Award on a Friday night. After lengthy discussions with his family and advisor, Gaudreau agreed to terms with the Flames late that Friday evening.

Gaudreau and teammate (and fellow Flames draft choice) Bill Arnold flew to Vancouver and made their NHL debuts together two days later, on the final night of the 2013–14 regular season. The Flames lost by a 5–1 score. Gaudreau scored the only goal for the Flames, the first of his NHL career.

From that point onward, aside from a five-game stint where he struggled at the start of his rookie season, Gaudreau was one of the most consistent offensive players in Flames franchise history. He went on to score 210 goals and amass 609 points over nine seasons with the Flames before his departure in free agency in the summer of 2022. During his tenure with the Flames, he was consistently their most important offensive player, leading the team in points in six of his nine seasons in Calgary.

Outside of Gaudreau, the remainder of the 2011 draft class performed well, with all five players selected by the Flames over that draft weekend spending time in the NHL. Button cited the 2011 crop as one of the best in his time with the club.

Baertschi joined the Flames briefly in 2011–12 on an emergency recall basis, being summoned from junior after the NHL club was already missing several regulars. He impressed in his five-game stint, scoring three goals. But his Flames performances in subsequent seasons were inconsistent, and his superb play in the AHL was followed by less impressive work on the big club as he struggled with the increased size and strength of NHL opposition, so he bounced between the two levels for parts of three seasons. He established himself as too good for the AHL level of competition but couldn't gain any traction at the NHL level. In retrospect, his impressive emergency recall performance may have set expectations too high for the remainder of his run in Calgary.

Blessed with speed, smarts, and creativity, Johnny Gaudreau was one of the top collegiate players of the 2010s and emerged as the Flames' most consistent offensive weapon during his seven seasons with the club.

At the time, Feaster may have also been guilty of not trying to recalibrate expectations when fans and media pondered if Baertschi was the heir apparent to Iginla. Feaster also exhibited some missteps in expectations management following his selection of Canadian prep school forward Mark Jankowski in the first round of the 2012 NHL Draft. Following the pick, he touted Jankowski as "a franchise guy" and "someone you can build around," and he infamously declared that 10 years after his selection, "Jankowski will be viewed as the best player in the 2012 draft." Jankowski ended up being a fairly effective fourth line and AHL centre, both in Calgary and elsewhere, but he wasn't anywhere close to being the best selection from his draft year.

Baertschi was traded to Vancouver prior to the 2016 trade deadline for a second-round pick, and he played well in a depth role for the Canucks before his NHL career was derailed by concussion issues. He went on to continue his playing career in Europe.

Granlund didn't end up as successful in the NHL as his old brother, but he played parts of seven seasons in the big league, amassing 335 games at that level. He spent parts of three seasons with the Flames, bouncing between the NHL and AHL levels, before being traded to Vancouver midway through the 2015–16 season in exchange for forward Hunter Shinkaruk. Granlund also briefly played in Edmonton before moving his playing career to Europe.

After returning to Portland and representing Canada at the World Juniors, Wotherspoon played just 30 NHL games, all with the Flames. He departed as a free agent following the 2017–18 season, but he's carved out a niche for himself as a strong AHL blueliner in several different organizations.

Brossoit wasn't in the Flames' organization for too long. After two breakthrough seasons as a star goalie for the Oil

Kings, he went pro but was traded early in his first pro season to the Edmonton Oilers—one of just three trades ever made between the two rival Alberta teams. Brossoit slowly developed into a strong goaltender, working his way up through the second-tier ECHL and the AHL before carving out a niche for himself as a strong backup goaltender. He's played 117 NHL games, split between the Oilers, Winnipeg Jets, and Vegas Golden Knights.

Feaster wasn't in an ideal situation when he took over for Sutter in late 2010. The farm system had depth issues. The NHL team was on the outside of the playoff picture—and unbeknownst to them at the time, they were a few seasons away from a full-on rebuild. And the looming Erixon signing deadline could have blown up on the club. But Feaster and his staff deftly navigated the Erixon situation in a way that landed them extra draft capital, then they embarked upon one of the more productive drafts in club history.

All five of the players the Flames selected in the 2011 draft played NHL games, and they found a franchise ace in the fourth round in the form of Gaudreau by taking a calculated risk on a small player who had perpetually defied criticisms of his size.

21

BRING ON THE REBUILD: THE FLAMES' MONUMENTAL 2013 DRAFT

JAROME IGINLA WAS a heck of a hockey player.

It goes without saying that the 2022 Hockey Hall of Fame inductee was a significant player throughout his playing career, but there was a period of several seasons—roughly between 2001 and 2006—when he might have been the best goal-scorer in hockey. Similarly, Miikka Kiprusoff had one of the best runs of any goaltender in league history during his early years with the Calgary Flames, setting a modern-day NHL goals-against average record (1.69) in 2003–04 and then winning the Vezina Trophy in 2005–06, becoming the first Flame to ever capture that trophy.

When your hockey club has the league's best goal-scorer and best goaltender, and your team went to a Stanley Cup Final recently, it's easy to convince yourself that the group is one or two pieces away from winning it all. So for virtually the entirety of Darryl Sutter's tenure as Flames general manager, he was in full "burn the boats" mode in an attempt to get his club to a championship. Out went draft selections, and in came a slew of veteran free agent and trade acquisitions designed to push the Flames over the top.

Even after Sutter's resignation from his post in 2010 and the installation of his assistant, Jay Feaster, in the big chair, the instructions seemed fairly simple: do what can be done to maximize the contention window enabled by Iginla and Kiprusoff's presences on the team. The adding continued, even with the Flames failing to qualify for the postseason in 2010, 2011, and 2012. Finally, on a western road trip during the lockout-shortened 2012–13 season that saw the Flames lose all three games—pushing them below the .500 mark in the standings—Iginla, who held a no-move clause in his contract, told Feaster that he could explore trade options. The Flames were given a list of a handful of teams that Iginla would accept a move to and went to work.

On March 27, 2013, following a Flames win over Colorado where Iginla was a healthy scratch, his time with the Flames came to a close. Shortly after the final horn, the Flames announced that Iginla had been traded to the Pittsburgh Penguins in exchange for college forwards Kenny Agostino and Ben Hanowski, and a first-round pick in the 2013 NHL

Draft. The trade had originally been reported on social media by multiple sources as being to the Boston Bruins, leading to momentary confusion when Feaster revealed the details of the trade with Pittsburgh.

The Flames also explored other moves to leverage existing assets for futures. Blueliner Jay Bouwmeester was sent to St. Louis in exchange for minor league defenceman Mark Cundari, Swiss goaltending prospect Reto Berra, and a first-round pick in the 2013 NHL Draft.

The Flames discussed a potential move with Kiprusoff, who had a year remaining on his contract, and Toronto general manager Dave Nonis told reporters that his club had a deal in place with Calgary for Kiprusoff prior to the trade deadline. However, Kiprusoff told Flames brass that his preference was to remain with the Flames as he mulled his playing future—that he and his wife had welcomed a new child just a month prior also contributed to his desire not to be moved. As a result, the Flames held onto Kiprusoff. He decided to retire at the end of the season and, after a summer at peace with his decision, the club announced his retirement at the end of the offseason.

As a result of their swaps, the Flames entered the draft with multiple first-round selections: sixth overall (their own pick), 22nd overall (from the Blues in the Bouwmeester trade), and 28th overall (from the Penguins in the Iginla trade). It was the third time in franchise history that they selected multiple times in the first round—they had two selections in both 1973 and 1976—and the first time they had ever selected three times.

The Flames could have lost their own first-round pick, though. They got off to a fairly uneven start to begin the 2012–13 campaign and with the schedule truncated to just 48 games due to the lockout, teams had little margin for error. So looking for a boost, the Flames came to an agreement on an offer sheet for unsigned restricted free agent Ryan O'Reilly of the Colorado Avalanche—at the time, O'Reilly and the Avalanche were at a stalemate in their contract negotiations and trade talks hadn't translated into any moves. The Flames announced the two sides had agreed to terms on February 28, ironically the day of a game between the Flames and Avalanche.

Midway through the game, roughly two hours after the offer sheet had been announced, the Avalanche announced that they would match the offer sheet, keeping O'Reilly on their roster under the terms of a deal negotiated with the player by the Flames. However, days later it emerged via a report from Sportsnet reporter Chris Johnston that under the terms of the recently negotiated collective bargaining agreement, because O'Reilly had played in Russia's Kontinental Hockey League after the beginning of the 2012–13 NHL season and because he would have been changing teams via the offer sheet (leaving Colorado for Calgary), he would have had to go through the waiver process to be added to the Flames roster. (Had Colorado signed O'Reilly directly, since he was already their property, no waivers would have been involved.)

According to Johnston, had Colorado not opted to match Calgary's offer sheet, the Flames would have given up their first- and third-round picks to the Avalanche for O'Reilly's rights and then likely lost the player on the waiver wire as his services were offered up to the league's 29 other teams— including Colorado. Reportedly the NHL was unaware that

O'Reilly had played in the KHL after the NHL season began, and O'Reilly's own agent, Pat Morris, wasn't aware that the waiver rule would apply.

The Flames disputed Johnston's contentions, with Feaster releasing a statement shortly after his report was published: "Our interpretation of the Article 13 transition rules governing restricted free agents, and the applicability of Article 13.23 under the new Collective Bargaining Agreement to such RFA's was, and continues to be, different than the NHL's current interpretation as articulated to us this morning. Moreover, throughout our discussions, the player's representative [Patrick Morris] shared our interpretation and position with respect to the non-applicability of Article 13.23. While we were prepared to advance our position with the NHL, in light of Colorado's having matched the offer sheet it is now an academic point. As such, we will have no further comment on the matter, the player, or the offer sheet process."

As stated by Feaster, the point became merely an academic curiosity after Colorado opted to match the offer sheet, but it was almost a very important point of interpretation— and could have cost the Flames a very valuable draft selection.

In the first major step of the club's long-anticipated rebuilding process, the Flames went into the 2013 draft with three first-round selections and used all of them, selecting a trio of forwards from different parts of the Canadian Hockey League.

A centre from Brampton, Ontario, sixth-overall pick Sean Monahan impressed in major junior with the Ontario Hockey League's Ottawa 67's, making the team in his 16-year-old season. By the time he entered his draft-eligible season, 2012–13, he already had 127 OHL games under his belt. He served as captain in 2012–13, posting 31 goals and 78 points. He ended the season ranked fifth among North American skaters on the final Central Scouting Service ranking. Monahan was seen as the logical pick at sixth overall, boasting maturity in several facets of his game, as well as a mature temperament and physique.

At 22nd overall, the Flames selected winger Emile Poirier from the Quebec Major Junior Hockey League's Gatineau Olympiques. A speedy offensive-minded player, Poirier had a big draft season, with 32 goals and 70 points, while he drew some criticism from scouts for his under-developed defensive game. He was ranked 39th among North American skaters, though he had more buzz by the summer due to a strong postseason performance with Gatineau. Poirier was seen as a bit of a project pick by the Flames because of his play away from the puck, but his scoring potential made him an attractive gamble.

At 28th overall, the Flames went to the Western Hockey League's Regina Pats and selected winger Morgan Klimchuk. A savvy two-way forward, Klimchuk was ranked 25th among North American skaters and seen as a fairly low risk, low reward pick. His offensive game numbers weren't scintillating—36 goals and 72 points in his draft year—and he was only averaged-sized at 6'0" and 185 pounds, but his hockey sense and skating were seen as big assets by scouts.

After the first round, the Flames leaned heavy on adding blueline depth. They selected towering Victoria Royals blueliner Keegan Kanzig—listed at 6'7" and 235 pounds—in the third round (67th overall). Brandon Wheat Kings defender Eric

Roy was taken in the fourth round (135th overall). Prep school winger Tim Harrison, an over-age player bound for Colgate University, was selected in the sixth round (157th overall). Russian defender Rushan Rafikov went in the seventh round (187th overall), along with Providence College freshman blue-liner John Gilmour (198th overall). Aside from a goaltender, the Flames got a little of everything in the 2013 class.

Monahan showed up to his first NHL camp in the fall of 2013 and, quite simply, stuck around for years and years. Coming into camp precisely as advertised as an NHL-ready player, Monahan was a smart, reliable centre who used his stout frame to get to the area around the net and score goals.

"Sean Monahan put on like 12 pounds between the draft and the start of the season," said Flames director of scouting Tod Button. "He went from 185 to 197, which allowed him to play."

Monahan established himself as one of the most consistent goal-scorers in club history before injuries—many of them sustained while he was scoring those goals around the net area—slowed him down. He scored 212 goals over 656 games during his nine seasons with the Flames, ranking ninth all-time in games played and eighth all-time in goals at the time of his departure via trade to Montreal in the 2022 off-season.

Poirier played the 2013–14 season in the QMJHL before moving onto the Flames' farm system for the 2014–15 season. Poirier had a superb initial pro season, with 42 points in 55 games for the Flames' farm team, the Adirondack Flames, and he earned a six-game call-up to the NHL as well. However, Poirier's progression stalled, notably due to some

injury challenges that cost him developmental time, and by
the end of the 2017–18 season the Flames opted not to retain
him, allowing him to leave as a free agent after just eight
NHL appearances.

Like Poirier, Klimchuk returned to junior for the 2013–
14, but he also spent the 2014–15 season in the WHL, split
between Regina and Brandon. He went pro in 2015–16, joining the AHL's Stockton Heat and playing primarily on the
lower lines for the Heat as he built up his defensive responsibilities, where he scored just nine points in 55 games. In the
2016–17 season he received more opportunities in offensive
situations, boosting his production to 43 points in 66 games.
Klimchuk spent another season with the Flames organization
before being traded to Toronto early in the 2018–19 campaign
in exchange for minor league defenceman Andrew Nielsen.
At the time Klimchuk was performing reliably at the AHL
level, but the addition of other prospects in the Flames system—including some that progressed quickly to the NHL
level—kept him from rising up the club's depth chart.

Of the five players the Flames selected after the first
round, only one—Kanzig—spent any time playing in the
Flames' system. Kanzig spent one season (2016–17) playing
in the minor leagues, primarily the second-tier ECHL, before
being traded to Carolina in a swap that brought backup goalie
Eddie Lack to Calgary. Gilmour and the Flames couldn't
come to terms on a contract, and he became a free agent
after finishing college. He established himself as a reliable
blueliner at the AHL level and played 37 games between the
New York Rangers and Buffalo before heading to Europe to
continue his career.

Feaster didn't remain with the Flames long enough to see many of the 2013 draft class mature. He departed the organization, along with assistant general manager John Weisbrod, in December 2013. He was commended by president of hockey operations Brian Burke at the time of his departure, and in the years that followed, for setting the table for the organization's rebuild. In particular, his inquisitiveness regarding the reasoning for many of the club's scouting practices led to both the adoption of the "work the list" system, as well as the introduction of more sophisticated data into the process through the work of Chris Snow and other staff members.

However, it would take a little while for those new practices in scouting, player evaluation, and development to really start paying off for the organization.

22

HOW BRAD TRELIVING MADE HIS MARK ON THE FLAMES IN THE 2015 DRAFT

AFTER JAY FEASTER'S dismissal in December 2013, president of hockey operations Brian Burke—hired three months earlier by team president Ken King with an aim of getting the franchise on track—opted to serve as interim general manager until he found the right person to hire as Feaster's replacement. On April 28, 2014, the Flames announced their new GM: Brad Treliving, son of Boston Pizza founder Jim Treliving (of Dragon's Den fame), and long-time assistant general manager of the Phoenix Coyotes.

Like Burke, Treliving had spent time as a player before moving into front office roles. Treliving played junior hockey

as a defenceman in the Western Hockey League for two sea-
sons, spending short stints with the Portland Winterhawks,
Brandon Wheat Kings, Spokane Chiefs, and Regina Pats.
He followed his junior career with six seasons of minor
league pro hockey, spending time with the International
Hockey League's Indianapolis Ice, the American Hockey
League's New Haven Senators and Prince Edward Island
Senators, and the East Coast Hockey League's Winston-
Salem Thunderbirds, Greensboro Monarchs, Columbus
Chill, Louisville Icehawks, and Charlotte Checkers. The
majority of Treliving's pro hockey was played in the sec-
ond-tier ECHL.

After learning a bit of the hockey business during
his ECHL tenure, Treliving hung up his skates at age 26
and crossed over to the front office. Treliving went on to
team with some business partners to establish the Western
Professional Hockey League, establishing low-level pro
franchises across New Mexico, Texas, and Louisiana. The
WPHL merged with the Central Hockey League after
the 2000–01 season, and Treliving was soon recruited by
Coyotes general manager Don Maloney to work with him
in the NHL.

Treliving received an education on how to run a league
with the WPHL—and how to run a hockey club in Phoenix.
The Coyotes' existence as an NHL club has been tumultuous, to say the least, with frequent ownership turnover,
a small yet dedicated following in the market, and persistent
financial challenges. The NHL actually controlled the franchise between 2009 and 2013 due to ownership issues. As a
result, the Coyotes operated at the margins and their hockey

operations group had to be equal parts prudent, clever, and persistent when it came to operating the club. In part due to Treliving's extensive, diverse hockey resume and rave reviews from others in hockey, he was the only person Burke interviewed for the Flames' GM position.

"I looked at a bunch of candidates, because that's your job, but the only guy I interviewed was Brad," said Burke. "I told [team president] Ken King that I went through the list, I did my due diligence, I've done my homework, I only want to interview one guy."

When Treliving came to Calgary, he had experience running the club's farm system, in assisting Maloney in managing the salary cap, and in assisting their scouting team in viewing players. In a contrast to Craig Button's hiring in 2000, the Coyotes organization put no restrictions on Treliving's involvement with the Flames' drafting at the 2014 NHL Draft—held a couple months after Treliving's arrival in Calgary. Treliving was able to be a full participant and functionally ran the show for the club at the draft, but the majority of the scouting for the season had been completed by the time he joined the Flames—the only major event left on the calendar was the Memorial Cup tournament.

The 2014 draft was a watershed moment of sorts for the Flames. The Flames had gone through what was a generally painful season in 2013–14, going 35–40–7 and finishing fourth-last in the league's overall standings. It was the club's first season without Jarome Iginla (who had been traded) and Miikka Kiprusoff (who had retired), but the club had seemed to develop a workmanlike identity under new captain Mark Giordano and head coach Bob Hartley.

The 2013 first-round pick Sean Monahan had established himself as a full-time NHL player, and college star (and 2011 fourth-round pick) Johnny Gaudreau signed and made his NHL debut late in the season. Adding a high draft choice to the existing young core could help that group take a step forward.

After the draft lottery, the Flames had the fourth overall selection—their highest selection since moving to Calgary, with only the second-overall picks they had being during the Atlanta years in 1972 (Jacques Richard) and 1973 (Tom Lysiak). It had the potential to be a franchise-altering selection. The four top-ranked players in North America, according to Central Scouting, were Kingston Frontenacs centre Sam Bennett, Barrie Colts blueliner Aaron Ekblad, Kootenay Ice centre Sam Reinhart, and Prince Albert Raiders centre Leon Draisaitl.

All four players had their vocal supporters within the independent scouting communities, and they all boasted lots of talent and valuable attributes, albeit in very different packages. Bennett boasted tenacity and a high compete level. Ekblad was physically mature and played a very complete game as a blueliner. Reinhart had speed and offensive skill. Draisaitl looked to be a potential power forward if he could develop a bit more physically. The only real knock on any of the four came at the NHL's draft combine in late May, an annual event where players do interviews with teams and go through physical challenges. Bennett was unable to do a single pull-up at the event.

Weeks later, Bennett taped a segment with the Canadian broadcaster of the draft, TSN, where he went to a local playground on draft weekend in Philadelphia and did several pull-ups. Whether the pull-ups (or lack thereof) had anything to do with it, Bennett didn't end up going first overall. Ekblad went first to Florida, Reinhart went second to Buffalo, and Draisaitl went third to Edmonton. Bennett landed in Calgary's lap at fourth overall, the first-ever draft selection for Treliving as a general manager in the NHL.

Bennett attended Flames training camp in the fall of 2014 and impressed. However, he suffered a shoulder injury during a preseason game that required surgery. He recovered and went through rehabilitation for the injury in Calgary, then returned to Kingston in mid-February. He played out the OHL season, scoring 11 goals and posting 24 points in just 11 games, but Kingston was swept in the playoffs. Rather than end his season prematurely, the Flames brought Bennett back to the NHL. He made his big-league debut on April 11, 2015, against the Winnipeg Jets, in the final game of the regular season for the playoff-bound Flames. Bennett set up a goal by Micheal Ferland just 33 seconds into the game, earning his first career NHL point.

Bennett impressed enough during training camp and his brief time back with the Flames that he was given a chance to play in the playoffs. He was a key role player during the Flames' two rounds in the 2015 postseason, bringing a combination of energy, physicality, and occasionally key goals or set-up. He earned the nickname "18-year-old Sam Bennett" from fans on social media for how mature and poised his game was, particularly given his youth. Faced with the choice of using up the first year of his entry-level contract or shutting down Bennett during the playoffs, Flames

brass decided to keep Bennett playing rather than lose what
he brought to their lineup.

In the following seasons, Bennett only occasionally
reached the levels of play that he did during the playoffs—
and when he did, it was usually during the postseason when
his boisterous physical play fit the intense tone of the games.
He spent parts of six subsequent regular seasons with the
Flames and was used in several different roles: top-six
winger, bottom-six winger, and centre on all four forward
lines. He was used in a shutdown role. He was used in an
offensive role. He was an appealing young player and could
do a lot of things well, but the combination of his "Jack of
all trades, master of none" skill set resulted in him bouncing
around the lineup and being used as a utility player to fix
line problems rather than being fit with players who max-
imized his effectiveness.

Bennett's most productive season was his 2015–16
rookie campaign, where he had 18 goals and 36 points playing primarily in a secondary role on a shutdown line with
Mikael Backlund and Michael Frolik. In subsequent seasons,
Bennett's role became less clear-cut, and his effectiveness
diminished on both sides of the puck. At the same time, new
young players like Matthew Tkachuk, Andrew Mangiapane,
and Dillon Dube entered the Flames' lineup and had their
roles carved out quickly, gradually establishing Bennett as
more of a complimentary piece rather than a prominent
player. Bennett was traded to the Florida Panthers prior to
the 2021 trade deadline.

The remainder of the 2014 class ended up being fairly
unimpressive. Mason McDonald, a promising goaltender

from the QMJHL's Charlottetown Islanders, was selected in the second round (34th overall) as part of a run of goaltenders selected. He never played his way up to the NHL level—Vancouver selected American netminder Thatcher Demko two picks later, and he became a reliable NHL goaltender. The McDonald–Demko situation had some parallels to the Flames selecting Trevor Kidd instead of Martin Brodeur or Felix Potvin in 1990. McDonald and Demko were both highly regarded by scouts in their draft year, but not only did Demko's NHL outcomes dwarf McDonald's, the Flames' selection failed to emerge as an impressive goaltender at the minor league level.

Towering forward Hunter Smith, listed at 6'7" and 200 pounds, was selected in the second round (54th overall) primarily due to his size and the hope he could become a power forward in the years ahead. He failed to impress in three seasons in the Flames' system, spending much of his time in the ECHL. Junior A defenceman Brandon Hickey, a smooth-skating, puck-moving defender, was selected in the third round (64th overall) and was traded to Arizona during his college career at Boston University. Tall Swedish defender Adam Ollas-Mattsson (sixth round, 175th overall) played briefly in the Flames system on a minor league deal but soon returned to Europe. Rugged over-age forward Austin Carroll (seventh round, 184th overall) was unremarkable in three seasons in the Flames system.

Aside from Bennett, no other player the Flames selected in the 2014 draft class played a game in the NHL. The team had an additional third-round selection but traded it to Chicago for depth forward Brandon Bollig, who played 116 games for the Flames. The Flames would have a more productive performance at the 2015 NHL Draft, using their picks effectively to select players and as assets in trades.

Notably, the Flames' performance at the 2015 draft came with almost the exact same staff Treliving had for the 2014 edition.

"Very few teams make major wholesale changes the first year because most of the staffs have a comfort level and understand the role of crossover scouts, and they do understand which European scouts know what they're doing and which don't," said Burke. "I've never cleaned house once. I've worked for six teams; I've never cleaned house. I will wait until the end of my first year and make one or two changes...and slowly build around the group that's there. Because the group that's there, unless they're totally inept, you can count on the group to give you good information. And look at the Flames, the group I inherited from Jay, and then Tree shortly thereafter inherited—they're a pretty solid group of scouts."

Treliving spent much of his first few seasons with the Flames assessing how the club was utilizing their existing resources and attempting to determine which resources they needed that they didn't have. He ended up adding a few area scouts to provide additional coverage in key areas, notably the United States junior and collegiate leagues, and also began building onto the club's data analysis and player development staff.

By the time the 2015 NHL Draft approached, the Flames were in a much better position than they had been the year prior. In Treliving's first season at the helm, the Flames had qualified for the playoffs and had beaten Vancouver in the first round, the club's first series victory since the 2004 Western Conference Final. More impressively, the Flames did it without their captain, Giordano—who had torn his bicep days before the trade deadline—and despite trading away a couple of players at the trade deadline.

In the midst of what he termed at the time an "asset accumulation phase," Treliving made two key trades prior to the 2015 trade deadline. Forward Sven Baertschi, a 2011 first-round selection that had requested a change of scenery, was traded to Vancouver for a second-round pick in 2015. Veteran forward Curtis Glencross, a pending unrestricted free agent, was sent to Washington for second- and third-round picks in 2015. As a result, the Flames headed to draft weekend in Sunrise, Florida, with momentum after a playoff appearance and several draft selections, especially early ones, with which to improve their team.

It would turn out to be one of the more eventful, productive weekends in terms of team building in franchise history.

Several hours before the hockey world convened in Florida, the Flames made a big splash, announcing that they had sent their own first and second-round picks (15th and 45th, respectively) and Washington's second-round pick (52nd) to Boston for restricted free agent defenceman Dougie Hamilton. Hamilton was a promising 22-year-old offensive blueliner at the time, and the Bruins were either unwilling or unable (from a salary cap perspective) to find common ground with Hamilton on a long-term contract. Treliving swooped in and was able to meet Boston's price for the player, consummating a deal before much of the league realized Hamilton was even available. The Flames signed Hamilton to a six-year contract just four days after completing the trade.

Having traded away three draft picks for Hamilton, the Flames didn't select for the first time until the 23rd pick of the second round, 53rd overall. They selected Swedish import defenceman Rasmus Andersson of the Barrie Colts. An offensive-minded blueliner in junior, Andersson was praised for his puck movement and booming shot but criticized a bit for his skating and defensive zone play. His fitness levels were also an area of concern for the Flames.

"When a player's drafted, there's no perfect player outside of one or two every year," said Treliving. "What are the things you can fix, or you can control or the player can control, or working in concert you can improve? In Rasmus' case, it was getting him into good physical condition. We felt that was a fixable defect."

Andersson played the 2015–16 season with Barrie, then prepared to go pro. At 2016's summer development camp, Treliving publicly acknowledged that Andersson's conditioning wasn't where it needed to be. Andersson received the message loud and clear and worked hard before training camp to get into better shape. He played the 2016–17 season with the Flames' top affiliate, the Stockton Heat, but was rewarded for his hard work with a month on the NHL roster. He played just once, but the idea was for him to get a sense of what the NHL lifestyle was all about.

Andersson split 2017–18 between Calgary and Stockton, getting into 10 NHL games and impressing. He made the

NHL roster out of training camp in 2018–19 and slowly but surely became a foundational piece of the Flames' defensive group. Ironically, the same player once criticized for his fitness (and publicly so) now leads the Flames in minutes played in nearly every game.

The Flames soon traded up into the second round, sending their own third-round pick (76th overall) and Washington's third-round pick (83rd overall) to Arizona for the second-to-last pick in the second round, 60th overall, which they used to select Swedish defenceman Oliver Kylington. Once touted as a potential top 10 pick in the draft and a player who played in the Swedish Hockey League at a very young age, Kylington had dealt with some consistency challenges while bouncing around Swedish hockey during his draft year—he made appearances in the Ivan Hlinka Memorial Tournament, the Under-18 Worlds, the SHL, the Swedish junior league, was loaned to the Allsvenskan, and attended Sweden's World Junior camp. Kylington was touted as a tremendous skater and puck-mover, but his defensive game needed work.

"People don't remember that draft, but there was talk of him being a top five pick the year before his draft year," said Treliving. "His issue was he played on a bunch of teams, there was a question of his ability to defend at the National Hockey League level. Everybody was concerned about, 'Great wheels, but can he defend?' To me, defending, checking, that's a learned trait. We thought we could fix that."

After Kylington's selection, there was debate regarding where he should play. He had the option of staying in Sweden, going to the Western Hockey League (he had been selected by the Brandon Wheat Kings in the import draft), or he could potentially play in the Flames' system. He opted to sign with the Flames and relocated to Stockton, where he went to work on his defensive zone play.

After three seasons of improvements with Stockton, Kylington began pushing for NHL duty in 2018–19. He kept improving his play away from the puck and minimizing his mistakes with the puck, eventually becoming an everyday NHL defender early in the 2021–22 season. Kylington's path to the NHL was not easy and involved several seasons of hard work tidying up his game, but the early returns have been promising for both him and the Flames.

The Flames selected Russian import forward Pavel Karnaukhov from the Calgary Hitmen in the fifth round (136th overall) and lanky North Bay Battalion blueliner Riley Bruce in the seventh round (196th overall). Neither player ever played in the Flames system, with Karnaukhov returning to Russia a year after being drafted and Bruce not being offered an NHL contract.

The real late-round gem was sixth-round pick Andrew Mangiapane, taken 166th overall in his second year of draft eligibility. A combination of a small OHL sample size and his small physical stature caused Mangiapane to be completely overlooked in the 2014 draft and mostly overlooked in the 2015 edition. The Flames saw Mangiapane's offensive performance, with 43 goals and 104 points, and felt he would be worth a late-round gamble.

"In Andrew's case, it was purely size," said Treliving. "And I don't look at Andrew as a small player. He's not a tall player, but he's not a small player. To me, when we talk about heaviness, that's the body type. Are you able to physically get inside? Are you strong enough to play an 82-game schedule? You don't necessarily have to be tall, but [it's about] his body, his ability to thicken up, get man strength. He's not tall, but he had a wide base. He was not a thin guy.... We didn't think size was going to be an issue with him at all. And he had a really high-end skill potential."

Mangiapane spent the 2015–16 season with Barrie, posting 51 goals and 106 points. He went pro the following season, joining Stockton of the AHL for the 2016–17 season. From that point, Mangiapane began a gradual stepwise progression in his game. He had 41 points as an AHL rookie over 66 games, then increased his production to 46 points in 39 games the following season.

Mangiapane's offensive progress earned him a few NHL call-ups. A strong start to 2018–19 in the AHL forced his way onto the NHL roster, where he found a niche on the Flames' fourth line as a tenacious forechecker that could contribute offensively as well. He's continued to increase his role with the Flames. He erupted for 35 goals in 2021–22, all while playing on the club's shutdown line with Mikael Backlund and Blake Coleman against the opposition's top players.

Over a two-day period in Florida in June 2015, the Flames drafted three players who turned into regular NHL players in Andersson, Kylington, and Mangiapane. They used picks they added at the trade deadline, which they received by trading a pair of expiring assets, to acquire a fourth regular NHL player in the form of Hamilton. Three years later, at the 2018 NHL Draft, they sent Hamilton to the Carolina

Hurricanes as part of a package deal—along with 2010 fifth-round pick Micheal Ferland and unsigned college prospect Adam Fox, a third-rounder from 2016—that landed them two other regular NHL players, defenceman Noah Hanifin and forward Elias Lindholm. Both Hanifin and Lindholm were, at the time, restricted free agents at contract impasses with the Hurricanes, and both players signed long-term deals with the Flames in the months following the trade.

Fox's inclusion in the trade with the Hurricanes raised a few eyebrows. At the time, Fox was one of the most promising prospects in the Flames system. He had recently completed his sophomore season at Harvard University and was considered one of the top collegiate players in the entire NCAA. But following the trade, Treliving explained in interviews that the team wasn't sure if they could get Fox under contract, and that they wanted players who wanted to be in Calgary. His inclusion in the offer to Carolina helped make the trade happen, as well as removed a bit of potential future anxiety for the club.

Johnny Gaudreau's selection by the Flames in the 2011 draft came on the heels of 2009 first-round pick Tim Erixon opting not to sign with the club, resulting in a trade to the Rangers. After Gaudreau's freshman season at Boston College, Anaheim Mighty Ducks prospect Justin Schultz left the University of Wisconsin and utilized a collective bargaining agreement loophole to become a free agent. As a result of those developments, there was significant fan anxiety that Gaudreau would spurn the Flames (like Erixon) and use the college loophole (like Schultz) that persisted until Gaudreau signed with the club in 2014. Fox's situation was a little bit different than Erixon's refusal to sign with the Flames.

"Adam Fox, I couldn't tell you what happened there," said Flames director of scouting Tod Button. "He was a third-round pick. He was excited to come to Calgary, was at our development camps. I don't think that was a before-the-draft thing. I think that was a situation where, and I'm guessing here, that the agent thought…. Every team passed on him two or three times, so it's not like he was a top 10 player who said he didn't want to go somewhere. He had the loophole, for sure, and I think he figured out he was a really good player. 'The next couple years, I'm a really good player, I can pick my spot.' Where a lot of these kids, they can't do that."

Button noted that the Flames do their due diligence with all prospects in terms of their willingness to eventually sign with the Flames, but the topic still bubbles up in fan and media discourse. The 2021 first-round selection Matt Coronato, who committed to Harvard when he was drafted by the Flames, was asked in his introductory Zoom press conference about his willingness to sign with the club. That the Flames selected him suggested the club received an answer that they liked when they brought it up in their pre-draft interview process. Coronato signed with the club in the spring of 2023.

Over one weekend in 2015, the Flames took advantage of having acquired extra draft picks by sending them to Boston for a high-end defenceman. They went into the entry draft with six selections and, after packaging two picks together to move up in the drafting order, made five selections. Three of those five selections became important NHL players for their team. Suffice it to say, Treliving really put his stamp on the Flames franchise in a major way at the 2015 NHL Draft.

"He analyses things so thoroughly," said Burke. "[He] gets the information you need to make smart decisions. I thought that was a masterful job, that draft."

23

EXPLOITING THE MARKET: HOW THE FLAMES FOUND LATE-ROUND DRAFT SUCCESS

ONE OF DARRYL Sutter's trademarks as Calgary Flames' general manager was leveraging draft selections to upgrade his club's roster as he chased a championship. During Brad Treliving's nine-year tenure, as the rebuild progressed and the Flames returned to the playoffs, an early phase of asset accumulation that saw expiring assets traded for picks and prospects soon turned into a phase of asset flipping as he tried to upgrade the club's roster.

From his arrival in April 2014 until his departure in April 2023, Treliving acquired 21 draft picks and traded away 35, for a net loss of 14 picks:

- Six first-round picks traded and three acquired, for a net loss of three.
- Seven second-round picks traded and six acquired, for a net loss of one.
- 10 third-round picks traded and five acquired, for a net loss of five.
- Five fourth-round picks traded and four acquired, for a net loss of one.
- Three fifth-round picks traded and four acquired, for a net gain of one.
- Two sixth-round picks traded and two acquired, for a net gain of zero.
- Two seventh-round picks traded and one acquired, for a net loss of one.

In the first three rounds of the draft, the Flames experienced a net loss of nine picks under Treliving.

But one of the reasons that Treliving was able to persist in trading away early draft selections to beef up his NHL roster without significantly depleting his farm system is that the Flames' scouting staff has become really adept at finding late-round gems, and their development staff has become quite skilled at helping mould them into NHL ready (or at least NHL-adjacent) players.

Despite his frequency in doing so, Treliving noted that his preference was to generally hold onto picks.

"I hate moving the picks," said Treliving. "People hear that and laugh because I've moved picks. You also come into a situation where the mandate is to get there quickly. You're not throwing away all your future, but we've made some decisions to add some pieces, some have worked, some haven't, to try to get our team to a certain spot. I have faith in the staff when they've shown they can find players outside the first round. But you hate doing it."

In nine seasons with the Flames, Treliving made several trades that sent early draft selections elsewhere. As he noted, some worked, some didn't.

At the 2015 draft, the Flames traded their first-round pick and two second-round picks to the Boston Bruins for restricted free agent blueliner Dougie Hamilton. The Flames had acquired additional picks through their moves prior to the trade deadline, though, and they ended up making two selections in the second round anyway, choosing defence-men Rasmus Andersson and Oliver Kylington. Hamilton was quickly signed to a long-term deal and was eventually traded to the Carolina Hurricanes as part of a larger trade that brought Elias Lindholm and Noah Hanfin to Calgary.

At the 2016 draft, the Flames traded a second-round pick to the St. Louis Blues in exchange for goaltender Brian Elliott. As in 2015, the Flames had added additional picks via trades, and they ended up making two selections in the second round once again, selecting goaltender Tyler Parsons and forward Dillon Dube. The Flames had strug-gled to find consistent goaltending. While Elliott ended up being just a single-season stop-gap, he performed well for the club.

Prior to the 2017 trade deadline, the Flames traded their 2017 second-round pick to the Ottawa Senators as part of a trade that brought forward Curtis Lazar to Calgary. Lazar had disappointed as a young player in Ottawa, even being placed on the waiver wire at one point, but the Flames had familiarity with the player due to him playing junior hockey with the Western Hockey League's Edmonton Oil Kings. The hope was that the club could kickstart his progress. It didn't pan out, though.

At the 2017 draft itself, they made a trade that impacted two years' worth of high draft picks. They traded a first-round pick in 2018 and second-round picks in 2018 and 2019 to the New York Islanders in exchange for defenceman Travis Hamonic. Hamonic was a well-regarded, stay-at-home blueliner under contract for three seasons when the Flames acquired him—which was likely the reason for the hefty acquisition cost.

Due to the Hamonic trade, and subsequent trade for goaltender Mike Smith involving their third-round pick, the 2018 draft was notable as having the latest initial Flames selection at a draft, at 105th overall in the fourth round. It was coincidentally the only time in franchise history that they didn't select a Canadian player at a draft.

Prior to the 2022 trade deadline, the Flames traded their 2022 first-round pick as part of a package to the Montreal Canadiens to acquire power forward Tyler Toffoli. Toffoli had two years remaining on his contract at a palatable cap hit and filled an organizational need as a right-shooting forward who scored goals, which he continued to do with Calgary. Toffoli's contract with the Flames was slated to expire following the 2023–24 season.

"That's the job, to make those decisions and move forward," said Treliving. "But you certainly have to find guys throughout the draft. And that's why every pick is important, right? Some people say oh well, it's a seventh-round pick, but they're really important...so any time you can add a pick in a deal or try to find one, you only get two days a year to add players, so they're valuable."

As are selections in the earlier rounds, draft picks made in the later rounds are only as valuable as the players acquired. Luckily for Treliving and the Flames, their scouting staff has been able to find promising players their developmental staff has helped morph into effective professionals.

In 2015, the Flames selected Barrie Colts winger Andrew Mangiapane in the sixth round. Mangiapane was in his second year of draft eligibility, having been overlooked the previous season due to a combination of his size (listed at 5′10″ and 170 pounds) and his small sample size in the OHL, with just 51 points in 68 OHL games on his resume as of the 2014 draft. A year later, Mangiapane was still small. His sample size was larger, and he had gone off for 43 goals and 104 points in his second full season in the OHL—enough to be ranked 85th among North American skaters by Central Scouting. But his size likely made a few teams nervous, and he slid to the sixth round, where the Flames selected him.

Mangiapane played one more season in the OHL, posting 51 goals and 106 points. He went pro in 2016–17, playing the entire season with the AHL's Stockton Heat and posting

20 goals and 41 points as a rookie, establishing himself as a reliable offensive forward. The following season, 2017–18, he had 21 goals and 46 points—scoring at higher than a point-per-game pace—and earned 10 games in the NHL during a mid-season call-up. Mangiapane didn't look out of place during his first NHL games, but he didn't stand out.

The following season, 2018–19, Mangiapane was recalled in November and slotted onto the Flames' fourth line alongside veteran centre Derek Ryan and checking winger Garnet Hathaway. The trio clicked immediately, with Mangiapane's forechecking complimenting Ryan's two-way play and Hathaway's crash-and-bang physicality. Mangiapane spent the remainder of the season in the NHL, simultaneously establishing himself as a useful NHL regular and helping his line establish itself as one of the top depth lines in the NHL.

The tenacity that helped Mangiapane get a foothold on the Flames' roster remained a key part of his game, as his willingness to go to the corners or the front of the net created turnovers to benefit his linemates and also led to him scoring a lot of key goals. He was promoted from the fourth line in 2019–20 and became increasingly used in high-leverage situations and alongside some of the Flames' top players, including Mikael Backlund and Blake Coleman. He emerged as a fixture of the Flames' lineup and a key part of their overall attack, relied upon to shut down and out-score the opposition's top offensive players.

In 2016, the Flames selected a local product in the sixth round that turned into a strong player within their farm system, though acquiring the pick used to select him was fairly complicated. The 2015–16 season didn't go terribly well for the Flames, with the team sliding back a bit in the standings after making the playoffs in the 2014–15 season. As a result, Treliving looked to move out some pending unrestricted free agents at the trade deadline in an effort to add some future draft selections. Veteran blueliner Kris Russell went to Dallas for young defenceman Jyrki Jokipakka, forward prospect Brett Pollock, and a conditional pick. Veteran forward Jiri Hudler was sent to Florida for second and fourth-round picks. A third trade that sent veteran forward David Jones to the Minnesota Wild almost didn't happen.

In 2015–16, the Minnesota Wild carried three goaltenders for the season: 29-year-old Devan Dubnyk, 25-year-old Darcy Kuemper, and 37-year-old Niklas Backstrom—confusingly, the NHL had two Backstroms with remarkably similar names for several seasons; Niklas (no C) was a Finnish goaltender, while Nicklas (with a C) was a Swedish offensive forward. Backstrom had been with the Wild since the 2006–07 season and was considered a franchise icon, but age and injuries had taken their toll on his game and the club was preparing to move in another direction. Simply put, Backstrom wasn't in their plans anymore. But a surgery over the summer prevented the Wild from buying out the final year of his contract, and his no-move clause meant he could block any move to the minors. So the Wild simply kept Backstrom on the roster and, aside from practices and occasionally dressing him as backup, he was never used in games.

The Flames were looking to add draft picks in the 2016 class and Jones, as an expiring contract, was prime for a move. But the Wild's cap situation was pretty tight, and to make the salary cap math work for Minnesota to take on

Jones' $4 million cap hit, they needed the Flames to take on Backstrom's $3.417 million cap hit. The Flames were good with the proposal, as goaltender Karri Ramo was out with a season-ending knee injury so the team was using Joni Ortio and Jonas Hiller as their tandem. With the deal nearly finalized, there was one last bit of business—they needed Backstrom to waive his no-move clause. There was one problem: when the Wild reached Backstrom by phone, he was at a suburban shopping mall near St. Cloud with his family, nearly an hour from his home.

"We had a game the night before the deadline and during the deadline day, there was a Bruce Springsteen show at the Xcel [Minnesota's arena] and I had some friends there who worked for the band, so I was planning on seeing them," said Backstrom. "Later that night there were a couple big Finnish bands playing in downtown Minneapolis who went to our game, so I was going to see them. So I had really planned out that day because everything was quiet."

Trade talks were quiet enough leading up to the trade deadline that Backstrom had planned out a busy day for himself. But when he was informed that there had been a trade set up for him to go to Calgary and eager for the chance to play games for the first time in over a year, Backstrom rushed home to send in his paperwork.

"We got back to the house and our printer didn't work," said Backstrom. "So I had to drive over to Mikko Koivu's house to scan and print my approval. It was a different journey; it wasn't really easy, and everything happened so late. But in the end, it got done."

Backstrom played four games for the Flames at the tail-end of the season. Two of his four games were played in Minnesota against his old team. His final appearance of the season—and the final game of his NHL career—was against the Wild, and he made 35 saves in a strong performance and was named first star in the building where he spent most of his NHL career. The win was bittersweet both for Backstrom and the Flames; the victory caused the Flames to pass the Columbus Blue Jackets in the standings, which moved them down in the lottery order for the upcoming NHL draft. Backstrom joked, years later, that he thought Treliving was a little bit upset with him for that.

"When you're on the management side or the hockey ops side, you understand what a big difference a couple spots in the draft is," said Backstrom.

The Flames dropped from fifth to sixth overall via the draft lottery. Columbus, who had switched spots with the Flames by virtue of their Backstrom-fueled win over Minnesota, won the third overall pick in the lottery. The scouting consensus was that the top three picks would be American forward Auston Matthews, followed by Finnish forwards Patrik Laine and Jesse Puljujarvi. After Toronto took Matthews first overall and Winnipeg nabbed Laine with the second pick, Columbus threw a curveball by selecting Canadian forward Pierre-Luc Dubois.

The ripple effect of Columbus going against the prevailing wisdom was that Puljujarvi went to Edmonton at fourth overall, Vancouver took Finnish defender Olli Juolevi at fifth overall, and American forward Matthew Tkachuk—son of long-time NHL star Keith Tkachuk—landed in the Flames' laps at sixth overall. Tkachuk was, by all accounts, the player the Flames most coveted in the top end of the draft and they ended up getting him, despite some hand-wringing due to how the draft lottery had turned out.

The other consequence of the Jones-for-Backstrom swap with the Wild was that the Flames got themselves an additional sixth-round selection. With that pick, they selected under-sized offensive forward Matthew Phillips from the Victoria Royals at 166th overall. Phillips was still available for the same reasons that Mangiapane fell to the Flames in the previous year: a combination of concerns about physical size and sample size. Phillips was listed by Central Scouting at 5'7" and 141 pounds and had played just a single season in the WHL, posting 76 points in 72 games and being named the league's top rookie.

The Flames area scouts thought he was a good gamble that late in the draft. Born and raised in the Calgary area, Phillips was on his way to an ice time when he found out he had been drafted by his hometown team.

"I actually had a spring ice time, a skill session, that I was going to," said Phillips. "I was watching the early rounds at home, and then I had to get going around the fourth round. I was halfway to the rink and then I got a call, and then my phone started blowing up."

Local news crews were waiting for Phillips when he got off the ice to do stories about his selection by the Flames.

While his NHL opportunities have yet to fully materialize, Phillips has emerged as a strong offensive player, standing out among the leaders not just in the Flames system but in the entire AHL. Even if he doesn't find a way to make the jump into the NHL, his excellent play in the AHL has helped his young teammates develop, so he's become a definite organizational asset.

In 2017, the Flames selected Slovakian forward Adam Ruzicka in the fourth round. The Flames had been idle since selecting Finnish blueliner Juuso Valimaki in the first round—they had traded their second- and third-round picks that year—and Ruzicka was seen as a "high ceiling" pick. Drafted from the OHL's Sarnia Sting, Ruzicka scored 25 goals and 46 points in 61 games in his draft year, and the only knock on his game was his consistency. Ruzicka had been one of the most-skilled players on his team or in his league for most of his youth, so he was being challenged in an environment, the OHL, where the skill level was much higher, and he would need to find ways to out-work and out-battle the opposition.

Ruzicka played two more seasons in junior, continuing to impress offensively, and turned pro in the Flames organization with the 2019–20 season. He worked his way up through the ranks, working on his consistency, and cracked the Flames' NHL roster to begin the 2022–23 season. Even if his development plateaus, he'll have established himself, at the very least, as a reliable depth NHL player.

In 2018, the Flames selected Norwegian forward Mathias Emilio Pettersen in the sixth round. Selected from the United States Hockey League's Muskegon Lumberjacks, he wasn't a stranger to scouts. Pettersen had actually landed on hockey's radar when videos of his dazzling puck-handling appeared on YouTube before he was even a teenager. He migrated to North America as a 14-year-old to pursue his hockey dream and spent two seasons in the USHL and two seasons in college at the University of Denver before turning pro and joining the Flames' farm system.

In late June 2017, the Flames made a minor trade with the Carolina Hurricanes. The Flames sent minor league defenceman Keegan Kanzig and a 2019 sixth-round pick to the Hurricanes in exchange for backup goalie Eddie Lack, depth defenceman Ryan Murphy, and a 2019 seventh-round pick. They bought out Murphy's contract the next day and only briefly used Lack as backup before he was replaced on the NHL roster by minor league starter David Rittich. The most impactful acquisition that day for the Flames could end up being the seventh-round pick, though.

Almost two years after the trade, the Flames used that seventh-round pick to draft Everett Silvertips goaltender Dustin Wolf at 214th overall—the fourth-from-last pick at the event. Listed at 5'11.5" and 156 pounds by Central Scouting in his draft year, Wolf had everything but size—and he was only considered "small" relative to other goaltenders, as the 11 goalies ahead of him on the Central Scouting rankings were all listed as taller than him, some by only half an inch. Wolf's family had driven up from Seattle to Vancouver for the draft, and a big cheer erupted from a small pocket of the Rogers Arena stands when his selection was announced. He had spoken to a handful of teams prior to the draft but had no idea he was on Calgary's radar.

As Wolf arrived at the Flames' table on the draft floor, Treliving gave him a big hug and some words of encouragement.

"His message was just it didn't matter where you get picked," said Wolf. "I still try to show that now, and each and every day going forward, [that] you know what, it doesn't matter if I was fourth from last or whatever. I play games to win for my team and if I do that, I'm pretty happy with how I'm doing."

Wolf posted 41 wins and seven shutouts in his draft season, ranking among the WHL's leaders in all goaltending categories—his 1.69 goals against average was the fourth best in league history. His two post-draft seasons, albeit shortened by the COVID-19 pandemic, saw him outright attack the WHL leaderboard in goaltending statistics. He narrowly missed becoming the WHL's all-time shutout leader due to the shortened seasons, but he was named WHL goalie of the year in his two post-draft seasons (2019–20 and 2020–21).

Going pro in 2021–22, Wolf joined the Flames farm system and really impressed by adapting to the rigours of the pro game right away. His small stature—for a goaltender— proved to be no real roadblock to success, as he was named to the AHL's All-Rookie Team and was named the AHL's top goaltender in 2021–22 and 2022–23 and the league's MVP in 2022–23. He dressed twice for the Flames as backup goaltender during the 2021–22 season and made his NHL debut in the final game of the 2022–23 season. His future seems very bright.

Under Treliving, the Flames showed a slight tendency to diversify their reserve list through their drafting by taking a little bit of everything—they've taken a mixture of player sizes, styles, and positions. It's not necessarily something the club has gone out of their way to do consciously; rather, it's a by-product of the team focusing on getting players with the highest ceiling. Treliving noted that after taking Valimaki in the first round in

2017, the club went 15 picks and nearly three full drafts before taking another defenceman, Yan Kuznetsov, in 2020.

"You're still evaluating, at the end of the day, when these players top out and they've reached their peak and they hit their projection, who's going to have the greatest upside?" said Treliving. "Again, at the end of the day, you don't want to have a whole bunch of one thing. What you're hoping to have is a whole bunch of good players who maybe can fill different roles."

When weighing a player's upside, a factor that becomes significant as each draft wears on is a player's deficiencies. Simply put, players earlier in the draft have fewer known flaws than players available in the later rounds, so the challenge for clubs is finding players with flaws that the player development staff can help them overcome so they can become reliable pros.

"If you have maybe an area that's a defect, is there an area that's going to help overcome that?" Treliving said. "In our game, two things overcome a lot of other things, and that's competitiveness and a brain—hockey smarts, hockey sense. You've seen players who aren't good skaters that are high-end hockey sense players; they don't look as slow. You've seen guys that are high-end competitors...Those two traits are really, really important, we feel."

In this sense, the Flames' success converting late-round draft picks into players who contribute throughout the club's system is as much a product of astute scouting as it is crafting a development team that can help smooth out rough spots a player may have. Not only that, but the team keeps adding to a player's profile as it works its system and looks back to apply lessons learned during prior developmental cycles to future draft selections. Knowing what player defects can be overcome is as much a scouting problem as it is a development problem, and the Flames keep attempting to refine their processes to help lead players to developmental success, both on and off the ice.

During Treliving's tenure, he added to his club's roster of area scouts and emphasized the importance of an area scout being an expert on their region. He also added multiple developmental resources, including a skating coach, a skills coach, a mental skills performance coach, and a dedicated goaltending coach for the developmental system. Treliving's successor, Craig Conroy, continued the trend, adding a strength coach and developmental coach for defencemen upon his hiring in 2023.

"Ten years ago, we had one guy, that's why Darryl [Sutter] used to bring the pro scouts in to do a lot of the development," said Button. "All that stuff gives you more ways to build your profile and then after, when you get the feedback from the skating coach, maybe that wasn't right or maybe this is why he didn't make it, or Ray Edwards will say work ethic. Sometimes you know that ahead of time. Sometimes you'll say, 'I'm going to take a chance on him in the fourth round,' because we know he's got this and this wrong with him, but this and this are good enough to play in the NHL, so maybe you figure the other two out."

Generally, when a hockey club trades away a lot of high draft selections, their organizational depth suffers because it can be extremely difficult to fill a developmental system with players selected in the later rounds. The Flames have bucked this trend, routinely finding valuable organizational depth and bonafide NHL players (like Mangiapane or Ruzicka)—or high-end prospects (Wolf)—late in the draft. This phenomenon allowed Treliving to leverage the club's early picks to bolster the NHL roster without completely emptying the Flames' prospect cupboards—a true rarity in modern drafting and a credit to the Flames' scouting and development staff.

ACKNOWLEDGMENTS

LIKE SO MANY of the group that consider ourselves, on our better days, sports writers, I had vague ambitions of writing a book someday. In the summer of 2022, an email exchange with Bill Ames at Triumph Books turned that vague ambition into a tangible challenge to tackle. I'll always appreciate Bill and the folks at Triumph for taking a gamble on a first-time writer, and I'm similarly appreciative for the patience and stewardship of editor Michelle Bruton throughout the process.

When I received the email from Bill asking if I wanted to tackle this project, I touched base with a few members of my professional support network to determine if it was something I would be able to do. From Jay Downton, Mike Gagnon, and David Quadrelli at the Nation Network to Pat Steinberg and Art Factora at Sportsnet Radio, everyone was incredibly enthusiastic and supportive about the project and helped me believe that I could pull it off and still occasionally get some sleep. I'm also incredibly appreciative for the patience of my Calgary media colleagues as I cobbled this project together, occasionally shoehorning questions into scrums and press conferences, who also allowed me to bounce ideas off of them.

This book would be tremendously lean without the generosity of the many individuals who shared their memories and stories with me. I'm extremely grateful to Cliff Fletcher, David Poile, Doug Risebrough, Al Coates, Craig Button, Jay Feaster, Brian Burke, Brad Treliving, Tod Button, Kent Nilsson, Patrick Laprade, Mikael Backlund, Niklas Backstrom, Matthew Phillips, and Dustin Wolf, as well as many others who helped fill in several background details. I'm quite appreciative of the public relations staffs of the Calgary Flames, Pittsburgh Penguins, Nashville Predators, Columbus Blue Jackets, Toronto Maple Leafs, and the National Hockey League Players Association for all their help organizing interviews.

My mother and father, Pamela and Jeff, always encouraged my curiosity about all things sports and fostered my love of hockey from a young age. When it became clear that my talents lay not on the ice—my short time in Trails West minor hockey was defined by energetic but poor play—they were supportive and enthusiastic as I pursued writing. Finally, my wife, Jennifer, was equal parts supportive, patient, and nurturing during my writing process, all while planning our wedding. Quite simply, this book would not have been possible without her.

APPENDIX

COMPLETE FLAMES DRAFT LIST

(Games current through the 2022–23 season)

2023

Rd.	No.	Name	Pos.	Country	Games
1	16	Samuel Honzek	LW	Slovakia	0
2	48	Etienne Morin	D	Canada	0
3	80	Aydar Suniev	LW	Russia	0
4	112	Jaden Lipinski	C	U.S.	0
6	176	Yegor Yegorov	G	Russia	0
7	208	Axel Hurtig	D	Sweden	0

2022

Rd.	No.	Name	Pos.	Country	Games
2	59	Topi Ronni	C	Finland	0
5	155	Parker Bell	LW	Canada	0
7	219	Cade Littler	C	U.S.	0

2021

Rd.	No.	Name	Pos.	Country	Games
1	13	Matt Coronato	RW	U.S.	1
2	45	William Stromgren	LW	Sweden	0
3	77	Cole Huckins	C	Canada	0
3	89	Cameron Whynot	D	Canada	0
5	141	Cole Jordan	D	Canada	0
6	168	Jack Beck	RW	Canada	0
6	173	Lucas Ciona	LW	Canada	0
7	205	Arsenii Sergeev	G	Russia	0

2020

Rd.	No.	Name	Pos.	Country	Games
1	24	Connor Zary	C	Canada	0
2	50	Yan Kuznetsov	D	Russia	0
3	72	Jeremie Poirier	D	Canada	0
3	80	Jake Boltmann	D	U.S.	0
4	96	Daniil Chechelev	G	Russia	0
5	143	Ryan Francis	RW	Canada	0
6	174	Rory Kerins	C	Canada	0
7	205	Ilya Solovyov	D	Belarus	0

2019

Rd.	No.	Name	Pos.	Country	Games
1	26	Jakob Pelletier	LW	Canada	24
3	88	Ilya Nikolaev	C	Russia	0
4	116	Lucas Feuk	LW	Sweden	0
5	150	Josh Nodler	C	U.S.	0
7	214	Dustin Wolf	G	U.S.	1

2018

Rd.	No.	Name	Pos.	Country	Games
4	105	Martin Pospisil	C	Slovakia	0
4	108	Demetrios Koumontzis	LW	U.S.	0
4	122	Milos Roman	C	Slovakia	0
6	167	Emilio Pettersen	C	Norway	0
7	198	Dmitry Zavgorodniy	LW	Russia	0

2017

Rd.	No.	Name	Pos.	Country	Games
1	16	Juuso Valimaki	D	Finland	160
4	109	Adam Ruzicka	C	Slovakia	75
5	140	Zach Fischer	RW	Canada	0
6	171	D'Artagnan Joly	RW	Canada	0
7	202	Filip Sveningsson	LW	Sweden	0

2016

Rd.	No.	Name	Pos.	Country	Games
1	6	Matthew Tkachuk	LW	U.S.	510
2	54	Tyler Parsons	G	U.S.	0
2	56	Dillon Dube	C	Canada	282
3	66	Adam Fox	D	U.S.	285
4	96	Linus Lindstrom	C	Sweden	0
5	126	Mitchell Mattson	C	U.S.	0
6	156	Eetu Tuulola	RW	Finland	0
6	166	Matthew Phillips	C	Canada	3
7	186	Stepan Falkovsky	D	Belarus	0

2015

Rd.	No.	Name	Pos.	Country	Games
2	53	Rasmus Andersson	D	Sweden	377
2	60	Oliver Kylington	D	Sweden	168
5	136	Pavel Karnaukhov	LW	Russia	0
6	166	Andrew Mangiapane	LW	Canada	342
7	196	Riley Bruce	D	Canada	0

2014

Rd.	No.	Name	Pos.	Country	Games
1	4	Sam Bennett	C	Canada	546
2	34	Mason McDonald	G	Canada	0
2	54	Hunter Smith	RW	Canada	0
3	64	Brandon Hickey	D	Canada	0
6	175	Adam Ollas-Mattsson	D	Sweden	0
7	184	Austin Carroll	RW	U.S.	0

2013

Rd.	No.	Name	Pos.	Country	Games
1	6	Sean Monahan	C	Canada	681
1	22	Emile Poirier	LW	Canada	8
1	28	Morgan Klimchuk	LW	Canada	1
3	67	Keegan Kanzig	D	Canada	0
5	135	Eric Roy	D	Canada	0
6	157	Tim Harrison	RW	U.S.	0
7	187	Rushan Rafikov	D	Russia	0
7	198	John Gilmour	D	Canada	37

2012

Rd.	No.	Name	Pos.	Country	Games
1	21	Mark Jankowski	C	Canada	322
2	42	Patrick Sieloff	D	U.S.	2
3	75	Jon Gillies	G	U.S.	35
4	105	Brett Kulak	D	Canada	416
5	124	Ryan Culkin	D	Canada	0
6	165	Coda Gordon	LW	Canada	0
7	186	Matthew Deblouw	C	U.S.	0

2011

Rd.	No.	Name	Pos.	Country	Games
1	13	Sven Baertschi	LW	Switzerland	292
2	45	Markus Granlund	C	Finland	335
2	57	Tyler Wotherspoon	D	Canada	30
4	104	Johnny Gaudreau	LW	U.S.	682
6	164	Laurent Brossoit	G	Canada	117

2010

Rd.	No.	Name	Pos.	Country	Games
3	64	Max Reinhart	C	Canada	23
3	73	Joey Leach	D	Canada	0
4	103	John Ramage	D	U.S.	2
4	108	Bill Arnold	C	U.S.	1
5	133	Micheal Ferland	LW	Canada	335
7	193	Patrick Holland	RW	Canada	5

2009

Rd.	No.	Name	Pos.	Country	Games
1	23	Tim Erixon	D	Sweden	93
3	74	Ryan Howse	LW	Canada	0
4	111	Henrik Bjorklund	RW	Sweden	0
5	141	Spencer Bennett	LW	Canada	0
6	171	Joni Ortio	G	Finland	37
7	201	Gaelan Patterson	C	Canada	0

2008

Rd.	No.	Name	Pos.	Country	Games
1	25	Greg Nemisz	C	Canada	15
2	48	Mitch Wahl	C	U.S.	0
3	78	Lance Bouma	C	Canada	357
4	108	Nick Larson	LW	U.S.	0
4	114	T.J. Brodie	D	Canada	830
6	168	Ryley Grantham	C	Canada	0
7	198	Alexander Deilert	D	Sweden	0

2007

Rd.	No.	Name	Pos.	Country	Games
1	24	Mikael Backlund	C	Sweden	908
3	70	John Negrin	D	Canada	3
4	116	Keith Aulie	D	Canada	167
5	143	Mickey Renaud	C	Canada	0
7	186	C.J. Severyn	LW	U.S.	0

2006

Rd.	No.	Name	Pos.	Country	Games
1	26	Leland Irving	G	Canada	13
3	87	John Armstrong	C	Canada	0
3	89	Aaron Marvin	RW	U.S.	0
4	118	Hugo Carpentier	C	Canada	0
5	149	Juuso Puustinen	RW	Finland	0
6	179	Jordan Fulton	C	U.S.	0
7	187	Devin Didiomete	LW	Canada	0
7	209	Per Jonsson	D	Sweden	0

2005

Rd.	No.	Name	Pos.	Country	Games
1	26	Matt Pelech	D	Canada	13
3	69	Gord Baldwin	D	Canada	0
3	74	Dan Ryder	C	Canada	0
4	111	J.D. Watt	RW	Canada	0
5	128	Kevin Lalande	G	Canada	0
5	158	Matt Keetley	G	Canada	1
6	179	Brett Sutter	LW	Canada	60
7	221	Myles Rumsey	D	Canada	0

2004

Rd.	No.	Name	Pos.	Country	Games
1	24	Kris Chucko	LW	Canada	2
3	70	Brandon Prust	LW	Canada	486
3	98	Dustin Boyd	C	Canada	220
4	118	Aki Seitsonen	C	Finland	0
4	121	Kris Hogg	LW	Canada	0
6	173	Adam Pardy	D	Canada	342

6	182	Fred Wikner	LW	Sweden	0
7	200	Matt Schneider	C	Canada	0
7	213	James Spratt	G	U.S.	0
9	279	Adam Cracknell	RW	Canada	210

2003

Rd.	No.	Name	Pos.	Country	Games
1	9	Dion Phaneuf	D	Canada	1,048
2	39	Tim Ramholt	D	Switzerland	1
3	97	Ryan Donally	LW	Canada	0
4	112	Jamie Tardif	RW	Canada	2
5	143	Greg Moore	RW	U.S.	10
6	173	Tyler Johnson	C	Canada	0
7	206	Thomas Bellemare	RW	Canada	0
8	240	Cam Cunning	LW	Canada	0
9	270	Kevin Harvey	LW	Canada	0

2002

Rd.	No.	Name	Pos.	Country	Games
1	10	Eric Nystrom	LW	U.S.	593
2	39	Brian McConnell	C	U.S.	0
3	90	Matthew Lombardi	C	Canada	536
4	112	Yuri Artemenkov	RW	Russia	0
5	141	Jiri Cetkovsky	C	Czech Republic	0
5	142	Emanuel Peter	C	Switzerland	0
5	159	Kristofer Persson	RW	Sweden	0
6	176	Curtis McElhinney	G	Canada	249
7	206	David van der Gulik	RW	Canada	49
7	207	Pierre Johnsson	D	Sweden	0
8	238	Jyrki Marttinen	D	Finland	0

2001

Rd.	No.	Name	Pos.	Country	Games
1	14	Chuck Kobasew	RW	Canada	601
2	41	Andrei Taratukhkin	C	Russia	0
2	56	Andrei Medvedev	G	Russia	0
4	108	Tomi Maki	RW	Finland	1
4	124	Yegor Shastin	LW	Ukraine	0
5	145	James Hakewill	D	U.S.	0
5	164	Yuri Trubachev	C	Russia	0
7	207	Garrett Bembridge	RW	Canada	0
7	220	David Moss	LW	U.S.	501
8	233	Joe Campbell	D	U.S.	0
8	251	Ville Hamalainen	LW	Finland	0

2000

Rd.	No.	Name	Pos.	Country	Games
1	9	Brent Krahn	G	Canada	1
2	40	Kurtis Foster	D	Canada	405
2	46	Jarret Stoll	C	Canada	872
4	116	Levente Szuper	G	Hungary	0
5	141	Wade Davis	D	Canada	0
5	155	Travis Moen	LW	Canada	747
6	176	Jukka Hentunen	RW	Finland	38
8	239	David Hajek	D	Czech Republic	0
9	270	Micki DuPont	D	Canada	23

1999

Rd.	No.	Name	Pos.	Country	Games
1	11	Oleg Saprykin	LW	Russia	325
2	38	Dan Cavanaugh	C	U.S.	0
3	77	Craig Anderson	G	U.S.	709
4	106	Roman Rozakov	D	Russia	0
5	135	Matt Doman	RW	U.S.	0
5	153	Jesse Cook	D	U.S.	0
6	166	Cory Pecker	C	Canada	0
6	170	Matt Underhill	G	Canada	1
7	190	Blair Stayzer	LW	Canada	0
9	252	Dmitri Kirilenko	C	Russia	0

1998

Rd.	No.	Name	Pos.	Country	Games
1	6	Rico Fata	RW	Canada	230
2	33	Blair Betts	C	Canada	477
3	62	Paul Manning	D	Canada	8
4	102	Shaun Sutter	RW	Canada	0
4	108	Dany Sabourin	G	Canada	57
5	120	Brent Gauvreau	RW	Canada	0
7	192	Radek Duda	RW	Czech Republic	0
8	206	Jonas Frogren	D	Finland	41
9	234	Kevin Mitchell	D	U.S.	0

1997

Rd.	No.	Name	Pos.	Country	Games
1	6	Daniel Tkaczuk	C	Canada	19
2	32	Evan Lindsay	G	Canada	0
2	42	John Tripp	RW	Canada	43

2	51	Dmitri Kokorev	D	Russia	0
3	60	Derek Schutz	C	Canada	0
3	70	Erik Andersson	C	Sweden	12
4	92	Chris St. Croix	D	U.S.	0
4	100	Ryan Ready	LW	Canada	7
5	113	Martin Moise	LW	Canada	0
6	140	Ilja Demidov	D	Russia	0
7	167	Jeremy Rondeau	LW	Canada	0
9	223	Dustin Paul	RW	Canada	0

1996

Rd.	No.	Name	Pos.	Country	Games
1	13	Derek Morris	D	Canada	1,107
2	39	Travis Brigley	LW	Canada	55
2	40	Steve Begin	C	Canada	524
3	73	Dmitri Vlasenkov	LW	Russia	0
4	89	Toni Lydman	D	Finland	847
4	94	Christian Lefebvre	D	Canada	0
5	122	Josef Straka	C	Czech Republic	0
8	202	Ryan Wade	RW	Canada	0
9	228	Ronald Petrovicky	RW	Slovakia	342

1995

Rd.	No.	Name	Pos.	Country	Games
1	20	Denis Gauthier	D	Canada	554
2	46	Pavel Smirnov	C	Russia	0
3	72	Rocky Thompson	D	Canada	25
4	98	Jan Labraaten	LW	Sweden	0
6	150	Clarke Wilm	C	Canada	455
7	176	Ryan Gillis	D	Canada	0
9	233	Steve Shirreffs	D	U.S.	0

1994

Rd.	No.	Name	Pos.	Country	Games
1	19	Chris Dingman	LW	Canada	385
2	45	Dmitri Riabykin	D	Russia	0
3	77	Chris Clark	RW	U.S.	607
4	91	Ryan Duthie	C	Canada	0
4	97	Johan Finnstrom	D	Sweden	0
5	107	Nils Ekman	LW	Sweden	264
5	123	Frank Appel	D	Germany	0
6	149	Patrick Haltia	G	Sweden	0
7	175	Ladislav Kohn	RW	Czech Republic	186
8	201	Keith McCambridge	D	Canada	0
9	227	Jorgen Jonsson	LW	Sweden	81
10	253	Mike Peluso	RW	U.S.	38
11	279	Pavel Torgaev	LW	Russia	55

1993

Rd.	No.	Name	Pos.	Country	Games
1	18	Jesper Mattsson	C	Sweden	0
2	44	Jamie Allison	D	Canada	372
3	70	Dan Tompkins	LW	U.S.	0
4	95	Jason Smith	D	U.S.	0
4	96	Marty Murray	C	Canada	261
5	121	Darryl Lafrance	C	Canada	0
5	122	John Emmons	C	U.S.	85
6	148	Andreas Karlsson	C	Sweden	264
8	200	Derek Sylvester	RW	U.S.	0
10	252	German Titov	LW	Russia	624
11	278	Blake Murphy	LW	Canada	0

1992

Rd.	No.	Name	Pos.	Country	Games
1	6	Cory Stillman	C	Canada	1,025
2	30	Chris O'Sullivan	D	U.S.	62
3	54	Mathias Johansson	C	Sweden	58
4	78	Robert Svehla	D	Slovakia	655
5	102	Sami Helenius	D	Finland	155
6	126	Ravil Yakubov	C	Russia	0
6	129	Joel Bouchard	D	Canada	364
7	150	Pavel Rajnoha	D	Czech Republic	0
8	174	Ryan Mulhern	C	U.S.	3
9	198	Brandon Carper	D	U.S.	0
10	222	Jonas Hoglund	LW	Sweden	545
11	246	Andrei Potaichuk	RW	Russia	0

1991

Rd.	No.	Name	Pos.	Country	Games
1	19	Niklas Sundblad	RW	Sweden	2
2	41	Francois Groleau	D	Canada	8
3	52	Sandy McCarthy	RW	Canada	736
3	63	Brian Caruso	LW	Canada	0
4	85	Steven Magnusson	C	U.S.	0
5	107	Jerome Butler	G	U.S.	0
6	129	Bobby Marshall	D	Canada	0
7	140	Matt Hoffman	LW	U.S.	0
7	151	Kelly Harper	C	Canada	0
8	173	David St-Pierre	C	Canada	0
9	195	David Struch	C	Canada	4
10	217	Sergei Zolotov	LW	Russia	0
11	239	Marko Jantunen	C	Finland	3
12	261	Andrei Trefilov	G	Russia	54

1990

Rd.	No.	Name	Pos.	Country	Games
1	11	Trevor Kidd	G	Canada	387
2	26	Nicolas Perreault	D	Canada	0
2	32	Vesa Viitakoski	LW	Finland	23
2	41	Etienne Belzile	D	Canada	0
3	62	Glen Mears	D	U.S.	0
4	83	Paul Kruse	LW	Canada	423
6	125	Chris Tschupp	C	U.S.	0
7	146	Dmitri Frolov	D	Russia	0
8	167	Shawn Murray	G	U.S.	0
9	188	Mike Murray	RW	U.S.	0
10	209	Rob Sumner	D	Canada	0
11	230	Invalid Pick	-	-	-
12	251	Leo Gudas	D	Czech Republic	0

1989

Rd.	No.	Name	Pos.	Country	Games
2	24	Kent Manderville	C	Canada	646
2	42	Ted Drury	C	U.S.	414
3	50	Veli-Pekka Kautonen	D	Finland	0
3	63	Corey Lyons	RW	Canada	0
4	70	Robert Reichel	C	Czech Republic	830
4	84	Ryan O'Leary	C	U.S.	0
5	105	Toby Kearney	LW	U.S.	0
7	147	Alex Nikolic	LW	Canada	0
8	168	Kevin Wortman	D	U.S.	5
9	189	Sergei Gomolyako	C	Russia	0
10	210	Dan Sawyer	D	U.S.	0
11	231	Alexander Yudin	D	Russia	0
12	252	Kenneth Kennholt	D	Sweden	0

1988

Rd.	No.	Name	Pos.	Country	Games
1	21	Jason Muzzatti	G	Canada	62
2	42	Todd Harkins	C	U.S.	48
4	84	Gary Socha	C	U.S.	0
5	85	Tomas Forslund	RW	Sweden	44
5	90	Scott Matusovich	D	U.S.	0
6	126	Jonas Bergqvist	RW	Sweden	22
7	147	Stefan Nilsson	C	Sweden	0
8	168	Troy Kennedy	RW	Canada	0
9	189	Brett Peterson	D	U.S.	0
10	210	Guy Darveau	D	Canada	0
11	231	Dave Tretowicz	D	U.S.	0
12	252	Sergei Priakin	RW	Russia	46

1987

Rd.	No.	Name	Pos.	Country	Games
1	19	Bryan Deasley	LW	Canada	0
2	25	Stephane Matteau	LW	Canada	848
2	40	Kevin Grant	D	Canada	0
3	61	Scott Mahoney	LW	Canada	0
4	70	Tim Harris	RW	Canada	0
5	103	Tim Corkery	D	Canada	0
6	124	Joe Aloi	D	U.S.	0
7	145	Peter Ciavaglia	C	U.S.	5
8	166	Theoren Fleury	RW	Canada	1,084
9	187	Mark Osiecki	D	U.S.	93
10	208	William Sedergren	D	U.S.	0
11	229	Peter Hasselblad	D	Sweden	0
12	250	Magnus Svensson	D	Sweden	46

1986

Rd.	No.	Name	Pos.	Country	Games
1	16	George Pelawa	RW	U.S.	0
2	37	Brian Glynn	D	Germany	431
4	79	Tom Quinlan	RW	U.S.	0
5	100	Scott Bloom	LW	U.S.	0
6	121	John Parker	C	U.S.	0
7	142	Rick Lessard	D	Canada	15
8	163	Mark Olsen	D	U.S.	0
9	184	Scott Sharples	G	Canada	1
10	205	Doug Pickell	LW	Canada	0
11	226	Anders Lindstrom	C	Sweden	0
12	247	Antonin Stavjana	D	Czech Republic	0

1985

Rd.	No.	Name	Pos.	Country	Games
1	17	Chris Biotti	D	Canada	0
2	27	Joe Nieuwendyk	C	Canada	1,257
2	38	Jeff Wenaas	C	Canada	0
3	59	Lane MacDonald	LW	U.S.	0
4	80	Roger Johansson	D	Sweden	161
5	101	Esa Keskinen	C	Finland	0
6	122	Tim Sweeney	LW	U.S.	291
7	143	Stu Grimson	LW	Canada	729
8	164	Nate Smith	D	U.S.	0
9	185	Darryl Olsen	D	Canada	1
10	206	Peter Romberg	D	Germany	0
11	227	Alexander Kozhevnikov	LW	Russia	0
12	248	Bill Gregoire	D	Canada	0

APPENDIX 277

1984

Rd.	No.	Name	Pos.	Country	Games
1	12	Gary Roberts	LW	Canada	1,224
2	33	Ken Sabourin	D	Canada	74
2	38	Paul Ranheim	LW	U.S.	1,013
4	75	Petr Rosol	LW	Czech Republic	0
5	96	Joel Paunio	LW	Finland	0
6	117	Brett Hull	RW	U.S.	1,269
7	138	Kevan Melrose	D	Canada	0
8	159	Jiri Hrdina	C	Czech Republic	250
9	180	Gary Suter	D	U.S.	1,145
10	200	Petr Rucka	C	Czech Republic	0
11	221	Stefan Jonsson	D	Sweden	0
12	241	Rudolf Suchanek	D	Czech Republic	0

1983

Rd.	No.	Name	Pos.	Country	Games
1	13	Dan Quinn	C	Canada	805
3	51	Brian Bradley	C	Canada	651
3	55	Perry Berezan	C	Canada	378
4	66	John Bekkers	C	Canada	0
4	71	Kevan Guy	D	Canada	156
4	77	Bill Claviter	LW	U.S.	0
5	91	Igor Liba	LW	Slovakia	37
6	111	Grant Blair	G	Canada	0
7	131	Jeff Hogg	G	Canada	0
8	151	Chris MacDonald	D	Canada	0
9	171	Rob Kivell	D	Canada	0
10	191	Tom Pratt	D	U.S.	0
11	211	Jaroslav Benak	LW	Czech Republic	0
12	231	Sergei Makarov	RW	Russia	424

1982

Rd.	No.	Name	Pos.	Country	Games
2	29	Dave Reierson	D	Canada	2
2	37	Richard Kromm	LW	Canada	372
3	51	Jim Laing	D	U.S.	0
4	65	Dave Meszaros	G	Canada	0
4	72	Mark Lamb	C	Canada	403
5	93	Lou Kiriakou	D	Canada	0
6	114	Jeff Vaive	C	Canada	0
6	118	Mats Kihlstrom	D	Sweden	0
7	135	Brad Ramsden	RW	Canada	0
8	156	Roy Myllari	D	Canada	0
9	177	Ted Pearson	LW	Canada	0
10	198	Jim Uens	C	Canada	0
11	219	Rick Erdall	C	U.S.	0
12	240	Dale Thompson	RW	Canada	0

1981

Rd.	No.	Name	Pos.	Country	Games
1	15	Al MacInnis	D	Canada	1,416
3	56	Mike Vernon	G	Canada	782
4	78	Peter Madach	C	Sweden	0
5	99	Mario Simioni	RW	Canada	0
6	120	Todd Hooey	RW	Canada	0
7	141	Rick Heppner	D	U.S.	0
8	162	Dale DeGray	D	Canada	153
9	183	George Boudreau	D	U.S.	0
10	204	Bruce Eakin	C	Canada	13

1980

Rd.	No.	Name	Pos.	Country	Games
1	13	Denis Cyr	RW	Canada	193
2	31	Tony Curtale	D	U.S.	2
2	32	Kevin LaVallee	LW	Canada	366
2	39	Steve Konroyd	D	Canada	895
4	76	Marc Roy	RW	Canada	0
5	97	Randy Turnbull	D	Canada	1
6	118	John Multan	RW	Canada	0
7	139	Dave Newsom	LW	Canada	0
8	160	Claude Drouin	C	Canada	0
9	181	Hakan Loob	RW	Sweden	450
10	202	Steven Fletcher	D	Canada	1

1979

Rd.	No.	Name	Pos.	Country	Games
1	12	Paul Reinhart	D	Canada	648
2	23	Mike Perovich	D	Canada	0
2	33	Pat Riggin	G	Canada	350
3	54	Tim Hunter	RW	Canada	815
4	75	Jim Peplinski	RW	Canada	711
5	96	Brad Kempthorne	C	Canada	0
6	117	Glenn Johnson	C	Canada	0

1978

Rd.	No.	Name	Pos.	Country	Games
1	11	Brad Marsh	D	Canada	1,086
3	47	Tim Bernhardt	G	Canada	67
4	64	Jim MacRae	LW	Canada	0
5	80	Gord Wappel	D	Canada	20

6	97	Greg Meredith	RW	Canada	38
7	114	Dave Hindmarch	RW	Canada	99
8	131	Dave Morrison	RW	Canada	0
9	148	Doug Todd	RW	Canada	0
10	165	Mark Green	C	U.S.	0
11	180	Robert Sullivan	C	Canada	0
12	196	Bernhard Englbrecht	G	Germany	0

1977

Rd.	No.	Name	Pos.	Country	Games
2	20	Miles Zaharko	D	Canada	129
2	28	Don Laurence	C	Canada	79
2	31	Brian Hill	RW	Canada	19
4	72	Jim Craig	G	U.S.	30
5	82	Curt Christopherson	D	U.S.	0
6	100	Bernard Harbec	C	Canada	0
7	118	Bobby Gould	RW	Canada	697
8	133	Jim Bennett	LW	U.S.	0
9	148	Tim Harrer	RW	U.S.	3

1976

Rd.	No.	Name	Pos.	Country	Games
1	8	Dave Shand	D	Canada	421
1	10	Harold Phillipoff	LW	Canada	141
2	28	Bobby Simpson	LW	Canada	175
3	46	Rick Hodgson	D	Canada	6
4	64	Kent Nilsson	C	Sweden	553
5	82	Mark Earp	G	Canada	0

1975

Rd.	No.	Name	Pos.	Country	Games
1	8	Richard Mulhern	D	Canada	303
2	26	Rick Bowness	RW	Canada	173
4	62	Dale Ross	LW	Canada	0
5	80	Willi Plett	RW	Paraguay	834
6	98	Paul Heaver	D	Great Britain	0
7	116	Dale McMullin	LW	Canada	0
8	134	Rick Piche	D	Canada	0
9	150	Nick Sanza	G	Canada	0
10	167	Brian O'Connell	G	Canada	0
11	181	Joe Augustine	D	U.S.	0
12	192	Torbjorn Nilsson	RW	Sweden	0
18	216	Gary Gill	LW	Canada	0

1974

Rd.	No.	Name	Pos.	Country	Games
2	28	Guy Chouinard	C	Canada	578
3	46	Dick Spannbauer	D	U.S.	0
4	58	Pat Ribble	D	Canada	349
4	64	Cam Botting	RW	Canada	2
5	82	Jerry Badiuk	D	Canada	0
6	100	Bill Moen	G	U.S.	0
7	118	Peter Brown	D	U.S.	0
8	135	Tom Linskog	D	Canada	0
9	152	Larry Hopkins	LW	Canada	60
10	167	Louis Loranger	C	Canada	0
11	182	Randy Montgomery	LW	Canada	0

1973

Rd.	No.	Name	Pos.	Country	Games
1	2	Tom Lysiak	C	Canada	919
1	16	Vic Mercredi	C	Canada	2
2	21	Eric Vail	LW	Canada	591
4	53	Dean Talafous	RW	U.S.	497
5	69	John Flesch	LW	Canada	124
6	85	Ken Houston	RW	Canada	570
7	101	Tom Machowski	D	U.S.	0
8	117	Bob Law	RW	Canada	0
9	133	Bob Bilodeau	D	Canada	0
10	148	Glen Surbey	D	Canada	0
10	149	Guy Ross	D	Canada	0
11	162	Greg Fox	D	Canada	494

1972

Rd.	No.	Name	Pos.	Country	Games
1	2	Jacques Richard	LW	Canada	556
2	18	Dwight Bialowas	D	Canada	164
3	34	Jean Lemieux	D	Canada	204
4	50	Don Martineau	RW	Canada	90
5	78	Jean-Paul Martin	C	Canada	0
6	82	Frank Blum	G	Canada	0
7	98	Scott Smith	LW	Canada	0
8	114	Dave Murphy	C	Canada	0
9	130	Pierre Roy	D	Canada	0
9	132	Jean Lamarre	RW	Canada	0